D1501041

Ring-Necked Pheasants
THRIVING IN SOUTH DAKOTA

On front cover: Cock pheasant in winter (Courtesy of Doug Backlund).

On back cover: Ring-necked pheasant male on territory in late winter (Courtesy of Scott Weins). Hen pheasant in early spring (Courtesy of Scott Weins).

Ring-Necked Pheasants
THRIVING IN SOUTH DAKOTA

Lester D. Flake
South Dakota State University, Brookings

Andy E. Gabbert
South Dakota Department of Game, Fish and Parks

Thomas R. Kirschenmann
South Dakota Department of Game, Fish and Parks

Anthony P. Leif
South Dakota Department of Game, Fish and Parks

Chad T. Switzer
South Dakota Department of Game, Fish and Parks

Published by the South Dakota Department of Game, Fish and Parks, Pierre.

Library of Congress Control Number: 2012909974
ISBN 978-0-9857132-1-8 (Hardback) — ISBN 978-0-9857132-0-1 (Paperback)

This publication may be cited as:
Flake, L.D., A.E. Gabbert, T.R. Kirschenmann, A.P. Leif, and C.T. Switzer. 2012. Ring-Necked Pheasants: Thriving in South Dakota. South Dakota Department of Game, Fish and Parks, Pierre.

Copies may be ordered from:
South Dakota Department of Game, Fish and Parks
523 E. Capitol Avenue, Foss Building
Pierre SD 57501
(gfp.sd.gov; Look under online shopping for merchandise or books)

Pheasants Forever assisted in covering printing costs.

ABOUT THE AUTHORS

Les Flake is Distinguished Professor Emeritus in the Department of Natural Resource Management, South Dakota State University, Brookings, where he was a faculty member for over 31 years. Les has a Ph.D. in zoology from Washington State University and an M.S. in biology from Brigham Young University. He currently lives in Springville, Utah, and has spent the past 9 years working on wildlife publications (wild turkeys, grouse, pheasants, and nesting ducks) for the South Dakota Department of Game, Fish and Parks.

Andy Gabbert is a habitat biologist for the South Dakota Department of Game, Fish and Parks (SDGFP) in Sioux Falls. He earned his B.S. in wildlife biology from Kansas State University and an M.S. from South Dakota State University where he studied pheasant use of habitats during winter. Andy has been developing and managing wildlife habitat on public hunting lands for over 12 years while working for the U.S. Fish and Wildlife Service, Nebraska Game and Parks Commission, and currently the SDGFP. Andy has a strong research interest in wildlife-habitat relationships in agricultural landscapes.

Tom Kirschenmann is Chief of Terrestrial Resources with the South Dakota Department of Game, Fish and Parks (SDGFP) in Pierre. Tom completed his B.S. in wildlife and fisheries sciences and his M.S. in wildlife sciences at South Dakota State University. Prior to accepting his current position he served as the Wildlife Program Administrator for Game Management in Pierre and, before that, as Senior Upland Game Biologist with SDGFP and as a Regional Biologist with Pheasants Forever.

Tony Leif is the Director of the Division of Wildlife for the South Dakota Department of Game, Fish and Parks (SDGFP), Pierre. Tony began his career with SDGFP as a conservation officer after earning a B.S. degree in wildlife and fisheries sciences from South Dakota State University and an M.S. in wildlife ecology from Texas Tech University. He conducted upland game bird research and led the upland game management program as a senior wildlife biologist for SDGFP and then administered the statewide game management program prior to his appointment as director in 2007.

Chad Switzer is a Wildlife Program Administrator with the South Dakota Department of Game, Fish and Parks (SDGFP) in Pierre. Chad graduated with a B.S. degree in fish and wildlife management from the University of Nebraska-Lincoln. Prior to his current position, Chad served as the Senior Upland Game Biologist and as a Habitat Biologist with SDGFP in Huron after employment as a Wildlife Management Biologist for the Nebraska Game and Parks Commission in North Platte. Chad has a strong interest in habitat development and management, land-use and wildlife relationships, and the influence of federal farm bill conservation programs on wildlife populations.

Each of the authors has multiple years' experience in research and/or management related to ring-necked pheasants in South Dakota. All are avid pheasant hunters and look forward to South Dakota's outstanding pheasant hunting each year.

ACKNOWLEDGEMENTS

We acknowledge the support of the South Dakota Department of Game, Fish and Parks (SDGFP) in encouraging the writing of this book and in providing financial support. We thank Pheasants Forever for assisting with printing costs and for photo assistance. Thanks to Kenneth F. Higgins (Professor Emeritus, South Dakota State University), Randy Rodgers (Kansas Department of Wildlife and Parks [retired]), and George Vandel III (Wildlife Division, South Dakota Department of Game, Fish and Parks [retired]) for reviewing an earlier draft of this book and for their many excellent comments and recommendations.

We especially thank Scott Weins (U.S. Forest Service, Spearfish, S.D.) and Doug Backlund (Wild Photos Photography, Pierre, S.D.) for their contributions of professional wildlife photographs for the book. Bill Lee and Dawn Stephens (curators, Agricultural Heritage Museum, South Dakota State University) helped us locate important historical photographs. We thank several others who have contributed photos and acknowledge these persons in the photo captions. Initials are given in parentheses for photos taken by the authors.

Several SDGFP personnel assisted us by reviewing quarterly reports and providing information. For this assistance we thank Corey Huxoll, Larry Gigliotti, Andy Lindbloom, Scott Stolz, Dale Gates, Spencer Vaa (retired), Travis Runia, Mark Norton, John Kanta, Scott Lindgren, Ron Schauer, and Emmett Keyser. Dave Dahlgren (Kansas Department of Wildife and Parks) and Todd Bogenschutz (Iowa Department of Natural Resources) provided further insight into pheasant ecology in their particular states. Boyd Schulz and Kurt Forman with the U.S. Fish and Wildlife Service (Brookings office) assisted with information on federal conservation programs that protect and restore grasslands and wetlands. We also appreciate information from personal communications with several other biologists cited in the text and from the many researchers cited in the book.

Several people provided assistance and encouragement from South Dakota State University (SDSU). We appreciate assistance from Gary Larson on plant identification questions. Several others from SDSU including Dave Willis, Carter Johnson, Kent Jensen, Chuck Dieter, and Arvid Boe provided information or otherwise assisted and encouraged completion of this book in various ways.

Dwayne Beck (manager of the Dakota Lakes Research Center and professor, SDSU) was of much help in providing information on the expansion of no-till agriculture and potential influences on cropping practices and wildlife; we appreciate his efforts to provide wildlife cover and improve soil and water conservation through no-till practices.

Robert Klaver (U.S. Geological Survey National Center for Earth Resources, Sioux Falls, S.D.) provided valuable satellite photos showing changes in pheasant wintering habitat associated with Lake Thompson and other large wetlands over the past several decades.

Mary Brashier provided editing assistance. We were also fortunate to retain the services of Terry Molengraaf (South Dakota State University) as our publication layout specialist.

We are appreciative of the many landowners who have worked to protect undisturbed grasslands, to protect and restore wetlands, and to otherwise support pheasants and pheasant habitat on their lands. We are also appreciative, as are thousands of hunters, of the many landowners who graciously allow hunting of pheasants on their land. Lastly, we recognize the role of hunters in supporting habitat programs and in sustaining the hunting tradition so important to the long-term conservation of wild ring-necked pheasants.

CONTENTS

FIGURES

PHOTOS

FOREWORD

Of all the places on earth where ring-necked pheasants have been successfully introduced, none has consistently produced pheasant populations and harvest levels that match those in South Dakota over the past 90 years. Memories of pheasant cocks crowing and strutting in the countryside, hunting dogs, pheasants flushing from the cover, rural landscapes, and of friends and friendships often come to mind. The birds provide a major economic stimulus to the state each fall and were designated as the state bird by the legislature in 1943, replacing the meadowlark, which already served as the state bird in several other states. Each year thousands of hunters, including residents and nonresidents, look forward to hunting pheasants in South Dakota. Those hunter numbers averaged 169,000/year for the recent period from 2003–2010.

For all of you who enjoy watching, hearing, and hunting the ring-necked pheasant, and especially for the many landowners that provide habitat for pheasants and other wildlife — this book is for you. If you have an interest in managing for wild pheasants or in hunting these birds, you will find this book filled with useful information. This information can help us understand and meet the many challenges that private and public land managers will continue to face in maintaining healthy pheasant populations in South Dakota and the upper Midwest.

In writing this book we wish to acknowledge those who have made substantial contributions to our knowledge of ring-necked pheasants in South Dakota. The multiple contributions from biologist Carl Trautman (deceased) are of particular note. His excellent book published in 1982 (History, ecology, and management of the ring-necked pheasant) includes information from most of the research that Carl and others conducted in South Dakota. Another dedicated researcher, Robert Dahlgren (deceased), also contributed multiple reports and journal articles on South Dakota's pheasant populations. Readers interested in these reports and those of several other pheasant researchers in South Dakota will find many of them listed in the Literature Cited section of this book.

Scientific names, acronyms, literature cited, measurements, and pheasant chick age

Scientific names other than for the ring-necked pheasant are not included in the text but are instead listed alongside common names in Appendix 1 in the back of the book. We use the term native (or indigenous) for species or peoples that were originally found in South Dakota prior to European settlement.

Common acronyms used throughout the text include those such as SDGFP (South Dakota Department of Game, Fish and Parks), U.S. (United States), CRP (Conservation Reserve Program), and USDA (U.S. Department of Agriculture). Several others are also used. We attempt to periodically use the full name along with the acronym the first time and where we feel it is helpful to remind readers of what the acronym means.

Literature cited in the text is listed in a single Literature Cited section in the back of the book.

Because of the intended audience we use English measurements commonly used in the United States. These include Avoirdupois pounds (1 pound = 0.45 kilograms), ounces (1 ounce =28.35 grams), inches (1 inch = 2.54 centimeters), feet (1 foot = 0.30 meters), yards (1 yard = 0.91 meters), and miles (1 mile = 1.61 kilometers).

Age estimates of chicks used in photo captions were approximations based on feather characteristics and size—the actual age of these wild birds was unknown.

PART I: HISTORICAL INFORMATION AND PHEASANT BASICS

CHAPTER 1
FROM FIRST PHEASANT RELEASES INTO THE 21ST CENTURY

South Dakota's status as the premier hunting destination for ring-necked pheasants (*Phasianus colchicus*) is no secret to avid upland game hunters. No other state or province in North America has had such a history of success in producing and harvesting wild ring-necked pheasants. However, reaching and maintaining that status has been and continues to be a long, interesting, and challenging journey. From early introduction efforts to the best pheasant hunting in the world, the ring-necked pheasant story in South Dakota is one that needs to be shared. Thousands of hunters from North America and from other parts of the world annually travel to this quiet, rural plains state in pursuit of ring-necked pheasants. The importance of South Dakota to ring-necked pheasant hunting and hunters is exemplified by the average of 1.7 million birds harvested annually from 2000–2010.

For ring-necked pheasant enthusiasts, the journey through time from the earliest introductions in South Dakota through changing agricultural practices, modified landscapes, and finally through the first decade of the 2000s can be most interesting and enlightening. The past tells us much about how to manage for pheasants and what to expect in the coming decades.

Introduction of ring-necked pheasants

The common pheasant is indigenous to much of Asia from China and Japan west to the Black Sea and possibly into parts of southeastern Europe (Trautman 1982:1–9). The many subspecies and strains of the common pheasant, when brought together, freely interbreed. Successful introduction of various strains of common pheasant into areas of western Europe, including England, occurred many centuries ago and followed the development of agriculture.

When common pheasants with the white neck ring (China and Mongolia) and without the white neck ring (southeast Europe, western Asia, and Japan) have hybridized, the white ring has become dominant in the resulting hybrids (Trautman 1982:3, 11).

Ring-necked pheasants in North America originated primarily from a mixture of common pheasants from Asia and hybrid pheasants from Europe, especially England. The first significant success occurred after pheasants from China were released in the Willamette Valley of Oregon in the late 19th century by Judge Owen Denny who had served as Consulate General in Shanghai (Trautman 1982:12). By 1910, pheasants from various Asian strains and English hybrids had been successfully introduced in most areas of North America with suitable agricultural landscapes and climate.

Most early releases in South Dakota were from wild birds obtained from previously established stocks in North America along with pheasants obtained from game farms (Trautman 1982:13–14). The first known release was near Sioux Falls as early as 1898 by a Dr. Zetlitz. Later, in 1908 and 1909, wild-captured pheasants of unknown origin were released by A. E. Cooper and E. L. Ebbert on their adjoining farms in Spink County near Doland. Some of the wild birds released in 1908 and 1909 are believed to be progenitors of wild populations established in Spink County. In 1911, the Department of Game and Fish as well as the Redfield Chamber of Commerce released substantial numbers of pheasants in Beadle and Spink counties that were also likely progenitors of later wild populations. Numbers of pheasants released in most early stocking efforts, where records are available, varied from only a few birds to several hundred (Trautman 1982:13–14). Sources of birds and pen-reared or wild status were not recorded in most cases.

Over the next several years, stocking efforts were continued and in 1919 the first South Dakota pheasant hunting season was implemented. The 1-day season was restricted to Spink County and allowed two roosters per hunter. The statewide pheasant population spread and increased rapidly over the next 25 years with the assistance of trapping and relocation. In recent years, relocation of pheasants has not occurred as wild pheasants can be found in virtually all areas of the state with suitable habitat (Photo 1-1).

Many of the early efforts and successes in introducing pheasants to South Dakota occurred in the James River corridor. Interestingly enough, this area still remains a stronghold for both pheasant production and hunter harvest. Details of the dates, number of birds, locations, and origin of birds for early introduction efforts are documented in Trautman (1982:13–14) and in the South Dakota Pheasant Management Plan (Switzer 2010).

Changes in farming practices
General landscape changes

A landscape can be thought of as a land area that includes the many land-use and habitat types in the general area or region. For example, the view of the coun-

Photo 1-1. Ed, Henry, and Wes Gehring found good pheasant hunting in Miner County near Howard around 1925. (Courtesy of South Dakota Agricultural Heritage Museum)

tryside east of Mitchell from a small airplane would be a landscape-level view. Such a view would include a mosaic of many square miles with croplands, grasslands, shelterbelts, wetlands, farmsteads, and other vegetation and land-use types.

Over the past century, farming methods, crops, and farming equipment have changed dramatically. So has the landscape (Photo 1-2). The primary pheasant range, which consists of eastern South Dakota and the counties in the south-central portion of the state, was once characterized by smaller fields with a diverse mixture of agricultural crops such as cereal grains (i.e., wheat, barley, oats), corn, hay, and pasture. Changes to the landscape primarily include larger

Photo 1-2. A powerful Case steam traction engine pulling three four-bottom plows and the horses pulling a disk in the background provide an image of changes coming to South Dakota's prairie landscape in the year 1900. (Courtesy of South Dakota Agricultural Heritage Museum)

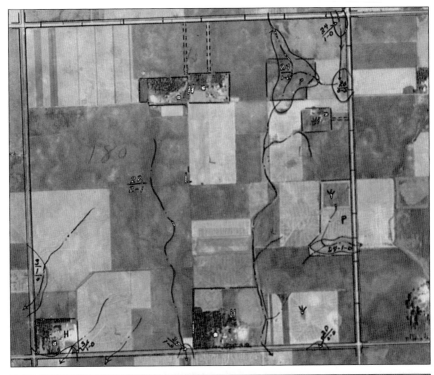

Figure 1-1. Section of land from Clay County, South Dakota (1937 top and 2008 bottom). Notice the difference in the number and size of fields.

fields (Figure 1-1), a predominance of row crops (especially in the eastern portion of the state), and more chemical weed control. Often included is loss of weedy fence lines, roadside cover, cover associated with small wetlands, and other small unfarmed areas important to pheasants. The quality of cover types important to pheasants also can change. For example, compared to 50 years ago, roadsides and alfalfa tend to be mowed earlier, and smooth bromegrass (or smooth brome) now crowds out valuable forbs in many grasslands and unfarmed edges or corners (i.e., roadsides, other unfarmed odd areas) (Vandel and Linder 1981).

Not only has the landscape changed to larger field sizes, the number of farms has declined by more than 50% statewide (Figure 1-2). In eastern South Dakota, agricultural fields near larger cities have increasingly been converted from production fields to urban development (Figure 1-3).

The response of pheasant populations to landscape changes has been well documented. The continued trend of increasingly larger fields and more acres planted to row crops is a concern as they both can lead to less suitable habitat and reduced pheasant production. Since 1900, the amount of land in oats, a once common crop that provided brood-rearing cover (Chapter 6), has dropped to almost nothing (Figure 1-4). Oats also provided safe nesting cover for late-nesting hens although the nest densities were relatively low (Baskett 1947). In contrast, since the mid to late 1970s row-crop acres for both corn and particularly soybeans (usually grouped with row crops) have continued to increase (National Agricultural Statistics Service 2010).

Wheat acreage in the state has remained relatively stable due to its ability to thrive in the drier portions of the pheasant range in central and western South Dakota. Winter wheat, a much better nesting cover than spring wheat because of earlier development, has increased in relation to spring wheat and may increase further as a crop in South Dakota in the future (Chapter 14). U.S. Department of Agriculture (USDA) land-retirement programs have also played a major role

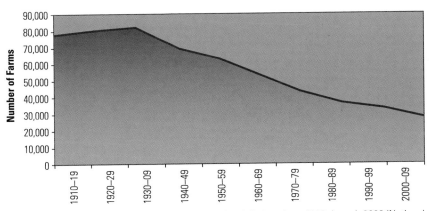

Figure 1-2. Average number of farms per decade in South Dakota from 1910 through 2009 (National Agricultural Statistics Services 2010).

Figure 1-3. Aerial view comparing the west side of Sioux Falls from 1940 (top) to 2008 (bottom). Notice the development and movement west, the addition of Interstate 29, and the change in the riparian habitat along the Big Sioux River.

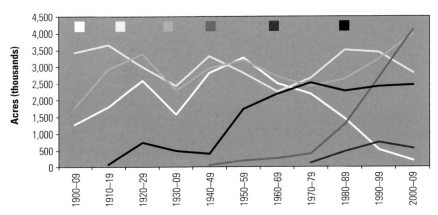

Figure 1-4. Average number of crop acreages (in thousands) per decade in South Dakota (National Agricultural Statistics Services 2010).

influencing pheasant populations through establishment of perennial herbaceous cover (grasses and forbs) on millions of acres of retired cropland under multi-year contracts with landowners (Bartmann 1969, Erickson and Wiebe 1973, Haroldson et al. 2006). Annual land-retirement programs through the USDA are of little value to pheasants and most other wildlife because they generally lack adequate herbaceous cover and are often mowed or plowed in mid summer (Harmon and Nelson 1973).

Equipment, herbicides, and land-use changes

Since the 1920s, hay and alfalfa have been a continuing and important component of farming in South Dakota. However, the method of harvesting hay and alfalfa has gone through major changes, particularly in the equipment used and the development of alfalfa varieties that enable earlier and multiple cuttings per season. From sickle mowers and small square bales to haybines and large bales, the evolution of larger and more efficient hay-harvesting machinery continues.

First cuttings of alfalfa are normally harvested by early bloom to provide the highest quality feed source. However, first cuttings often coincide with the period when the majority of pheasant hens are in the later stages of incubation, usually around late May to early June (Chapter 5). Nests are often destroyed and hens killed or injured due to contact with harvest equipment (Baxter and Wolfe 1973:22). Pheasant chicks, especially in the first 2 or 3 weeks post hatch, can also be killed by mowing equipment.

Many farmers are avid sportsmen themselves and are conscious of pheasant reproduction in alfalfa; these landowners sometimes delay their first cutting as long as possible to protect nesting pheasants. A few have gone so far as to use devices (flushing bars and/or suspended chains) to help reduce hen mortality by flushing hens off the nest before being caught in haying equipment. The success of flushing bars in protecting hen pheasants is better in years with lower mois-

Photo 1-3. A flushing bar with suspended chains may induce some nesting hens to escape before they are injured or killed by mowing equipment. Hen pheasants that flush before being hit by the mower will usually renest. (Courtesy of Chris Dekker)

ture when the hay is not as dense (Green 2011) (Photo 1-3).

Four-bottom plows and small seed drills for planting crops have been replaced by large seed drills and row-crop planters pulled by huge tractors guided by global positioning system (GPS) technology (Photos 1-4). With the larger, more efficient machinery one person can farm several thousand acres each year compared to several hundred just a few decades ago. However, larger equipment leads to landscape changes, particularly changes in field sizes, that can result in a loss of habitat for pheasants and other wildlife (Figures 1-1 and 1-3).

The rapid expansion of more sustainable no-till farming is becoming an

Photos 1-4. Even though the potential was there for much larger, more powerful tractors, small tractors (1959, inset 1948) and small farms remained the norm through the 1950s. In the ensuing years, much larger equipment and larger fields have had major influences on rural landscapes and availability of pheasant habitat. (Courtesy of South Dakota Agricultural Heritage Museum)

important factor influencing the landscape in South Dakota. No-till farming and resultant stubble and residual plant matter on the ground moderate soil temperatures and make it possible to grow winter wheat more successfully (by reducing winter kill) in South Dakota, as explained in Chapter 14. Winter wheat and tall wheat stubble (>15 inches) are both positive additions for pheasants.

Equipment changes will continue to be accompanied by genetic changes in crop seeds. Corn that ripens in a shorter growing season and drought-resistant corn and soybeans are genetic changes that can influence crop distribution. Drought resistance is one factor associated with expansion of soybeans into more xeric (drier) central regions of South Dakota.

Herbicide-resistant corn and soybeans have also resulted in significant agricultural and habitat changes. Fields planted with herbicide-resistant row crops can reduce or eliminate the amount of mechanical cultivation needed to control weeds. While reduction of mechanical cultivation has several positives for soil and water, the heavy use of herbicides on herbicide-resistant crops results in "clean" fields and virtually eliminates annual weeds. Removal of annual weeds in crops and on cropland edges further reduces cover and food sources, especially for pheasant chicks.

Unfortunately for wildlife, herbicide-resistant crops have also provided the means to rapidly convert grassland habitat into agricultural production land. Sod can be treated with Roundup® or similar non-selective herbicides in the fall and planted directly the following spring without tilling the soil (Photo 1-5). The perfection of this method along with unintended effects of federal crop subsidies is leading to increased loss of grassland nesting and brood-rearing cover for pheasants as well as for valuable native wildlife species such as sharp-tailed grouse and greater prairie-chickens. Much of this grassland being converted to cropland was once considered marginal soil unsuitable for cropping.

Photo 1-5. This former grassland (nesting and brood cover) was treated with a nonselective herbicide in the fall and planted directly to sunflowers in the following spring. Unfortunately, crops such as sunflowers, soybeans, and corn are seldom used for nesting by pheasants, grouse, or other ground-nesting birds. (TRK)

Historical highlights—changes in habitat and pheasant populations

Since the initial efforts to establish pheasants in South Dakota, nothing has had a more significant influence on pheasant population increases and decreases than landscape-level habitat changes. Habitat is the foundation that supports regional and local pheasant populations. Smaller, local efforts to improve cover are important and do make a difference. However, since World War II, the highest pheasant populations have always been associated with major landscape changes that are heavily influenced by national agricultural policies. Such policies establish large acreages of high quality, undisturbed herbaceous cover for nesting and brood rearing through federal land-retirement programs (Photo 1-6).

Obvious peaks and valleys have been recorded in South Dakota's pheasant populations since the 1920s (Figure 1-5). It is no surprise that the peaks coincided with four specific eras that featured landscape-level increases in pheasant cover: the Great Depression of the 1930s, World War II in the early to mid 1940s, the Soil Bank Era of the late 1950s and early 1960s, and most recently the Conservation Reserve Program (CRP) beginning in 1986 and continuing through publication of this book (2012).

The 1930s were difficult economic times, both nationally and in South Dakota. However, the inability to produce crops due to prolonged drought conditions and the tough economic atmosphere resulted in good habitat conditions for pheasants. Idle farmland, low-intensity farming, and a subsidized federal farm-retirement program resulted in high quality cover for pheasant populations (Trautman 1982:59). Scarcity of pooled or running water (water bodies) for pheasant use did not deter population growth in this abundant cover (Trautman

Photo 1-6. South Dakota's ring-necked pheasant populations have been most impressive in periods when undisturbed herbaceous cover has been well distributed across the landscape. (Courtesy of Doug Backlund)

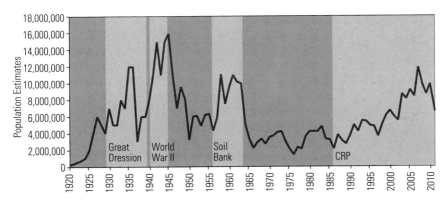

Figure 1-5. Preseason population estimates of South Dakota's pheasant population. Landscape-level increases and improvements in pheasant habitat during the Great Depression, World War II, the Soil Bank, and the Conservation Reserve Program played a primary role in population explosions (see Chapter 12 and Appendix 2 for survey information used in estimate).

1982:58). Once the persistent drought broke, much of the idle farmland went back into production. Loss of this idle farmland, coupled with a hard winter (1936–1937), led to a major decline in pheasant numbers (Figure 1-5).

A few years later, landscape changes associated with World War II again positively affected pheasant populations. With men going to war and women entering the workforce, much farmland remained idle. Provided with good cover and favorable weather, pheasant populations increased rapidly and again reached extremely high levels by the mid 1940s. In fact, population estimates in the mid 1940s reached all-time highs, somewhere in the range of 16 to 17 million birds (Figure 1-5). However, as in the 1930s, bird numbers began to drop dramatically around 1946 to a level less than one-third that of the all-time high of just a few years earlier (Photo 1-7).

A short decade later pheasant populations again responded to a significant landscape habitat program called the federal Conservation Reserve Program, better known as the Soil Bank (1956 Soil Bank Act). During the late 1950s, farmers could enroll agricultural land into the USDA Soil Bank Program that created hundreds of thousands of acres of idle grass, legumes, or grassland-legume habitat (Dahlgren 1962). At its highest level in 1961, South Dakota had just over 1.8 million acres of Soil Bank (Trautman 1982:101). The undisturbed habitat mixed within agricultural land provided ideal conditions for pheasant populations to explode, reaching levels of over 11 million birds (Photo 1-8). The Soil Bank program demonstrated that a federal conservation program could be implemented at a landscape level, providing benefits to landowners and wildlife alike (Bartmann 1969, Erickson and Wiebe 1973).

After loss of undisturbed herbaceous cover from the Soil Bank Program, legislation was passed creating another multi-year land-retirement program called the Cropland Adjustment Program (1965 Food and Agriculture Act).

Photo 1-7. These hunters came each year from Indiana to hunt pheasants near Columbia (northeast of Aberdeen) and to stay at Daly Corners (owned by Dick Daly) in the 1940s. (Courtesy of the South Dakota Agricultural Heritage Museum)

Photo 1-8. Undisturbed herbaceous cover associated with the Soil Bank years produced phenomenal numbers of pheasants. In this 1958 photo near Colman, Robert V. Lee (foreground) stands by his 1950 Chevy pickup with Ben Bishman in the background. (Courtesy of the South Dakota Agricultural Heritage Museum)

Unfortunately, due to inadequate funding, this program influenced only limited acreage in South Dakota and had minimal influence on the pheasant population when compared to the Soil Bank Program (Trautman 1982:101).

With the loss of undisturbed herbaceous cover on retired farmland and increases in farming intensity, pheasant populations declined to much lower levels, reaching estimated preseason populations near 2 million birds in the mid

1970s. Losses of pheasant habitat throughout the Midwest were spurred by a massive grain deal with the former Soviet Union in 1973, high prices on grain, and encouragement of "fence row to fence row" farming; unfortunately, the fence rows and much additional pheasant habitat were often removed or tilled to make larger fields (Rodgers 2005). Pheasant populations in South Dakota during this period were the lowest since the birds became strongly established in the 1920s. Within a decade, a new USDA program would again establish extensive herbaceous cover on retired cropland.

In 1986, the federal Farm Bill added the most recent USDA Conservation Reserve Program (CRP), a program in decline after 2007 but still operational and with new sign-up opportunities as of publication of this book (2012). During the first 10 years, much of the CRP was established in western South Dakota. Contracts were awarded to private landowners on the basis of an Environmental Benefits Index (EBI) that ranked applications on projected conservation values such as reduced soil erosion, improved water quality, and wildlife habitat. In 1996 the Environmental Benefits Index (EBI) ranking was modified and a shift in CRP enrollments moved from the western to the eastern part of the state, the traditional stronghold of the state's pheasant population. Accompanied by a string of mild, open winters between 2003 and 2008 and good nesting and brood-rearing conditions, pheasant numbers reached levels comparable to those experienced during the Soil Bank at approximately 12 million birds (Figure 1-5) (South Dakota Game, Fish and Parks, unpublished data).

Like the earlier program popularly known as the Soil Bank, the current CRP program is a voluntary conservation program that allows landowners to take highly erodible land out of production and place it into idle conservation land (Photo 1-9). Peak enrollment in the most recent CRP for South Dakota was the same as for the earlier Soil Bank at about 1.8 million acres. Pheasants as well as sharp-tailed grouse, greater prairie-chickens, and a number of other wildlife species benefited from this addition of extensive and long-term herbaceous cover to the landscape. Like the previous three time periods of high pheasant numbers, undisturbed habitat at a landscape level provided the conditions for the prolific ring-necked pheasant to respond.

Early 2000s—where we stand

For most pheasant hunters, the first decade of the 21st century was nothing short of phenomenal. The habitat established on a landscape level, largely due to the Conservation Reserve Program (CRP), was the cornerstone supporting the good reproduction responsible for impressive pheasant populations. It should be cautioned that since the fall of 2007, as contracts began expiring, hundreds of thousands of acres of CRP grasslands have been converted to cropland and rapid losses of this excellent pheasant habitat may continue. These losses will only be partially offset by new enrollments for CRP or similar land retirement programs (Chapter 15).

Photo 1-9. The Conservation Reserve Program added a variety of perennial grass cover (forbs may be included) such as this field of intermediate wheatgrass to former croplands across the South Dakota landscape, providing abundant nesting, brood rearing, and other seasonal cover on private lands. (LDF)

Pheasant populations in South Dakota are tracked by three main methods: August roadside brood surveys, harvest estimates, and preseason population estimates (Chapter 12).

Although there are annual fluctuations in pheasant numbers, the overall trend from 2000 through 2007 was upward. Most impressively, the pheasants per mile index (PPM) for 2007 and 2008 (7.9 and 8.6 respectively) were the highest since those experienced in 1958, 1961, and 1963 during the Soil Bank era (Figure 1-6). The PPM index reflects the results of brood counts along with counts of hens and roosters that are seen along the brood survey routes. An example of how the PPM index is calculated is provided in Chapter 12.

There may be no better indicator of a pheasant population than harvest statistics. Not surprisingly, harvest data during the 2000s depict trends similar to those of the population estimates (Figure 1-7).

A color-coded map of brood survey data provides an intriguing way to visualize the spatial distribution of pheasant abundance in South Dakota in recent years (Figure 1-8). The James River corridor and south-central South Dakota are clearly areas with some of the highest pheasant populations. Similarly, counties with high average harvest numbers reflect those areas with strong pheasant numbers as indicated by brood surveys (Figures 1-8, 1-9).

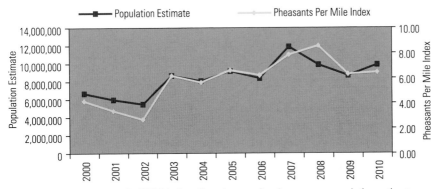

Figure 1-6. Pheasants per mile (PPM) indices (brood surveys) and preseason population estimates during a period (2000–2010) of abundant habitat and predominately favorable weather in South Dakota.

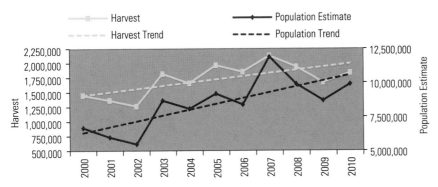

Figure 1-7. Preseason population estimates and harvest trends during a period of pheasant abundance from 2000-2010 in South Dakota.

Chapter thoughts

Many of us have wonderful memories of pheasant hunting, friends, and related happenings in beautiful and expansive South Dakota. While the introduction and history of this exotic bird in South Dakota has been a monumental success, pheasant populations have fluctuated with major peaks and valleys closely associated with landscape-level changes in farm size, cropping practices, and availability of permanent herbaceous cover for reproduction and other needs. The abundance of pheasants and hunting opportunities in the future will continue to depend primarily on the availability of nesting, brood rearing, and other seasonal habitats on a landscape level. As each of the authors can enthusiastically attest, pheasant numbers and pheasant hunting remain excellent in much of South Dakota's pheasant range as of the writing of this book.

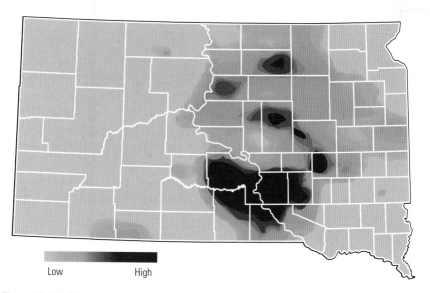

Figure 1-8. This "thunderstorm map" provides a visual of distribution and abundance of pheasants in South Dakota during a recent period of pheasant abundance from 2000 through 2009 based on brood survey data (PPM). Due to differences in habitat quality, local areas may support pheasant populations higher or lower than those shown.

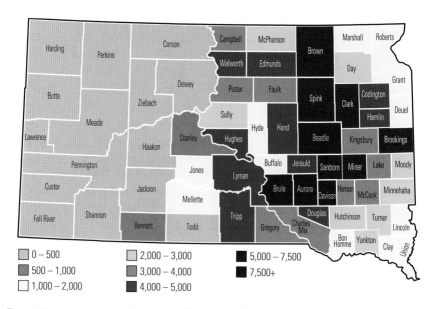

Figure 1-9. Average pheasant harvest per 100 square miles for each county in South Dakota during a recent period of pheasant abundance from 2000 through 2010.

CHAPTER 2
PHEASANT BIOLOGY: A FEW BASICS

Many questions and discussions arise related to the biology and ecology of the ring-necked pheasant. Hunters and landowners are often interested in determining the age of harvested roosters as a means of estimating reproductive success during the spring and summer. Others may ask: At what age do roosters get their full coloration? How much do hens and roosters weigh? How far do pheasants move to winter cover? We address these questions and several others in this chapter. Major topics related to pheasant biology and ecology such as male breeding territories, feeding, nesting, and brood rearing are discussed in later chapters.

Age terminology

When referring to age we have defined chicks and juveniles in the same manner as used for grouse (Connelly et al. 2003). Age terminology used in this book is defined as follows:

Chicks: Young pheasants from hatch to 10 weeks of age.

Juveniles: Pheasants from 10 weeks of age until the following breeding season. The term juvenal ("al" suffix) is used for plumage, not as an age category.

Adolescents: A general term for mid to late stage chicks and early stage juveniles. For example, 7–12-week-old pheasants would be adolescents.

Yearlings: Pheasants during their first breeding season (spring and summer following previous year's hatch). In most cases, as in the literature, we have grouped yearlings with adults.

Adults: Pheasants reaching their first breeding season or older. Some authors may separate yearlings from adults.

Sequence of molts and plumages

Pheasants have a relatively simple sequence of molts and plumages. Chicks hatch with a covering of wet natal down that soon dries to a fluffy covering (Photo 2-1). Natal down provides the primary insulation for the chick into the second week of life but is quite inadequate without regular protection from the hen at night and during other cold, wet periods (Chapter 6).

By 2 weeks of age chicks are losing their downy appearance (Westerskov 1957). The natal down is lost in the prejuvenal molt (sometimes called post natal molt) and almost fully replaced with hen-like juvenal plumage (note "al" suffix used for plumage stage) by about 6 weeks. The early replacement of natal down with juvenal plumage is even evident at hatch when several flight feathers (remiges) are beginning to emerge (Westerskov 1957) (Photo 2-2).

Photo 2-1. Note the plumage (natal down) of this chick that probably hatched less than 12 hours earlier. The remnant of the egg tooth used to help break the eggshell at hatch is still visible at the end of the upper mandible (beak). (Courtesy of Josh Jensen)

Photo 2-2. Between 2 and 3 weeks of age chicks still have downy heads; considerable down still showing on the breast, belly, and legs; and short tails. Juvenal plumage is rapidly replacing the natal down. (Courtesy of Scott Weins)

For chicks older than 6 weeks and in juveniles and adults, the visible plumage on the surface of the bird is composed of contour feathers. Contour feathers have a main shaft and interlocking side branches (barbs) and can vary in size and shape from small feathers on the back, breast, and top of the head to the large flight feathers (remiges) on the wing and the unusually long and pointed tail feathers (rectrices) (Photos 2-3, 2-4).

The drab juvenal plumage is of short duration and is replaced in the first prebasic molt (sometimes called post juvenal molt) which begins while the chicks are still just getting their juvenal plumage. Juvenal plumage is gradually replaced with the first basic plumage (sometimes called adult plumage) by early to mid fall. The replacement of juvenal plumage involves a complete molt, including the sequential replacement of all flight feathers. Pheasants do not lose their flight capabilities during molt.

Photo 2-3. By roughly 5 weeks chicks are nearly covered by juvenal contour feathers and their tails reach about 3 inches in length. (Courtesy of Scott Weins)

Photo 2-4. These pheasant chicks are around 8 to 9 weeks. Both chicks are beginning to show distinctive male coloration on the neck and breast plus the development of what will become attractive red wattles around the eyes. (Courtesy of Doug Backlund)

The juvenile hens' first basic plumage is an attractive but subdued tannish (mottled) brown with some chestnut in the neck, back, and other areas. Juvenile males obtain most of their colorful first basic plumage by 16–18 weeks of age and have the same general appearance as adults; however, the outermost flight feather (primary 10) is not fully grown until 24 weeks (Westerskov 1957). The first basic plumage is sometimes called adult plumage but, as described above, it is obtained by juveniles during their first fall (Photos 2-5, 2-6).

The first basic plumage in adult males is replaced by the almost identical definitive basic plumage during the second prebasic molt. The second prebasic molt and replacement with definitive basic plumage begin in June for males and last about 3–4 months (Giudice and Ratti 2001). Molting is heaviest in July and August. Cock pheasants with short tail feathers in late summer may have molted the rectrices.

Photo 2-5. The colorful red skin and wattle around the eye (orbital region) and the initial replacement of juvenal plumage with the more striking colors of the 1st basic plumage are evident by the time males reach 10 to 12 weeks of age. (Courtesy of Scott Weins)

Photo 2-6. Juvenile males show the greenish black and mottled neck and head, prominent red wattles, pinnae, and other characteristics of the 1st basic plumage by around 12 to 13 weeks of age. (Courtesy of Scott Weins)

Annual molting in the adult hen is delayed due to energy requirements for nesting until after the young hatch or the unsuccessful female abandons her nesting efforts for the year. The second prebasic molt and replacement with definitive basic plumage in hens take place over about a 3-month period. Both the cocks and hens continue this same molt pattern (prebasic molt) each year through the remainder of their relatively short lives, remaining in one plumage (basic plumage) throughout the year (Photo 2-7).

Although there are some small differences in colors and shapes of a few feathers, the differences between first basic plumage and the definitive basic plumage, even in males, is not readily apparent (Photo 2-8).

Photo 2-7. This hen is in either 1st basic plumage or definitive basic plumage; they are very similar. Note that even hens have some red on the bare skin around the eyes (orbital area). Also, note the attractive chestnut colors and dark markings worked into a tannish gray background. (Courtesy of Scott Weins)

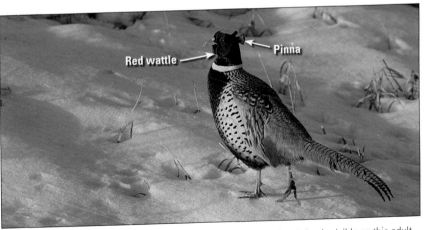

Photo 2-8. The pinnae and colorful red wattles are well developed and clearly visible on this adult cock pheasant during the courtship period starting in late winter. (Courtesy of Scott Weins)

A few specifics on feathers and function

Beneath the contour feathers on the surface of the body are down-like feathers needed for insulation. These down-like feathers include the common afterfeathers branching from the base of many larger feathers as well as other down-like plumage. If you pull out a few contour feathers from the belly you will note the presence of an afterfeather branching off from the base — the insulative value is obvious.

Contour feathers may have more specific names based on their size, shape, and function. For example, the secondaries and primaries are large, stiff contour feathers on the wing that are essential for flight (Photo 2-9). The secondaries arise between the elbow and wrist of the wing while the primaries, 10 in number, arise from beyond the wrist. The small contour feathers overlying or anterior to the flight feathers both on the top (dorsal) of the wing and underneath (ventral) are called coverts and have various names such as greater secondary coverts, greater primary coverts, or lesser secondary coverts.

The pointed tail of a pheasant is made up of long rectrices near the center with progressively shorter rectrices on the sides and is especially attractive in males. Even hen pheasants have relatively long tail feathers compared to most birds. The rectrices of males are important in courtship and threat displays (Chapter 4). The rectrices are also important in steering the bird and helping soften and slow the landing, acting similar to the wing flaps on an airplane.

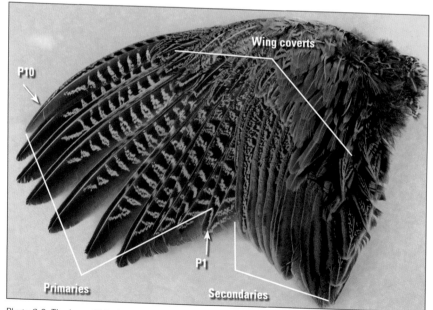

Photo 2-9. The large flight feathers (remiges) include the primaries on the outer or hand portion of the wing and the secondaries of the forearm portion of the wing. The primaries are numbered from primary 1 (P1) closest to the body (most proximal) to primary 10 (most distal). The overlying smaller feathers are coverts of various types. (LDF)

Age determination: are they juveniles or adults?

In the fall, ring-necked pheasant males can be separated into juvenile and adult categories, but mistakes are easily made on some birds. Hunters and landowners are understandably interested in determining the number of young versus adult pheasants they have harvested, both as a means of evaluating that year's reproduction and for cooking (culinary) purposes.

Bursa of Fabricius

Measurement of bursa depth is the most accurate method to determine age category in harvested pheasants but is seldom used by hunters because of the difficulty in initially locating the bursa (Photo 2-10). Juvenile and adult pheasants in the fall through mid winter can be accurately separated by measuring the depth of the Bursa of Fabricius (bursa). The bursa is located on the upper wall (dorsally) of the cloaca (chamber receiving waste and reproductive material) near the anal opening; the bursa is involved in antibody production and fighting infections. During October through December the bursa in juveniles is likely to be over a half inch and often about 0.7–0.9 inch in depth (Kirkpatrick 1944; L.D. Flake, unpublished data). Adults have a bursa generally less than 0.25 inch in depth, much shallower than that of juveniles.

The unfeathered base of a flight feather plucked from the wing is handy and can be used to probe the bursa by bending the tail back and exposing the anus. The V- or U-shaped opening of the bursa can be difficult to locate, and assistance from a biologist can be helpful until you learn the technique.

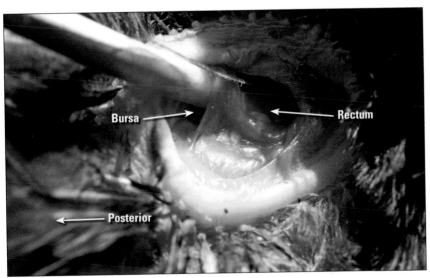

Photo 2-10. The depth of the bursa of Fabricius is reduced from around 0.7-0.9 inches in a young juvenile to only about 0.25 inches or less in pheasants surviving to the following breeding season. Here, the bare end of a feather (handy in the field) is used to probe the bursa to determine the age. The tail of the bird (posterior) is oriented towards the bottom left. (LDF)

A major source of error with this method is the incorrect identification of the bursa. Be careful not to thrust the feather shaft through the wall of the bursa. Biologists recommend use of a more rounded probe to reduce this problem, but such a probe is usually not as readily available as a flight feather. If you can accurately determine age, it can be interesting to record the bursa depth and attach this to the lower leg with a label so it can be compared with spur length and appearance.

Spurs

Early in the hunting season into about mid November, adults with long, dark (usually), and impressively pointed spurs can be easily distinguished from juveniles that have shorter, cone-shaped, sometimes whitish spurs, even though a few birds with intermediate spur characteristics may be aged incorrectly (Robertson 1997:131) (Photos 2-11). By mid fall, spurs on older juveniles can be quite long and black although they are usually still identifiable by the cone shape. Spurs become more difficult to use and are less reliable for aging later in the fall and into winter as the juveniles mature (Gates 1966b).

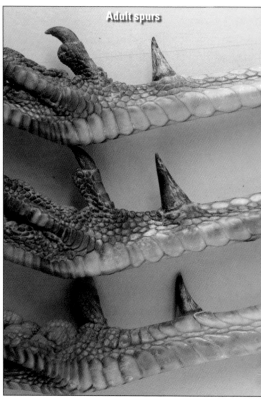

Photos 2-11. Juvenile spurs (left) from cock pheasants are generally shorter and more cone shaped while adult spurs (right) are longer, more streamlined, and less cone shaped. By mid to late season spurs of intermediate characteristics increasingly cause errors in the use of spurs for aging. (LDF)

Lower mandible (jaw)

Juvenile or adult status in pheasants can generally be determined until about mid November by the strength of the lower mandible, which grows progressively stronger as juveniles mature during the hunting season (Photos 2-12). If the dead rooster is held by the tip of the lower bill and lightly shaken, the bill generally bends or breaks in juveniles but remains rigid and holds up the body weight in adults (Robertson 1997:131). When tested on approximately 40 harvested pheasants between November 1 and November 12, only one older juvenile mandible (also aged by bursa depth) was able to hold up the body weight of the harvested rooster without noticeably bending or breaking. The lower mandibles (jaws) of all adults were strong enough to hold up the body weight (L.D. Flake, unpublished data).

Plumage

For roosters hatched later in the summer, age identification based on plumage early in the hunting season is not a problem because they have only partially replaced the drab juvenal plumage. However, juvenile males hatched earlier in the reproductive season can be around 18–20 weeks of age by early November, an age by which they are almost completely into their first basic plumage. Many hunters incorrectly assume that any fully colored male is an adult. Plumage coloration is not an accurate method for determining age in fall-harvested pheasants unless the juveniles are still showing and replacing juvenal plumage.

Pheasants generally replace all of their juvenal primaries by the first fall so the difference in shape of the outer two primaries (P9 and P10) cannot be used to estimate age as is done with grouse, wild turkeys, and most other galliform birds.

Photos 2-12. From the pheasant opener until about mid November almost all juveniles can be distinguished from adults based on the considerable flexibility (left) of the lower mandible (beak). The mandible remains rigid in adults (right) or juveniles later in the hunting season. (LDF)

The shape of some of the larger wing coverts in first basic plumage tends to be narrower and shorter than those in older males in definitive basic plumage, but these differences are difficult to recognize (Giudice and Ratti 2001). The appearance (shape and size) of primary 1 (P1; count in 10 primaries from the outermost primary) can be used for separating most juveniles from adults in both males and females (Robertson 1997:131). There is some error due to overlap in length and shaft diameter of P1 between juveniles and adults (Wishart 1969, Greenberg et al. 1972). Sequential molt and replacement of juvenal primaries with first basic primaries through summer and early fall is sometimes used by biologists to estimate age in weeks of older chicks and juvenile pheasants (Johnsgard 1986:23).

Although unusually long tail feathers may be associated with 2-year-old or older roosters, this approach has not been shown to be dependable for aging pheasants. You may want to collect the longest rectrices along with the spur on a number of roosters to make your own observations.

Growth and weight

The published weights of pheasant chicks at hatch are generally around 0.7 to 0.8 ounces with males averaging only slightly more than females. Pheasant chicks grow rapidly and approach adult size at about 20 weeks of age. Chick weights increase most rapidly from the first to the second week (61% increase) and from the second to third week (67% increase) (Westerskov 1957). Between 42 and 138 days post hatch the weight of both sexes increases approximately fourfold (Kirkpatrick 1944). By the time chicks have reached full weight at around 24 weeks, males have increased their weight from hatch by roughly 6,000%, females around 5,000%. Voracious and persistent feeding is obviously needed for this type of growth.

The average weight of 177 hens captured in January, February, and March (1999–2001) in Beadle County, South Dakota, was 2.1 pounds. Weights of juvenile and adult hens were similar (A.P. Leif, unpublished data). Weights of 39 juvenile cocks in this same area averaged 2.7 pounds, while 44 adult males weighed an average of 2.9 pounds. Studies in other regions of North America indicate weights of hen pheasants often fall between 1.9 and 2.3 pounds, while males are generally just under 3 pounds (Edwards et al. 1964, Snyder 1985) (Photo 2-13).

Weights of both male and female adults tend to peak in mid to late fall or early winter. Weights of hens peak again in mid to late spring and males have a second peak in weight around late winter or early spring (Havasi 1992). Adult males generally reach their lowest weights in mid winter. It is not unusual for pheasants to gain weight from mid winter to spring if the winter is not severe (Edwards et al. 1964, Gates and Woehler 1968); they can also lose weight during this period in severe winters. Adults of both genders normally lose weight by mid summer due to the energy demands of reproductive activities (Edwards et al. 1964, Havasi 1992).

Photo 2-13. Pheasant weights can vary throughout the year, but generally mature hens weigh a little over 2 pounds and roosters just under 3 pounds. (Courtesy of Doug Backlund)

Seasonal movements

Movements of pheasants are usually studied using small radio transmitters that enable researchers to periodically determine the location of an animal from data collected with a directional antenna and radio receiver along with triangulation procedures. Transmitters and antennas weighing less than 3% of the bird are usually placed around the neck on adult pheasants (necklace mount) (Photo 2-14). On pheasant chicks, transmitters (along with antennas) the size of small coins are either sutured to or implanted under the skin (subcutaneous implants) on the back.

Ring-necked pheasants make only minimal seasonal movements if they can find food and cover near habitats used during the breeding season. Female ring-necked pheasants made cumulative directional movements to winter cover that averaged 0.7 miles in southeastern Wisconsin (Gatti et al. 1989). However, if necessary, pheasant hens will move 2 to 3 miles to find secure wetland or woody cover in severe winters (Gabbert et al. 1999).

There is a tendency for juvenile hens to move farther to winter cover than adult hens (Gatti et al. 1989, Homan et al. 2000). Longer dispersal distances in the young, a behavior found in many species, may benefit the species by reducing

Photo 2-14. Hen pheasants with necklace mounted radio transmitters can be closely monitored during key periods such as prenesting, nesting, and brood rearing. (Courtesy of Brian Pauly)

inbreeding and even colonizing new areas. These increased seasonal movements resulted in increased losses of juvenile hens to predation during late fall and winter (Gatti et al. 1989). Once pheasants reach good winter cover along with nearby food plots, waste grains, or unharvested crops, daily movements tend to remain quite limited (Gatti et al. 1989, Gabbert et al. 1999).

In Iowa, 70 to 83% of pheasants (both sexes) dispersed during spring from their wintering area into surrounding farmland, with remaining birds breeding on the wintering area. Distances moved from wintering areas by spring-dispersing hens and roosters averaged 1.4 miles during 2 years with the most adventuresome birds generally dispersing no more than 4 to 5 miles (Weston 1954). Spring dispersal of cock pheasants from wintering areas to breeding areas in South Dakota is discussed further in Chapter 4.

Home range

Biologists refer to the area used on a regular basis by an individual or flock as a home range. Rooster home ranges were studied in east-central South Dakota during the breeding period when they were on territories from mid March to mid June and are reported in Chapter 4. These home ranges of cock pheasants were markedly less than a quarter section (160 acres). The period with the least movement by hens is during incubation, especially close to hatch (Photo 2-15). During nesting, hens in eastern South Dakota confined their overall home ranges

Photo 2-15. Hen pheasants have smaller home ranges during nesting than in the remainder of the year, especially during late incubation when they typically confine activities to an area of less than 2 to 3 acres. (Courtesy of Scott Weins)

to areas of 20 to 52 acres (Kuck et al. 1970). Mobility declines greatly as incubation progresses and it is not unusual for incubating hens close to hatching to confine their nest recess (temporarily leaving the nest) movements to a home range area of 2 to 3 acres, less than the combined playing surface of three American football fields (Hanson and Progulske 1973). Movements of brood hens and broods are discussed in Chapter 6.

Most home range estimates for hens in fall and winter in Wisconsin fell between 42 and 156 acres (Gatti et al. 1989), while winter home ranges were generally less than 62 acres in southeastern North Dakota (Homan et al. 2000). Even outside of the breeding season, the distance hens move from the core of their home range (activity radius) during daily activities is generally less than one-third mile (Hanson and Progulske 1973). The core of the home range is an area of heavy use where the pheasants spend over half of their time.

Home ranges of pheasants are of various shapes and sizes to take advantage of needed resources such as cover for loafing and night roosting, food sources, protection from wind and snow, nesting, and other needs. Home range estimates increase if they are estimated for a longer time span. For example, as noted earlier, home ranges for broods during the entire brood-rearing period of 10 weeks is much larger than weekly estimates of home range because they include shifts to new areas as they grow older. Pheasant home ranges seem quite limited in size when you consider the actual area available to the birds.

Chapter thoughts

It is enjoyable and often of practical value to learn more about pheasants in relation to aspects of their biology such as age, plumage, weight, and mobility. In this chapter we have provided, through text and photos, specific information on several aspects of pheasant biology not covered in other chapters. The more you know about pheasant biology, the more you will enjoy watching and hunting these birds. Some of this information, particularly an understanding of movements and home ranges, is also important for managing pheasants.

PART II: PHEASANTS THROUGH THE YEAR

CHAPTER 3
NUTRITIONAL NEEDS

Food resources and general nutrition influence pheasant body condition, survival, and reproduction. Pheasant food habits have been well documented in a number of studies and show the broad adaptability of these birds. In North America as well as in Europe and Asia, waste grains from agricultural crops are important to pheasant populations throughout much of the year. Specific waste grains that pheasants use are related to availability. Other foods commonly eaten include weed seeds, leaves of forbs and grasses, berries or other fruits, and insects (Photos 3-1). Pheasants also consume small pebbles, soil particles, and other grit to assist grinding action in the gizzard and as a source of calcium and magnesium, particularly during the egg-laying period.

Photos 3-1. Pheasants, behaving almost like sharp-tailed grouse (inset), will occasionally feed on berries in shrubs or trees such as this Russian olive. (Courtesy of Doug Backlund, inset courtesy of Scott Weins)

We review the general food, water, and grit requirements of ring-necked pheasants as well as the more specific needs of hens during the reproductive period and of chicks during the first few weeks of life.

Water

Pheasants are sometimes attracted to open water sources or the lush habitat associated with them, but actual drinking water does not appear to be crucial to their survival and success in most cases (Photo 3-2). Pheasants will use open water from various sources but can normally obtain their water needs from dew, insects, fruits, and succulent leaves. Snow and moisture from grain kernels and wild seeds suffice for winter needs. During hot, dry years in the early 1930s, volunteer herbaceous habitat on idle farmland was abundant and open water sources were extremely scarce, yet huge numbers of pheasants thrived on these hot, dry lands (Trautman 1982:58–59).

Food needs—first weeks post hatch

The diet of pheasant chicks through their first 4 weeks of life requires more insect protein than that of older chicks, juveniles, and adults (Photo 3-3). Older chicks transition from this early dependence on insects to a diet dominated by seeds and leafy material. The need for a high protein diet during the early weeks of life is satisfied by feeding heavily on a variety of insects along with some small

Photo 3-2. Pheasants will drink from water bodies but they normally get all the water they need from succulent insects, dew, and plant parts. Pheasants are attracted to the herbaceous cover associated with wetlands. (Courtesy of Doug Backlund)

Photo 3-3. These newly hatched pheasant chicks will soon follow the brood hen from the nest to brood-rearing habitat where they must be able to find abundant insects for food. (Courtesy of Josh Jensen)

invertebrates such as spiders and sow bugs (Trautman 1982: 54, Hill 1985). For brevity through the text, we often just refer to insects since they greatly dominate the diet.

Pheasant chicks are precocial at hatch, meaning they exit the egg with open eyes, well-developed legs, and covered with down. Chicks imprint on the hen as a parental object (filial imprinting) and must follow the hen to sites with abundant food when she leads them away from the nest (Chapter 6). The down-covered young do not need training from the female to recognize insects or other food sources. Their quick reflexes are readily evident as they dart about, seizing and eating small prey such as leafhoppers, small beetles, insect larvae, immature grasshoppers, various flies, ants, spiders, and other small invertebrates (Trautman 1982:54, Hill 1985, Whitmore et al. 1986). Chicks in the first few weeks post hatch show a preference for the largest insects they can ingest. Insects less than 0.12 inches in diameter are seldom eaten (Whitmore et al. 1986) (Photo 3-4).

Grass-forb cover, field edges, marsh edges, alfalfa fields, weed patches, and other vegetation types that support abundant insects are critical habitat for these young broods. In Illinois, broods hatched in landscapes with varied farming practices (smaller fields, more diverse crop plantings, and more edge) had smaller home ranges (areas of daily movement) than those hatched in more monotypic farmland dominated by large fields such as corn and soybeans (Warner 1984).

Photo 3-4. Good pheasant brood habitat in the first few weeks post hatch must have an abundance of food for chicks. Such areas usually have a mixture of grasses and forbs along with a relatively open understory for chick movement. (Courtesy of Matt Grunig)

Broods have to work harder and move greater distances to find food in more monotypic farmland, exposing themselves to greater dangers and higher mortality. Row crops sprayed for insects and/or weeds, especially if in large fields with minimal edge habitat, are generally rather sterile habitats of minimal value to young pheasant broods (Photo 3-5). Research in England showed that broods with smaller home ranges had better survival than those with larger home ranges; the authors suggested that availability of adequate insect food sources enabled brood hens to rear the young within a smaller area (Hill 1985).

Brood habitat with abundant insects for chicks clearly has a positive influence on chick survival in the first few weeks post hatch. Lack of adequate protein in the diet during the first 3 weeks post hatch may have persistent physical effects on pheasants as adults (Ohlsson and Smith 2001). Low protein in the diet of male chicks causes them to develop smaller and less colorful wattles and likely reduces their ability to compete for territories and females (Ohlsson et al. 2001).

General food habits of juveniles and adults

Juvenile (10 weeks until following breeding season) and adult pheasants eat a wide variety of plant foods along with some insects (Swenk 1930; Fried 1940; Trautman 1952, 1982:55). In most pheasant populations, agricultural waste grains (or seeds) such as corn, sorghum, wheat, oats, sunflowers, and soybeans make up over 70% (by dry weight) of the food eaten annually (Photo 3-6).

Photo 3-5. These pheasant chicks (over 6 weeks) are now able to run and fly with considerable skill and are no longer as dependent on insects as in the first few weeks of life. The soybeans are tall enough to provide protective overhead concealment near the field edge of grasses and forbs where seeds, leaves, insects and other food items are available for food. (CTS)

Photo 3-6. Harvested corn near good winter cover provides an excellent food source for pheasants throughout most of South Dakota's pheasant range. (CTS)

Additional foods include seeds of wild plants, foliage of both wild and agricultural plants, various fruits such as those of chokecherries or Russian olive, and insects.

The types of waste grains available for pheasants are influenced by agricultural commodity markets and the general landscape where pheasants live. For that reason, domestic sunflower or sorghum seeds often dominate the diet where those crops are common (Photo 3-7). Even in summer months, waste grains sometimes average over 70% of the diet (Trautman 1952, 1982:55).

Seeds of volunteer plants such as green foxtail, barnyardgrass (wild millet), ragweed, annual sunflowers, and a number of other species are found in pheasant crops and are most common in the late summer and early fall (Trautman 1952, 1982:55). Perhaps you have observed an old or unused feedlot with tall, dense kochia providing winter cover and seeds for wintering pheasants — pheasants love these areas for protective cover from wind and cold and for the kochia and other weed seeds (Photo 3-8).

Leaves (and flowers) of plants such as alfalfa, common dandelion, clover, and various grasses are consumed by pheasants but make up a much lower percentage of the spring through fall diet than for sharp-tailed grouse or greater prairie-chickens. Except for young chicks, insects are usually not as abundant in the summer and fall diet of pheasants as in greater prairie-chickens and sharp-tailed grouse. As with prairie grouse, grasshoppers are the most common insects ingested by pheasants (Trautman 1982:55). Insect use peaks for hen pheasants at around 15–16% in May and June when laying hens are in need of invertebrates.

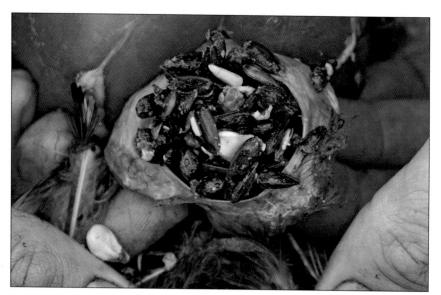

Photo 3-7. The crop contents of this rooster harvested in north-central South Dakota in early November show it had been feeding on sunflowers and corn. Sunflowers were the predominant crop in the area. (LDF)

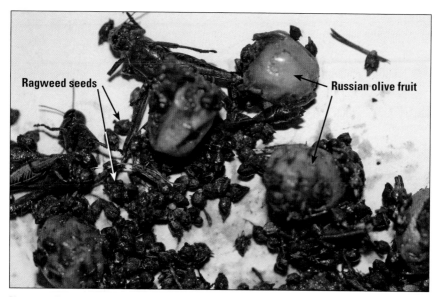

Photo 3-8. The crop of this November harvested rooster from north-central South Dakota (near the Missouri River) was filled with ragweed seeds, Russian olive fruit, and grasshoppers. This pheasant was harvested over a half mile from the nearest grain field. (LDF)

Grit

In addition to food items, pheasants also ingest snails, small pebbles, and soil particles that are important in providing minerals such as calcium and magnesium and, secondarily, for improving the grinding action of the gizzard (McCann 1939) (Photo 3-9). The gizzard of pheasants is highly effective at fragmenting and eroding ingested pebbles, soil particles, and other grit (Vance 1971). As noted in the following section, calcium and magnesium are particularly important to laying hens. Young birds undergoing growth also require more calcium from grit than more mature birds. In winter when grit may be difficult to find, pheasants are able to greatly reduce the passage of grit through the system and retain the grit in the gizzard (McCann 1939).

Nutritional needs of reproducing hens

During the reproductive period hen pheasants need to call upon stored fats and proteins and also often need to supplement their diet with extra energy and protein. Female condition during the pre-laying and laying period is important to ring-necked pheasants because of the influence it has on their reproductive performance and even on the females' chances of survival (Gates and Woehler 1968).

Pheasant hens producing eggs during pre-laying and laying need increased amounts of calcium. These hens ingest grit containing about four times as much calcium as grit ingested by non-laying hens (Kopischke and Nelson 1966). Laying hens can apparently detect high calcium content in grit and selectively choose

Photo 3-9. This young rooster, about 13 or14 weeks of age, is seeking grit along a gravel road. (Courtesy of Scott Weins)

those sources. Placement of crushed limestone on roads and liming of fields as an agricultural practice add to the availability of calcium. Calcium for nesting hens may also be obtained from snail shells or small bone fragments. Soil particles ingested for calcium often contain magnesium, an element used in small quantities for egg formation (Kopischke and Nelson 1966).

Experiments have shown that captive pheasants in good condition with higher calcium diets (3.2 %) can produce an initial clutch as well as a second clutch when the first clutch has failed; hens placed on a limited calcium diet (0.5%) can only produce one clutch and show evidence of osteoporosis in the leg bones (Chambers et al. 1966). In another study, the highest rate of egg production in hens fed an otherwise excellent diet (26% protein, 0.6 % phosphorus) was obtained on a diet containing 2.5% calcium. Egg production was markedly lower for hens fed on diets of only 0.9% calcium and for hens with excessive calcium (3.7%) in the diet (Hinkson et al. 1970).

Lack of calcium in the diet does not appear to be a problem for pheasants in South Dakota or most other areas, particularly in the upper Midwest (Kopischke and Nelson 1966). Thus, we do not consider calcium availability as a concern for those managing for pheasants on private or public lands in South Dakota.

The condition of overwintering hen pheasants can be important to subsequent nesting efforts. Captive ring-necked pheasants placed on high quality diets (26% protein plus unlimited water and grit) gained weight from February through the egg laying period in April (Breitenbach et al. 1963). Egg laying in hen pheasants limited to poor diets was only 9% of that in pheasants with unlimited food available; hens on this limited diet maintained their body weight until they began laying eggs but then lost weight (Breitenbach et al. 1963). Additionally, the period of egg laying was greatly delayed and shortened in pheasants with limited food.

In a separate study, below-normal winter weights in captive pheasants fed limited diets caused delayed weight gains in spring compared to hens fed unlimited amounts (Gates and Woehler 1968). This reduction in weight during the reproductive period led to a delay in the start of egg laying, a phenomenon that would reduce the opportunities for renesting if the initial nest was destroyed in the wild. Studies have not shown a reduction in egg weight or hatchability of eggs in hens entering the nesting season at below-normal weights.

These research studies tell us that the condition of wild pheasants during winter and into the reproductive period is an important factor influencing reproductive success (Photo 3-10). Normally, hen pheasant weights peak annually in late March or early April at the time the oviduct and ovary are greatly enlarging in size in preparation for egg laying. If hens are stressed in winter they may fail to reach normal weights needed to withstand the energy and nutrient demands of egg laying, incubation, and early brood rearing. For example, during two moderate Wisconsin winters, pheasants reached peak weights averaging 2.3 pounds in late March, while in the more severe winters hen weights were 10% lower, averaging only 2.0 pounds at the end of winter (Gates and Woehler 1968). After the severe winters, hen pheasants had depleted body reserves and, consequently, egg laying was delayed, clutch sizes were smaller, and the number of nesting attempts declined.

Poor hen condition upon entering the breeding season may also cause increased mortality. In Wisconsin, May through October survival of hens averaged only 37% following two winters that caused unusual weight loss compared

Photo 3-10. The body condition of overwintering hens can influence their potential for nesting success in the following spring. This hen appears to be in good condition and is prepared for the demands of nesting. (Courtesy of Scott Weins)

to 54% after more normal winter weight losses in 5 different years (Gates and Woehler 1968).

For landowners and others managing pheasants these results indicate the importance of adequate nutrition for hens. Experimental studies on pheasants in England in areas lacking adequate winter foods have clearly shown that management to improve winter food availability can greatly increase hen fat reserves (Draycott et al. 1998). Good winter cover near reliable food sources can assist hen pheasants in reaching peak weights in late winter or early spring in time for the start of nesting. Food plots may play a role by providing readily available food when snow cover is deep and waste grains and weed seeds become unavailable (Chapter 10).

Crop depredation

During peak pheasant years, South Dakota landowners have sometimes contacted the South Dakota Department of Game, Fish and Parks (SDGFP) to report problems with pheasants damaging crops, especially corn seeds or sprouts in the spring. With the increase in pheasants in the late 1990s and early 2000s, damage reports on recently planted row crops again increased. Pheasant depredation primarily occurs on emerging corn, and most complaints are from areas of the state with high pheasant densities. Tolerance of pheasant depredation varies among landowners and it appears that they report more damage during years of higher commodity prices and increased agricultural input costs. During 2000–2010, SDGFP annually responded to approximately 75 to 125 different complaint sites, primarily in eastern South Dakota (Switzer 2010).

Corn treated with anthraquinone has been approved in South Dakota and has been found to reduce corn depredation by pheasants (Hodne-Fischer 2009). A nonchemical approach, the broadcasting of cracked corn on fields planted to corn, will also buffer the amount of depredation by pheasants. The best deterrent to date is a combination of the two treatments, particularly in areas with extremely high pheasant densities.

Chapter thoughts

Adequate amounts of food to meet nutritional needs are essential to health, reproduction, and survival in pheasant populations. Reproduction in hens and survival in chicks can be influenced by food availability and resulting nutritional condition. Foods can vary from primarily insects for young chicks to heavy dependence on waste grains for juveniles and adults from fall through early spring. An important part of habitat selection in pheasants throughout much of the year is related to the nearby availability of abundant and nutritious foods. A diversity of vegetation in a landscape, such as uncut grasslands, weedy edges of fields and wetlands, and intermixed crop fields contributes to healthy pheasant populations by providing needed food sources throughout the year.

CHAPTER 4
TERRITORIES AND COURTSHIP

Warming temperatures and lengthening days of late winter bring about new sights and sounds to South Dakota's diverse agricultural landscapes. The spring strutting and courtship calls of cock pheasants begin as the first hint of sunlight breaks the darkness of late-winter nights. The camaraderie of winter flocks shifts to intolerance as male pheasants look to stake their claim to a piece of property, warning potential trespassers that they are unwelcome.

It is the stimulation of the upcoming breeding season that causes this shift in the roosters' dispositions and subsequent changes in their daily habits. It will be a few more weeks yet before hens feel a similar desire to reproduce, but they too will eventually feel the urge to shift their attention away from winter survival to spring breeding. The sights and sounds of territorial establishment and courtship that have come about with the introduction of pheasants a century ago are now commonplace in landscapes of eastern South Dakota and portions of western South Dakota that have been largely or partially transformed from sod prairies into agricultural production (Photo 4-1).

Spring dispersal

The hormonal response to lengthening days and the associated discontent that cocks feel toward each other stimulate them to move about the landscape in search of a suitable place to establish breeding territories. Movements from wintering areas to breeding areas are termed spring dispersal. In a 5-year radio telemetry study conducted south of Huron, most (73%) male pheasants dispersed at least one-third mile from where they were captured to their spring breeding ranges. Some males (27%) remained on the same area where they wintered through the breeding season without any dispersal movement. Of the cocks that

Photo 4-1. This territorial male is walking with a distinct attitude and showing his best apparel, typical characteristics by late winter or early spring. (Courtesy of Scott Weins)

dispersed, the average distance from the winter capture site to the center of activity during breeding was 2 miles and the longest dispersal distance documented was a straight-line distance of 8 miles (Leif 2003, 2005) (Figure 4-1).

Pheasants, like most wild creatures, have a tendency to return to a familiar place if they have made appreciable movements between seasonal areas of habitat. Spring dispersal (movements of more than one-third of a mile) is more common and of a greater average distance if the severity of the preceding winter forced birds to congregate in larger flocks due to restrictions in the amount of suitable habitat. Almost all (93%) cocks dispersed in 1997 and 2001 when the amount of winter snowfall ranked among the highest and winter temperatures ranked among the coldest on record in the last 100 years. On the other hand, only 58% of males dispersed following relatively mild winters (Leif 2003).

The timing of dispersal in South Dakota is closely related to March temperatures. During the relatively warm late-winter weather in 1999 and 2000, all male pheasants dispersed from winter flocks prior to the end of March. In contrast, most cock pheasants remained in winter flocks until early April (1 or 2 weeks later) during the years of 1997, 1998, and 2001 when March temperatures were colder than average (Leif 2003).

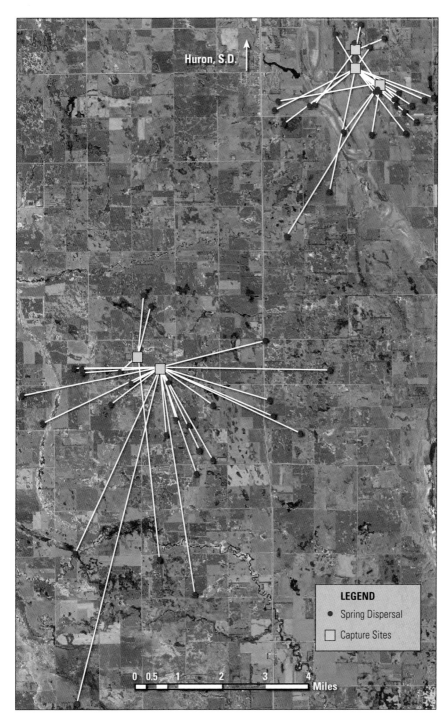

Figure 4-1. Spring dispersal from wintering areas (winter capture site) to breeding areas (center of spring activity) for male pheasants on a landscape near Huron. Sections (often marked by roads) represent 1 square mile (640 acres) of land.

While cock pheasants get the urge to leave winter flocks before winter has ended its grip on South Dakota, hen pheasants remain in winter flocks well into April. Some hens even wait until early May to make their way out from wintering ranges to seek breeding areas. Similar to cock pheasants, winter weather severity influences the timing of hen pheasant dispersal. The median date of hen dispersal (April 26) was a week later following the severe 2000–2001 winter than in springs following the relatively mild winters of 1998–1999 and 1999–2000. A similar relationship between winter severity and spring dispersal was found in a Wisconsin study (Gates and Hale 1974).

In addition to the desire to return to familiar breeding areas, longer pheasant movements in springs after cold, snowy winters are probably related to habitat conditions. Deep snow has a degrading effect on some herbaceous habitats, particularly stands of smooth brome.

Shallow wetlands scattered over much of eastern South Dakota provide excellent pheasant breeding habitat during dry years. These same wetlands are rendered mostly unusable for breeding pheasants when spring runoff from abundant snow pack fills them to near capacity (Figure 4-2); as a result, the availability of pheasant breeding habitat can be altered quite drastically in wet versus dry years.

Territorial and courtship behavior

Much of what we know about the pheasant courtship period comes from research conducted in the United Kingdom (Great Britain). As a likely result of repeated stockings of domestic pheasants, much of the movement and home range information for male pheasants in the United Kingdom is quite different from that in South Dakota. Cock pheasants in the United Kingdom are more sedentary and occupy substantially smaller home ranges than in South Dakota (Hill and Robertson 1988b:61, Leif 2005). Despite these differences, research into pheasant breeding ecology in the United Kingdom can help us understand the behavior of breeding pheasants in South Dakota. The breeding system of pheasants is termed "territorial harem defense polygyny" (Hill and Robertson 1988b:54). Dominant male pheasants defend an area of land (territory) that includes or is near habitats that are also attractive to hen pheasants. Males are polygynous (multiple female mates), in that they will breed with any and all hens that they can coax into becoming members of their harems.

Male pheasants establish territories where the male and hens will have access to food and cover during the breeding season. These territories are exclusive of other males but inclusive to any hen pheasant wanting to use the area. Males attract hens with audio and visual displays (Photo 4-2).

The hoarse two-syllable crowing call that is so prevalent during spring in much of South Dakota is intended to repel other males and lure hens. Crowing calls can be heard for over a mile on calm mornings. Cock pheasants follow each crowing call by making a deep vibrating noise with their wings in a somewhat

2000

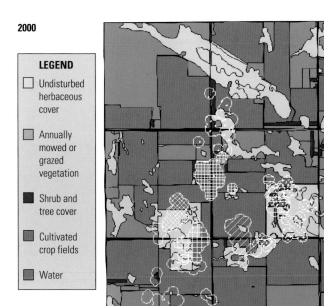

LEGEND

☐ Undisturbed herbaceous cover

▨ Annually mowed or grazed vegetation

■ Shrub and tree cover

▨ Cultivated crop fields

▨ Water

2001

Figure 4-2. Land cover types and locations of radio-marked male pheasant home ranges during the breeding season on a 9-square mile study area in a relatively dry year (2000) and a relatively wet year (2001) in Beadle County, South Dakota. Home ranges of individual males are represented by unique cross hatching or other patterns.

Photo 4-2. Each spring, especially early in the morning, the scenes and sounds associated with territorial male pheasants are common across the primary pheasant range in South Dakota. (Courtesy of Scott Weins)

abbreviated version of the wing drumming of ruffed grouse (Flake et al. 2010:52–53). Crowing calls provide long-range advertisement of male locations to both hens and other cocks while the wing beating is likely intended to be an act of intimidation. The warning is meant to tell nearby potentially intruding males that a mighty opponent awaits if they choose to violate the boundaries of the territory (Photos 4-3).

While crowing calls and subsequent wing drumming are the most prominent displays of breeding male pheasants, cocks defending their territories also use a series of aggressive behaviors toward intruding males (Hill and Robertson 1988b:68). The initial action toward an intruding male is termed a "walk threat" whereby the resident male boldly approaches a trespasser with head and tail held high and pinnae (ear tufts) feathers held fully erect. The featherless orbital wattles on his head redden and protrude, inflated with blood. If the intruder stands his ground, the "walk threat" becomes an aggressive charge. If the intruder still declines to retreat, the resident male will often peck the ground while continuing to approach. In a last aggressive display to thwart a physical confrontation, the resident male may stretch one wing and erect and spread his tail feathers, holding both in full view of the trespasser (Taber 1949, Hill and Robertson 1988b:68).

Aggressive displays are nature's way of reducing or limiting physical conflict and possible injury. However, the lack of a submissive retreat in response to aggressive breeding rituals will cause the territorial dispute to escalate into a physical confrontation.

Photos 4-3. Crowing and subsequent wing-flapping display (drumming) of a territorial cock pheasant on the edge of wetland escape cover. This cock is advertising to hen pheasants and sending a warning to other males. (Courtesy of Scott Weins)

Fights between breeding cock pheasants typically begin with the two opponents crouching inches away from each other beak-to-beak, keeping their wings tucked away but often fanning wide their tail feathers. The opponents begin to spar with a series of flinching head bobs that seem to provoke the imminent scuffle. In an instant, both birds will spring into the air, brace against each other with their wings, and slap their spurs in lightning-fast punches. The aerial joust lasts less than a second. As the brawling birds drop to the ground, they immediately return to their crouched sparring positions and resume provocation of each other with jerky head bobs (Photo 4-4). A victor may begin to emerge as one bird makes a brief charge that can cause the other to make a short retreat before returning to the sparring position.

Skirmishes between male pheasants seldom result in injuries to the combatants. The length of 15 confrontations observed by researchers on a study area in the United Kingdom lasted an average of 18 minutes (Hill and Robertson 1988b:68). Fights end when the apparent loser retreats in flight with the victor in close aerial pursuit. Quite often, an aerial chase also follows confrontations that do not escalate into fights.

Photo 4-4. These two roosters are resting between jousts of fighting as is evident from the ruffled feathers on the bird on the right. (Courtesy of Doug Backlund)

The aggressive behavior of male pheasants has been used as a method of capturing cocks in the spring (Smith et al. 2002, Leif 2003). The technique employs placing a caged tame cock in the territory of a wild pheasant and luring the wild bird to the location by playing a recording of the crowing call. The urge to expel the intruder seduces the wild male pheasant to enter a wire trap set on either side of the tame bird. On one occasion the researchers targeted a displaying male, set the trap, and came back 30 minutes later to find a wild male pheasant in each of the two traps on both sides of the stool pheasant!

Hen pheasants that are attracted to the territory of a breeding male by his advertising call and wing drumming likely choose to join a harem if they find the food and protective cover that they are seeking. Availability of nesting habitat does not appear to be a factor contributing to the selection. Choosing to occupy the habitats within a male pheasant territory brings with it the protective services of the territorial male (Hill and Robertson 1988b:77). Mate guarding during this prenesting period allows hens to feed without disruption from neighboring or transient male pheasants (Photo 4-5).

As the breeding season progresses and hens join a male's harem, cocks shift their attention to courtship. There are three acts of courtship that male pheasants display to hens (Hill and Robertson 1988b:73–74), acts that are somewhat similar to those used to drive off unwelcome males. A male approaching a hen and seeking her receptiveness to copulation holds his head high and pinnae prominently

Photo 4-5. Territorial cock pheasants are polygynous, attempting to attract multiple hens to their harems. Hen pheasants have no difficulty locating males because of the cocks' advertising calls and wing drumming. (Courtesy of Roger Hill)

erect. As he nears a member of his harem, he will perform a lateral display by fanning his tail, extending the wing closest to her, and tilting his body toward her with his head held low (Photo 4-6).

Later in the spring as hens become increasingly receptive to copulation, males will use a ritual called "tid-bitting" along with the lateral display to entice copulation (Hill and Robertson 1988b:74). Tid-bitting is the ritualistic act of a male pheasant holding his head low while calling the female he is courting and pointing to a morsel of food. If the hen is ready to copulate she will squat down, putting her breast on the ground, and the male will step onto her back for a brief copulation that lasts no longer than a second or two (Photo 4-7). Although hens normally will have multiple copulations in the course of egg laying, they are capable of storing viable sperm in their bodies for an average of 3 weeks and do not need to copulate prior to laying each egg (Shick 1947).

Territorial and nomadic males

Male pheasants hatched the preceding year are capable of competing with older pheasants for territories and will participate in their first breeding season before they are even a year old. In areas with abundant pheasants such as in many parts of east-central South Dakota, availability of suitable locations for territories during the breeding season are likely insufficient for the numbers of

Photo 4-6. Cock pheasant spreading his tail and showing off his colorful feathers in a lateral display to an interested hen. (Courtesy of Roger Hill)

Photo 4-7. During the breeding season, cock pheasants mount receptive hens to copulate. Hens remain fertile for an average of about 3 weeks once they copulate with a male but may still copulate multiple times and sometimes with more than one male. (Courtesy of Scott Weins)

breeding males. As a result, some males are unable to find and defend territories with suitable habitat and become somewhat nomadic; these nomadic males still attempt to have active roles in the breeding population (Leif 2005). Research in eastern South Dakota (Beadle County) indicated that most (73%) second year or older (> 21 months) male pheasants established territories, while only 33% of yearling (9–10 month old) cocks were able to secure a territory (Leif 2003). The more sedentary, non-territorial males identified by researchers in the United Kingdom assumed inactive roles in the breeding population if they were unable to establish and defend a territory (Hill and Robertson 1988b:67). In the eastern South Dakota study, 39% of males were unable to establish and defend territories. These males exhibited nomadic breeding tendencies and maintained an average area of daily activity (home range) of 112 acres (Leif 2005). Home ranges of males that successfully established territories averaged less than half that at 45 acres.

Home ranges of hens during the breeding season (mid April through mid June) on these same eastern South Dakota study areas were similar in size to those of territorial males, averaging 55 acres (Schilowsky 2007). Hen pheasants do not exhibit territorial behavior and have home ranges that frequently overlap one another.

Linkage between courtship, habitat, and survival

Nesting habitat and survival throughout the year are discussed in Chapters 5 and 7. However, habitat and survival relationships during the breeding season relate directly to this chapter and deserve some attention here.

Habitats selected by male pheasants and subsequently by hen pheasants are of critical importance from post winter through the egg-laying period. The perils associated with spring dispersal and egg laying result in very low hen survival compared with other seasons (Chapter 7) (Snyder 1985, Riley et al. 1994, Leif 1996). In South Dakota, half of all hen pheasant mortality during a year normally occurs in April and May, all or almost all the result of predation (Leif 1996). The time period between breakup of winter flocks and the start of egg incubation was also the period of highest female pheasant mortality in Colorado (Snyder 1985). Cock pheasants also experience high rates of mortality during this period, second only to the period when the pheasant hunting season is open (Leif 2003) (Photo 4-8).

Since male pheasants disperse from winter flocks 3 to 4 weeks earlier than hens, the distribution of hens is at least partially driven by the distribution of

Photo 4-8. Territorial roosters can quickly disappear when danger approaches. A mixture of new growth and residual grasses makes up an important portion of this male's territory. (CTS)

breeding males. Pheasant home ranges are established in association with habitats that provide protective cover (Leif 2005). Territorial cocks assert their dominance by selecting and defending the best habitats, most notably dense woody cover and idle herbaceous habitats. Woody cover in eastern South Dakota refers primarily to planted shelterbelts that have mixtures of both trees and shrubs, dense shrub plantings, and volunteer sandbar willow patches. These territories provide both open display areas and nearby dense cover to allow escape from large raptors such as red-tailed hawks (Photo 4-9).

Male pheasants that are unable to secure a territory with preferred habitats use the residual cover (vegetative cover remaining from previous season) of fence lines or similar strip habitats; these males include more open habitats like pastures and hay fields in their home ranges than older, dominant males. The lower quality of open habitats in comparison to idled herbaceous cover results in enlarged home ranges of transient male pheasants when compared to resident territorial cocks. Since hen pheasants have home ranges that overlap those of territorial males, habitats selected by hen pheasants were very similar to that of territorial cocks (Schilowsky 2007).

During early morning hours, breeding pheasants spend more time out in pastures, mowed cover, and crop fields than during the midday hours. Male pheasants (both territorial and nomadic) likely use these open-type habitats in mornings to optimize their chances of being seen and heard by other pheasants. During midday, their preference shifts to habitats that provide concealment and escape cover (Leif 2003). Hen pheasants follow this same pattern of daily habitat selection, choosing to feed in early morning hours under the watchful guard of a

Photo 4-9. Woody cover, such as this multi-row belt dominated by dense rows of shrubs, provides ideal escape cover for courting males when interspersed across the landscape. Such areas also receive heavy pheasant use throughout the remainder of the year. (LDF)

territorial male and seeking concealment and protection of woody and residual herbaceous cover during the middle of the day (Photo 4-10).

Throughout the day, pheasants either need to occupy or have immediate access to some type of cover with the structure necessary to conceal them from predators and provide escape habitat if detected. Idle herbaceous habitats (fields of grasses and forbs, fence lines, dry wetlands, etc.), and woody habitats contain residual cover. As the breeding season progresses, protective habitats become more abundant as current-year growth reaches a usable height and density. Grass or legume hayfields provide minimal protective cover in March and April, but new growth in these predominately cool-season plant habitats usually reaches a sufficient height to conceal pheasants by early May; the same is true for pastures if they are not grazed by livestock during this period.

As a result of new growth across the landscape, pheasant use of woody and idle herbaceous habitats is highest in early spring relative to later on in the breeding season. Habitat selection gradually shifts to include pastures and hayfields as the growing season progresses and protective cover develops (Leif 2003). Row crops (corn and soybeans) offer very little, if any, habitat to pheasants during the courtship and breeding period. Consequently, pheasants use row crop fields in South Dakota at relatively low levels throughout the breeding period (Leif 2003, Schilowsky 2007). In contrast, fields of small grains, especially winter wheat, can contribute both a source of food and protective cover as they reach sufficient height for pheasant concealment earlier in the growing season (Rodgers 2005).

Photo 4-10. Courting males will sometimes use croplands in the early mornings to enhance their visibility. However, they must be close to more concealing herbaceous or woody cover for quick escape from predators. (Courtesy of Scott Weins)

It is important to note that not all woodland-type habitats are beneficial to breeding pheasants. Woody cover with high stem density at ground level (shrubs) is an attractive and beneficial component of pheasant breeding areas. Isolated mature trees and blocks or belts of tall trees may have a negative influence on pheasant survival in local areas. This is because tall trees serve as hunting perches for some predators such as great horned owls and red-tailed hawks. Likewise, egg predators such as American crows and black-billed magpies often nest and hunt near shelterbelts. Pheasants in Colorado experienced higher predation rates from hawks or other raptors on an area with trees than sites without trees (Snyder 1985). Older shelterbelts are also a preferred habitat for certain mammalian predators, in particular, raccoons (Pedlar et al. 1997, Kuehl and Clark 2002).

A lone tree on the edge of a wetland is a prime location for avian predators to perch and wait for prey to become available (Stafford et al. 2002). Together, great-horned owls and red-tailed hawks removed 36% of the springtime pheasant population in a Wisconsin study (Petersen 1979). Although it seems counterintuitive toward efforts to establish woody cover for wintering and territorial pheasants, a chainsaw to remove large deciduous trees, especially lone trees, can be a very important pheasant management tool.

Like woody cover, not all herbaceous habitats provide equal benefits to pheasants. Warm-season grasses such as big bluestem, switchgrass, and Indiangrass have a more rigid stalk and retain more of their residual vertical structure through winter and into spring than most cool-season grasses. Many volunteer weed species such as kochia and sunflowers are also able to remain erect and provide protective cover and food through harsh winters and into early spring (Photo 4-11).

Photo 4-11. Early spring residual cover is very effective in reducing prenesting hen losses to raptors. Pheasants use their long tail feathers like the wing flaps on an airplane to reduce speed at landing. (Courtesy of Scott Weins)

Cool-season grasses begin growing early in spring and can provide green cover sooner than warm-season grasses. Additionally, cool-season grasses provide both a direct food source of new green shoots similar to cereal grain fields in Great Britain (Robertson 1996) and a substrate for insect production, an important food of breeding pheasants and their broods (Trautman 1982:54–56). Both cool- and warm-season grasses meet different pheasant habitat requirements in the breeding season and managers will be most effective by establishing fields of both types within management units.

Complexes of habitat must be attractive to both male and female pheasants. In addition, habitats also must protect breeding pheasants from predators and enhance reproductive success if they are to ultimately benefit pheasant abundance. Idle herbaceous cover is the most important habitat type in row-crop regions of South Dakota because of the multiple benefits that this habitat type provides to breeding pheasants. Woody cover with high stem density at ground level also greatly enhances habitat suitability for breeding pheasants because of the superior predator avoidance cover that it provides.

Chapter thoughts

Spring is a time of change for pheasants: changes in the way they behave and in the way they select habitats. With these changes come increased risks. Cock pheasants no longer attempt to conceal themselves but in stark contrast, attempt to attract all the attention they can get. The most dominant males are able to secure the best breeding habitat and attract mates to share the protective and nutritional habitat elements in their territory. Cocks that face defeat in their attempts to establish territories will settle for less desirable habitats but remain vigilant, still desiring to breed. The best breeding habitats are found in blocks of idle herbaceous cover interspersed with shrub patches or other woody cover with high stem densities near the ground.

Hens stay in the collective protection of winter flocks longer than cocks but soon face increased risks of predation as they depart the security of their winter flocks and disseminate across the landscape in search of a mate and a suitable nesting site. Their bodies are stressed to produce eggs and they need a sufficient amount of high protein foods for the nutritional boost necessary to fulfill the pending requirements of nesting. For them to survive this dangerous period, they must have access to habitats that provide a place to hide and escape predators. These protective elements are found in woody and grass-forb habitats that were left undisturbed in the previous growing season.

The rituals of pheasant breeding behavior are truly intriguing and serve to attract the attention of hunters and nonhunters alike. The spectacle and accompanying chorus of the breeding season transform South Dakota's bountiful landscapes into a festive place, characterized by sights and sounds found in very few locations in North America and, for that matter, the world.

CHAPTER 5
NESTING—A CRITICAL TIME

Good nesting and brood-rearing success are critical to maintaining pheasant populations and to hunter success during the fall hunting season. For that reason, there is considerable interest from the public in how the pheasants are doing in any given reproductive season. While both nesting and brood-rearing success are critical to recruitment (adding new birds), we confine our topic to nesting in this chapter — discussion of chicks and broods follows in the next chapter.

Nesting behavior is mostly instinctive in nature. Hen pheasants, including yearling hens hatched the previous summer, generally attempt to nest each breeding season. The chances that a pheasant nest will hatch is usually called nest success while the chances that a hen will successfully hatch a clutch during the breeding season (even though previous attempts may fail) is termed hen success. We report both nest success and hen success as percentages.

A nest is considered successful if one or more eggs in a clutch hatch. Thus, if 25 out of 100 nests initiated by pheasants in an area hatch, nest success would be 25%. Likewise, if 50 out of 100 hens eventually hatched a clutch either on the first attempt or on renest attempts after an earlier clutch is destroyed or abandoned, hen success would be 50%.

Despite the pheasants' common occurrence and abundance throughout much of South Dakota and the upper Midwest, there is a great deal of misunderstanding concerning the habitats ring-necked pheasants need to be successful during the breeding season (spring and early summer). There is also considerable misunderstanding about other aspects of pheasant nesting behavior. Living around pheasants does not necessarily convey an understanding of their biology and the forces influencing their populations.

We can have about as many pheasants as we want if we supply the appropriate habitat — and nesting habitat is an integral part of those needs during the breeding period.

A few basics about pheasant nesting characteristics and behavior
Hen fertility

As spring approaches, pheasants disperse across the surrounding habitat and the more competitive males set up crowing territories (Chapter 4). Hens are attracted to the crowing and displays of the polygynous males (multiple females per male) and, after copulating, nest in sites dispersed throughout the available habitat. Males know nothing of where hens locate their nests and they are not directly involved with nesting other than in fertilizing the female.

Hens have no problem finding cock pheasants to copulate with no matter how heavy the hunting related mortality on the males in the previous hunting season. Studies across several states, including South Dakota, show that close to 90% or more of the eggs in pheasant nests are fertile (Dahlgren 1962, Trautman1982:43). As noted in Chapter 4, hens copulate multiple times but can produce fertile eggs for around 3 weeks after a single copulation (Shick 1947).

Basic nest site

The nest structure is rudimentary, basically composed of a scratched-out nest bowl that is sparsely lined with vegetation either already growing in the nesting spot or pulled into the nest from vegetation reached by the hen while on the nest. Residual vegetation from the previous year is especially important early in the season for concealing the nest site and it also makes up much of the grass lining the nest. As nesting progresses into incubation, small feathers from the female may be included in the nest lining.

Initial nests and renests

Initial nests represent the first nesting attempt during the reproductive season. Renesting is the laying of another clutch of eggs after a previous clutch has been destroyed or abandoned. Hen pheasants will often renest one or more times in the same reproductive season (Gates 1966a). Rarely, a hen will renest after hatching a first clutch if the chicks are lost in the first few days after hatch. In a Wisconsin study, surviving radio-transmittered females produced an average of 1.8 nests with a maximum of 4, including initial nests and renests. Renests produced 40% of the broods (Dumke and Pils 1979).

The variety of chick ages observed in late August resulting from renesting efforts has led some to the incorrect conclusion that pheasant hens rear multiple broods in a single summer. If a pheasant hatches her clutch and successfully rears the chicks, she is finished with nesting for the season. Radio-telemetry studies conducted in South Dakota and elsewhere in the upper Midwest have repeatedly documented that pheasant hens are only capable of rearing one brood of chicks each summer (Leif 1994).

Hens still laying their first clutch or in early incubation when the nest is destroyed or abandoned are more likely to renest than hens that lose their clutch in the late incubation stage. The same is true for pheasants laying subsequent clutches (renests). Multiple renesting efforts explain why a few hens finally hatch a brood and are found with fairly young chicks in August or September. In Wisconsin, 68% of hens with unsuccessful first nests renested while 41% of hens with unsuccessful second clutches renested (Dumke and Pils 1979).

Renesting hens may still be fertile from earlier copulations if the clutch is destroyed early in the nesting effort. If the nest is destroyed or abandoned later in incubation, the delay before starting a renest is usually longer and it is more critical that the hen copulate with a male again. Males remain sexually active through midsummer and are available to renesting hens.

Timing of laying and incubation, laying rate, clutch size

Egg laying usually begins in late April with peak nest initiation in May and peak hatching in mid to late June (Trautman 1982:40). In eastern South Dakota (Sinai Township, Brookings County), nest initiation peaked in the first half of May and hatching peaked in the last half of June (Olson and Flake 1975). In another eastern South Dakota study, the earliest nest initiation was April 26 and latest July 23 while the earliest hatch was June 12 and the latest August 26 (Purvis et al. 1999a). Biologists and citizens have occasionally reported newly hatched broods as early as the third or fourth week of May. Although some nest incubation occurs in April and August, most occurs during May, June, and July (Leif 1996). This is the critical period when nesting cover is needed most to protect incubating hens from disturbance (Figure 5-1).

The nesting season can be delayed by a cold, wet spring for a week or more, while warmer weather may encourage earlier nest initiation. Hen body condition also may influence the timing of laying. If hens are in poor condition after a severe winter, research indicates they may delay nesting and reduce renesting efforts (Gates and Woehler 1968, Draycott et al. 1998).

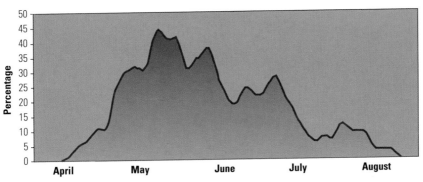

Figure 5-1. Proportion of hens incubating clutches from April through August in eastern South Dakota (Leif 1996).

Laying hens deposit slightly less than one egg per day (later each day) between 2 hours after sunrise and 2 hours before sunset (Baskett 1947). Most eggs are various shades of olive-brown. A hen will skip laying until the next day when egg laying gets too late in the day. On average an egg is laid about every 1.3 days. The hen stays at the nest for 1 to 2 hours during early egg laying with the amount of time spent on the nest increasing as incubation approaches (Kuck et al. 1970).

Ring-necked pheasants lay an average of 12 to 13 eggs in their first or initial nesting attempt and fewer eggs at renesting (Photo 5-1). If a hen renests repeatedly, each succeeding renest generally has fewer eggs. In Iowa, initial clutch size for pheasants fitted with necklace transmitters averaged 12.6 while renests averaged 9.9 eggs (Clark and Bogenschutz 1999). Laying a clutch of 12 eggs would take about 15–16 days.

The incubation period is approximately 23–24 days. Incubating hens remain on the nest except for one or two daily nest relief or recess periods generally of an hour or less. Pheasant hens, like most other birds, periodically stand and turn and rearrange the eggs with their bills. This behavior prevents premature adhesion (sticking together) of egg and shell membranes and allows the eggs more equal time in the warmer center and cooler edges of the clutch. Hens do not cover the nest when leaving for recess during incubation or during the laying stage.

If you know where a hen is nesting it is best to avoid flushing her from the nest. Early in the laying period the hen often abandons her nest if disturbed. As the nesting effort proceeds into incubation the hen tends to abandon less readily. Nevertheless, hens will sometimes abandon even in late incubation if flushed from the nest (Photo 5-2).

Photo 5-1. Note the blue colored pheasant egg among the more common olive brown eggs. This clutch of 14 eggs is close to the 12 to 13 eggs commonly found in initial nest attempts early in the nesting season. If this nest is successfully hatched, the hen is done nesting for the year. (Courtesy of Nick Docken)

Photo 5-2. Researchers can determine the approximate stage of incubation based on how high an egg floats in a water column. This egg near the top indicates it is at about 20 days incubation and should hatch in a few days. (Courtesy of Nick Docken)

Dump nests and nest parasitism

Pheasants have a propensity to lay eggs in nests that have been initiated by another pheasant, resulting in what appears to be a "super-sized" clutch of eggs. Such dump nests are generally made up of fertile eggs and are often abandoned by the hens. On occasion, hens will sit on one of these super-sized clutches and successfully hatch a large number of the eggs. In Brooking County in eastern South Dakota, a hen incubated a dump nest with 30 eggs of which the hen hatched at least 22 (L.D. Flake, personal observation). That would be an impressive parade of chicks! It seems quite a task to keep 22 out of 30 eggs warm during the incubation period, periodically turning and rearranging them, let alone actually hatching that many (Photo 5-3).

Hen pheasants will also lay eggs in duck nests or in those of sharp-tailed grouse or greater prairie-chickens. Laying eggs in the nests of other species is sometimes called nest parasitism. Pheasant nest parasitism can sometimes be a concern in greater prairie-chicken conservation efforts where the two species occur together (Westemeier et al. 1998) (Photo 5-4, 5-5).

Photo 5-3. With 22 visible eggs (one mostly hidden by feather), this is likely a pheasant dump nest with eggs from more than one female. A hen pheasant will sometimes incubate and successfully hatch a dump nest, but many are abandoned. (Courtesy of Mary Clawson)

Photo 5-4. Pheasants will sometimes lay eggs in other birds' nests such as in this duck nest. The pheasant eggs are olive brown and are smaller than the unidentified duck eggs. (Courtesy of Nick Docken)

Photo 5-5. Parasitism by laying hen pheasants on greater prairie-chicken nests is a matter of concern in some areas of the Midwest where both occur. The pheasant eggs are olive-brown and are noticeably larger than the prairie chicken eggs. (Courtesy of Nick Docken)

Early in the nesting season, it is common to find randomly deposited pheasant eggs nowhere near a nest bowl. These eggs are likely laid by hens that have yet to select a nest site.

Nesting habitat
What is not nesting habitat?

By late spring or early summer the landscape in South Dakota's agricultural regions seems covered with knee-high vegetation, much of it due to growth of agricultural crops. Don't assume that most of this landscape is suitable pheasant nesting habitat. After subtracting row-crop habitat such as corn, soybeans, sorghum, or sunflowers, a much more realistic picture of pheasant nesting habitat emerges. In some areas, there is actually little cover other than roadside ditches and other strip cover or limited odd areas for nesting pheasants. This can be a problem for pheasants, particularly in the state's eastern counties.

Pheasants avoid nesting in conventionally tilled corn. When corn was no-till planted into corn stubble or herbicide treated sod (grass) there was some nesting use but nest densities were only a small fraction of that in strip cover such as unmowed roadsides or fence lines (Basore et al. 1986).

Soybeans are of poor value compared to good herbaceous cover in terms of pheasant nest densities but success of the few pheasant nests (renest attempts) found in soybeans can be relatively high (Warnock and Joselyn 1964). Soybeans planted into no-till corn stubble and residue had extremely low pheasant nesting densities (Basore et al. 1986). In South Dakota, use of conventionally tilled or no-till soybeans for nesting is thought to be extremely low. Over several years of a study, radio-marked hen pheasants in east-central South Dakota made no use of available soybeans fields for nesting (A.P. Leif, unpublished data).

No-till planting of soybeans into dense, tall stubble (and volunteer weeds) will understandably destroy most early pheasant nests in the planted area. It is possible that soybeans planted into tall wheat, canola, or flax stubble (>15 inches) could still provide reasonable cover for renesting pheasants (later nests) but this practice will need to be evaluated, particularly if no-till planting into tall stubble continues to expand in South Dakota (Chapter 14).

Recently, a hunter purchased 240 acres in eastern South Dakota for the primary purpose of producing and hunting wild pheasants. Unfortunately, his only experience with pheasants was hunting cornfields with a line of hunters and blockers and flushing large numbers of birds. His view of pheasant habitat was a cornfield, and for that reason he had most of the grass cover tilled and replaced with a large cornfield to benefit the pheasants. In doing so he destroyed nesting and brood-rearing cover. He had only needed a few acres of food plot to go along with the much more valuable breeding cover. Reseeding of most of the tilled ground to a suitable grass and forb mixture was required to restore the habitat (A.E. Gabbert, personal experience).

The hunter's experience, unfortunately a rather common occurrence, is only one example of the surprising amount of misinformation and misunderstanding floating around about pheasant nesting and the importance of nesting cover. Biologists, land managers, and landowners with habitat development experience should be encouraged to share their success stories to help assure that appropriate habitat management is applied (Photo 5-6).

What is good nesting habitat?

Nesting habitat for ring-necked pheasants can be described as patches of cover, usually mixed grasses and forbs, that the birds will readily select for nesting and that will provide them with adequate visual screening from predators and protection from the elements. Any type of grass and forb cover (excluding row crops) in fields or adequately wide strips (like many undisturbed roadsides) that can conceal a hen and that is not mowed or harvested before most nests hatch can be suitable cover (Trautman 1960). Cover quality can vary greatly depending on density, height, and inclusion of forbs (Carter 1973, Vandel 1980, Vandel and Linder 1981) (Photos 5-7).

Photo 5-6. Here, corn has replaced expired Conservation Reserve Program grasslands and, unfortunately, is seldom used for pheasant nesting or by young broods. Replacement of undisturbed herbaceous nesting and brood-rearing cover with row crops will result in declining pheasant populations at local and regional levels. (CTS)

Photos 5-7. Hen pheasants remain motionless on the nest in an effort to avoid detection by predators. Both residual and new growth vegetation are important to concealment. The alfalfa mixed in with grasses in the right photo enhances concealment value of the cover. (Courtesy of Nick Docken)

An example of good nesting cover could include blocks (fields), wide strips (we suggest at least 50 feet wide), or other variable patches of grasses such as intermediate and tall wheatgrass along with intermixed legumes like alfalfa (Photo 5-8). Mixtures of vegetation dominated by native grasses such as switch-grass and big bluestem are also good nesting cover (George et al. 1979, Rohlfing 2004, Hankins 2007) (Chapter 9).

Areas dominated by smooth brome are common and can be good nesting cover, especially if intermixed with alfalfa. If these smooth brome-alfalfa fields are not mowed or grazed on an annual basis or are left intact until after about mid July (preferably after August 1) they can make excellent nesting areas. A grass such as Kentucky bluegrass falls over readily (lodges), provides inadequate cover, and is of little value as nesting cover for pheasants. It is important that nesting areas that are mowed or grazed later in the summer be allowed adequate

Photo 5-8. Intermediate wheatgrass and alfalfa in combination provide excellent nesting and brood-rearing area on this Game Production Area (GPA). Legumes and other forbs improve the value for nesting and young chicks. (CTS)

time for regrowth if they are to provide residual concealment for nesting hens in the following spring before new herbaceous growth has occurred.

Nesting cover can become stunted as litter and nutrients are tied up in dead plant material and the soil surface is shaded and cooled by a thick layer of litter. This is especially common after several years in areas planted or invaded by smooth brome. These sod-bound areas are often characterized by numerous paths of predators that feed on an abundance of small rodents (mostly voles) in the litter material (Carter 1973). While sufficient numbers of alternate prey in diverse areas with good nesting habitat are thought to buffer (lighten) the effects of predation on pheasant nests, an abundance of prey in combination with poor nesting cover and abundant predator trails is not a good situation. Treatments to improve these areas such as interseeding of legumes, burning, mowing, or grazing of sod-bound nesting cover are discussed in Chapter 9.

Research in Iowa indicated that nesting cover in larger tracts (or blocks) tended to reduce predation compared to small or linear areas of nesting cover; this will be further discussed in Chapter 7 (Clark et al. 1999). Small tracts of nesting cover, such as a 1-acre block of dense grasses and forbs, are still much better than no nesting cover. No relationship was found between size of nesting cover tracts (blocks of cover) and nesting success in South Dakota, but there was increased nesting success in landscapes with more grassland nesting cover, less cropland, and fewer farmsteads (Fisk 2010). Mammalian nest predators, such as striped skunks and red fox, may find it more difficult to locate nests in larger patches of cover or more cumulative areas of nesting cover on the landscape.

Wide fence lines or other wide strips of cover can be valuable nesting cover, but those of only a few feet (less than 6 feet, for example), are of questionable value. Roadsides planted to grass and legume mixtures or even voluntary herbaceous plants are valuable for pheasants (Joselyn and Tate 1972, Keyser 1986, Warner et al. 1987). In the Sinai Township near Brookings, roadsides produced 14% of hatched pheasant clutches in the early 1970s (Olson and Flake 1975).

Ungrazed multi-row tree belts that also feature good herbaceous cover in the understory are readily used by nesting pheasants with good success (Olson and Flake 1975). Other areas such as grass or weedy fringes around wetlands and odd field corners not plowed and planted to crops can all be valuable to pheasant nesting. As nesting cover becomes more restricted on the landscape, these narrow strips, small patches, and odd areas become more important in sustaining the pheasant population (Photo 5-9).

Occasionally an area with good breeding habitat (and even good winter habitat) can be hit by extremely deep snow and blizzards, killing much of the pheasant breeding stock. However, even in these areas, the survival and recovery of the pheasant population will be strongly related to the quantity and quality of cover during the breeding season. If available nesting cover is adequate, pheasants will recover at a remarkable rate and often return to normal population levels within 1 to 3 years. We observed such a winterkill (1996–1997) and rapid recov-

Photo 5-9. Road rights-of way are examples of strip cover that can be important as pheasant nesting and brood-rearing habitat if left unmowed until at least mid July. The landowner adjacent to the roadside had a strong interest in protecting this cover for pheasants. (Courtesy of Matt Grunig)

ery in eastern South Dakota (Gabbert et al. 1999). Where the breeding habitat is highly limited, pheasants will generally not thrive although the area may carry a minimal number of birds from year to year.

Precipitation and nesting cover

Nesting cover quality and nesting success in an area can vary from year to year with changes in precipitation and soil moisture. In years with adequate moisture, the herbaceous vegetation in potential nesting areas grows rapidly in spring and early summer and, along with residual cover, provides excellent concealment for nesting hens. When soil moisture is favorable in mid to late summer, regrowth of mowed or grazed haylands is often adequate to provide residual nesting cover the following spring.

Drought in South Dakota is accompanied by stunted growth of grasses and forbs and is often associated with intensive haying and grazing of available grasses for use as forage for livestock. Little cover is left for pheasants and this will be reflected in poor reproduction during the spring and summer of drought and poor survival of hens. Drought can also result in reduced reproduction the following year because of lack of residual cover for concealment of early nesting pheasants (Martinson and Grondahl 1966).

There are some exceptions to poor pheasant production in drought years. Pheasants thrived when much land was left untilled and in volunteer herbaceous cover as occurred in drought years during the Great Depression and during World War II (Chapter 1).

Agricultural crops used for nesting cover

In the early 1970s one could commonly observe fields of blue in eastern South Dakota—these were flax fields in flower. Pheasant nest densities in flax were low but the success of such nests was high (Olson and Flake 1975). Most appeared to be later nests, probably renests. Flax is no longer common as a crop in South Dakota.

Wheat and other small grains are still common in central and western portions of South Dakota's pheasant range. Small grains usually support a low to medium density of late pheasant nests but the success of those nests is relatively good (Olson and Flake 1975, Trautman 1982:50). Fall planting of winter wheat avoids the problem of destruction of early pheasant and waterfowl nests due to spring planting in tall stubble (>15 inches). Winter wheat also provides earlier concealment for nesting hens than spring wheat. It is much more valuable for nesting than spring wheat. In south-central Nebraska, winter wheat made up 25% of the landscape and provided safe nesting cover for pheasants (Linder et al. 1960, Baxter and Wolfe 1973:14). Predator activity and nest predation in winter wheat and other small grains is generally low, probably because of low success in finding scarce prey, lack of established predator trails, and large field sizes (Linder et al. 1960) (Photo 5-10).

In the more arid portions of the northern plains, stubble from winter wheat and spring wheat is sometimes left fallow and only planted in alternate years to accumulate soil moisture. Pheasants will readily use tall wheat stubble with intermixed weeds for general cover and for nesting and brood rearing during the fallow year (Rodgers 1983, Snyder 1984).

Cultivation of wheat stubble or herbicide application to reduce weed growth is highly destructive to pheasant use of this cover (Rodgers 2002). In fact, surface tillage for weed control can destroy all nests and many young chicks and hens in summer-fallowed wheat. Use of undercutters (without mulch treaders) for weed control in summer-fallowed wheat in place of surface tillage was found to save 53% of pheasant nests and to permit better survival of hens and flightless chicks (Rodgers 1983). The practice of summer fallowing wheat and planting in alternate years has largely been abandoned in South Dakota in favor of no-till practices and rotation of winter wheat and spring wheat with several other crops as further discussed in Chapter 14.

Photo 5-10. Winter wheat develops earlier and is much more valuable for nesting pheasants than spring wheat. (Courtesy of Josh Jensen)

Alfalfa is readily used by nesting pheasants but is basically a dangerous trap because the mowing periods are early enough and frequent enough that hens usually do not have time to hatch a clutch (Chapter 1). A variety of alfalfa that flowers later and can be harvested later than current varieties has been developed at South Dakota State University, and research is proceeding on testing and producing seed for this variety for the Dakotas (Boe et al. 1998). Landowners interested in producing alfalfa while benefiting pheasants may be interested in these late-blooming varieties. The first cutting would occur after most pheasant nests have hatched. The drawback for farmers is that there would be fewer cuttings per year.

Grass haylands, particularly those dominated by warm-season grasses, are generally mowed later than alfalfa and can be valuable for nesting pheasants if mowed after mid July, preferably after August 1. If mowed too early they can be a trap for nesting hens. These haylands can include plantings such as intermediate and tall wheatgrass, smooth brome, warm-season natives such as switchgrass or big bluestem, and mixtures of grasses and alfalfa. Native grasses and forbs harvested only for seed after mid July can also provide both live and residual nesting cover. Haylands often have sufficient regrowth to provide residual nesting cover the following spring if summer and fall precipitation is adequate.

Nest success and failure

Nests are considered successful if one or more chicks hatch from the clutch. If the clutch survives until hatching, most eggs normally hatch successfully; nest success is also sometimes called nest survival. We present nest success (or nest survival) as a percentage. Some of the complexities in correctly estimating nest success are not discussed but can be reviewed in Mayfield (1975).

Causes of nest failure

Pheasant nests fail due to a variety of causes and those failures are often followed by renesting attempts. Nests may be abandoned or destroyed due to unintentional disturbances such as cattle grazing or some other agricultural activities. A variety of predators such as red fox, striped skunks, eastern spotted skunks, raccoons, American badgers, Virginia opossums, coyotes, American crows, and black-billed magpies will prey on pheasant eggs (Photos 5-11, 5-12). Ground squirrels, particularly the Franklin's ground squirrel, will prey on the eggs of pheasants, mallards, sharp-tailed grouse, and other ground-nesting birds in the Midwest (Garrettson and Rohwer 2001). Some of the interesting complexities influencing predator populations and predation, such as coyote suppression of other predators, are discussed in Chapter 7. Other nest failures can be caused by mowing, spring tillage, flooding, and hailstorms. Infertility may cause some individual eggs to fail but is almost never the cause of nest failure.

A few vegetation and landscape effects

The characteristics of cover selected by hens for nesting can greatly influence the chances of a nest being successful. In east-central Wisconsin nest success was highest in unharvested grass hay and wetlands (peripheral cover and dry basins) and lowest in harvested hay, primarily alfalfa and red clover, and peas (Gates and Hale 1975:34). Some of the safest nesting areas for pheasants in eastern South Dakota in the early 1970s included idle farmland (with herbaceous cover), tame hay (excluding alfalfa), wheat, and flax (Olson and Flake 1975). Pheasant nests in continuously grazed pastures and narrow fencerows have low chances for success (Linder et al. 1960, Trautman 1982:49).

Researchers in Iowa determined that radio-transmittered pheasants had markedly better success hatching nests in a landscape with abundant nesting habitat (25% perennial grassland cover) than in a landscape more heavily dominated by cropland (only 9% perennial grassland cover) (Clark and Bogenschutz 1999). These perennial grassland areas included intermixed grasses and forbs

Photo 5-11. Badgers are one of a variety of mammalian predators that will prey on the eggs of pheasants and other ground-nesting birds. They are effective predators on rodent pests but can cause problems for landowners because of their digging activities. (Courtesy of Nick Docken)

that provided large blocks of concealing cover for nesting hens. It is clear that an abundance of larger blocks of permanent nesting cover on the landscapes provided by federal land-retirement programs such as the Conservation Reserve Program (CRP) and Soil Bank have proven valuable in providing excellent sites for pheasant mating (male territories), nesting, and brood rearing. Increases in permanent herbaceous cover associated with the CRP allowed for marked

Photo 5-12. Pheasant nests may be completely destroyed by a predator in a single visit or, as in this case, partially destroyed. This pheasant nest will probably fail as the egg predator will likely return to remove more eggs. (Courtesy of Nick Docken)

increases in populations of ring-necked pheasants in most of the upper Midwest since 1985 (King and Savidge 1995, Riley 1995, Clark and Bogenschutz 1999, Haroldson et al. 2006).

Examples of nest success rates

Even in areas with extensive nesting cover, pheasants initiating a nest almost always have less than a 50% chance of bringing the clutch to successful hatch. In many cases the actual nest success rates are below 30%. A few examples of nest survival from the Midwest may be helpful here.

Hatching success for pheasant nests (including initial and renests) located by nest searches in east-central Wisconsin ranged from 24 to 46% per year and averaged 30% from 1958 to 1966 (Gates and Hale 1975:42). Nests were classed as active, abandoned, or destroyed; also recorded were empty nest bowls where the eggs had been removed by a predator. In eastern South Dakota (Lake Sinai Township) searches for active, abandoned, and destroyed nests yielded estimates of 21% nest success in 1973 and 28% in 1974 (Olson and Flake 1975). Similar values of 20% nest success in 1958 and 24% in 1959 were recorded in eastern South Dakota by Trautman (1960). Near Huron, nest success for wild hens fitted with radio transmitters averaged an excellent 42%, with almost half of total losses due to nest predation from predators such as striped skunk and red fox (Leif 1994).

Hen success

Hen success or hen nesting success is the percentage of females that eventually succeed in hatching a clutch (at least one chick) during the reproductive season (Cowardin et al. 1985). Persistent renesting by pheasant hens that have their nests destroyed or that abandon their nests allows many of the surviving females to eventually hatch a clutch during the breeding season. Some hens die from various causes during the reproductive season before they can complete their nesting efforts and are not included in the estimate of hen success.

Hen success in hatching a clutch (one or more chicks hatched) during the reproductive season is variable by year and area but generally falls between 40 and 80% (Giudice and Ratti 2001). In northern Iowa, 71% of surviving hens in an area with excellent nesting habitat were successful in eventually hatching a clutch during the reproductive season, while 52% eventually hatched a clutch in a landscape with more cropland and much reduced nesting cover (Clark and Bogenschutz 1999). In eastern South Dakota near Huron, 63% of radio-marked wild hens that initiated incubation of a nest and survived the nesting season managed to hatch a clutch either in an initial or subsequent nesting attempt (Leif 1994) (Photo 5-13).

The persistence of pheasants in renesting after nest failure is highly important to the success of this bird. Production would be much lower if pheasant hens ceased nesting after an initial clutch was destroyed or abandoned.

Photo 5-13. Hatched clutch of pheasant eggs showing the white eggshell membranes and eggshell caps after the hen and chicks have departed the nest. (Courtesy of Nick Docken).

Chapter thoughts

Knowledge of pheasant nesting biology and habitat needs is essential to understanding and managing pheasant populations. Both yearling and older females are active nesters, with basically all hens attempting to nest each year. Nesting is a risky process for the hen and for eggs even in the best habitats. Of all the hen pheasants alive when winter breaks its grip in South Dakota, approximately one-third will be killed before they initiate incubation, another third will be unsuccessful in their attempts to nest and rear a brood, and a third will successfully recruit (hatch a clutch and successfully rear at least one chick) young pheasants into the pheasant population. In most areas, less than 35% of pheasant nests reach hatching, with many nests lost to causes such as abandonment, predation, flooding, and mowing. Because of persistent renesting, hen success in eventually hatching a clutch, often 60% or greater, is much higher than nest success. We can positively influence pheasant nesting success by providing sufficient amounts of quality nesting habitat.

CHAPTER 6
PHEASANT CHICKS: FROM HATCHING TO INDEPENDENCE

Pheasant chicks, temporarily helpless and covered with wet down, emerge from their life-sustaining egg chamber about 23–24 days after the hen begins incubation. The precocious (advanced in development) young enter a world no less dangerous than in the egg stage and now must soon feed themselves on a diet primarily composed of insects (Chapter 3). Although they carry a supply of yolk material from the egg in their gut, they cannot last long without the warmth of the brooding hen and without the hen leading them to secure habitat that provides abundant food. Chick survival is most precarious in those first hours, days, and weeks after hatch.

Here we cover basic information on brood hens and chicks that should be of value in managing pheasants during this important portion of the breeding season. We define the chick stage as pheasants from hatching to 10 weeks of age as is commonly used for grouse (Connelly et al. 2003:34). Food habits of chicks are treated in Chapter 3 but are at times mentioned in relation to habitat needs. As was the case with the nesting stage, the chick stage is a highly vulnerable period that greatly influences annual populations.

Hatching—the first day

The first signs of hatching occur when a chick begins to pip the eggshell (crack or chip the shell) on the blunt end of the egg. Even prior to hatching, the hen communicates with the young and helps coordinate the pipping activity through low clucking. Chicks are able to slowly rotate in the egg while chipping a circular cut in the blunt end of the egg using the transitory egg tooth on the top of the beak and a special, temporarily enlarged hatching muscle on the back of the neck. After the egg caps pop off, the hatched chicks remain somewhat helpless and immobile in the nest for an hour or two until their down feathers are dry. The hen carefully broods and tends to the chicks while in the nest. Hatching in a clutch is fairly synchronized and is generally completed within a few hours. Chicks soon begin to walk around in the nest and are ready to leave with the female in less than 12 hours (Photo 6-1). Even when newly hatched, the gender can be determined by careful observation of the shape and characteristics of the wattle or cheek patch tissue around the eye (Woehler and Gates 1970).

Chicks must strongly and quickly imprint to the brood hen (filial imprinting) as a parent object so they will automatically follow her closely without error if they are to survive. Filial imprinting begins when the hen softly clucks to the young during the pipping process and may continue to strengthen for a short time after the young leave the nest. Imprinting on the hen is especially important when the hen leads the vulnerable chicks from the nest, usually within 24 hours or less of hatch. If they do not scramble to closely follow the hen they will not last long on their own.

Because young pheasants leave the nest soon after hatching, a synchronized hatch is critical to their survival. The synchronized hatch only occurs because

Photo 6-1. Chicks are still breaking (pipping) their way out of at least two of the eggs. Eggshell caps from hatched eggs and a chick are visible. Other chicks that already hatched have moved outside the photo. (Courtesy of Nick Docken)

the hen does not incubate her clutch until the last egg in the clutch is laid — thus ensuring that all eggs develop and hatch together.

A nest with successfully hatched eggs can be identified by the presence of loose egg membranes, eggshell caps, and lack of excessive blood on the egg membranes and shells. It is not uncommon for an egg or sometimes a couple of eggs to be left behind and to be either infertile or non-term (chick has not hatched). If a chick hatches too far behind its brood mates, it may be unable to successfully follow when the hen and brood depart the nest.

First weeks after hatch

Upon departing the nest, the hen pheasant soon leads the chicks to safe cover and to feeding areas usually within about 100 yards of the nest for the first 2 days (Riley et al. 1998). Hens seek out brood-rearing areas with ample densities of insects and other invertebrates for the chicks to capture; thus, availability of insects can have a major influence on early chick survival (Hill 1985).

It is rare for a rooster to accompany a brood hen with her young chicks, even for a short time. Like nesting, rearing the chicks is strictly the job of the hen. Males have but one critical function in terms of maintaining the population — fertilization of the hens prior to nesting.

It is sometimes said that chicks are unable to maneuver through nesting cover to follow the hen if the cover is too thick, but there is no evidence that this is a real problem influencing chick survival. Chicks are amazingly adept at scrambling through, over, and around obstacles and seem to move through thick stands of grasses and forbs with a natural skill.

During the first couple of weeks the hen spends much of her time brooding the young under her body and wings when they are not feeding or on the move. Chicks burrow under the hen (nestle in breast or belly feathers) or under her wings to avoid the hot sun, rain, or the cool night air; the hen is somewhat like having a portable heater with a roof. Early post-hatch chicks maintain body temperatures lower than normal for older chicks, juveniles, and adults but gradually increase their body temperature and ability to thermoregulate through the first weeks of life (Ryser and Morrison 1954, Hissa et al. 1983).

The hen's predator-warning call is innately recognized by recently hatched chicks and causes them to scatter and hide. If a brood hen with young chicks is approached too closely by humans, she will usually fly or run a short distance and stay nearby. In some cases, hens will pretend to be injured (distraction display) to draw the predator away from the brood (Robertson 1997:82). The hen can be quite aggressive toward some predators. For example, hen pheasants have been observed flying at and into northern harriers to deter predation on their chicks (Carroll 1985). Northern harriers are often observed flying over intermediate to tall stands of grasses and forbs in search of mice and other prey. While these medium-sized hawks appear quite large and can prey on pheasant chicks, they are much less effective in taking juveniles and adults (Photo 6-2).

Photo 6-2. Northern harriers are medium-sized hawks with a large wingspan that often hunt for voles or other prey over grasslands and wetlands. Hen pheasants have been known to aggressively attack and successfully drive off this hawk in defense of their young. (Courtesy of Scott Weins)

Developing flight

Juveniles initiate short "grasshopper-like" flights by 2 weeks of age when their flight feathers (primaries and secondaries) have developed adequately (Trautman 1982:43). Flight development may begin a few days earlier or be delayed slightly, evidently in response to nutritional condition and rate of flight feather growth on chicks. By 3 weeks of age, chicks often fly for 50 yards or more when flushed (Photo 6-3). By 5 weeks of age they can fly over 200 yards and are well on their way to full flight capabilities.

Movements, brood breakup

In the first 3 weeks after hatching the brood usually remains in an area of less than 10 acres around the nest if food and cover are adequate (Kuck et al. 1970). (For comparison, an American football field playing surface covers 1.3 acres.) The home range of chicks continues to increase as they develop and their mobility improves. Research indicates that movements and home ranges (area of daily activity) of broods in diverse habitats with good brood-rearing cover tend to be smaller than in areas with less diversity of land use and more cropland. This difference in movements indicates that brood hens and their chicks must travel greater distances in poor habitat to find adequate food and cover (Warner 1984). Chicks forced to move over greater distances to find resources are prone to greater risks of mortality. If brood habitat is adequate, several broods can be reared to independence in overlapping home ranges (Hanson and Progulske 1973).

Photo 6-3. Even though around 3 weeks of age, this chick can fly about 50 yards if flushed by a predator such as a red fox. After the disturbance subsides the hen is able to use a brood-gathering call to rapidly gather the young. (Courtesy of Scott Weins)

Broods tend to remain intact with the brood hen until brood breakup, although banding together by more than one brood or adoption of some chicks from another brood is not uncommon as broods reach and surpass about 6 weeks of age (Baskett 1947, Gates and Hale 1975:57). Chicks flushed by predators, humans, or other causes will usually join back together with the hen in a brief period of time. Even if broods are scattered at night they can find each other readily. To bring the brood back together, the hen gives a brood-gathering call innately recognized by the chicks.

Broods normally remain with the hen until about 10 to 12 weeks of age after which they become independent of the hen and brood. A few late-hatched broods from renests may still be intact when the pheasant season starts in mid October.

What makes good brood habitat?

On departure from the nest, the hen attempts to lead the precocial chicks to nearby habitat with adequate overhead screening cover, an open understory where chicks can move about to feed, and with an abundance of insects. Such areas usually have a diversity of forbs and grasses to support insects (Hill and Robertson 1988b:117). Grass-legume fields and other areas commonly used for nesting and interspersed weedy areas within them usually provide good places for broods to feed, loaf, escape predators, night roost, and perform other daily activities (Carter 1971, Trautman 1982:51, Riley et al. 1998).

Weedy edges along agricultural fields, ungrazed shelterbelts, abandoned farmsteads, roadsides, railroad rights-of-way, and other undisturbed areas can be important to brood rearing. Rows of shrubs such as wild plum, hedge cotoneaster, and Nanking cherry associated with weedy understory or edges can provide edge-type habitat and attractive overhead cover. Strip cover along roadsides, fence lines, wetland margins, and other odd areas can be managed to provide good brood habitat especially where legumes (such as alfalfa or sweetclover) are interseeded to encourage a healthy diversity and abundance of insects for foraging chicks (Nelson et al. 1990) (Photo 6-4).

Some forage crops and small grains can also provide important brood habitat if not harvested during the early life stages when entire broods may be destroyed. In Illinois, alfalfa hayfields or alfalfa-red clover mixtures as well as oats served as important brood cover particularly in the first 4 to 5 weeks after hatch (Warner 1979). Alfalfa is sought out by brood hens and broods in eastern South Dakota (Carter 1971, Hanson and Progulske 1973) and is an important brood-rearing cover in Nebraska (Baxter and Wolfe 1973:32–33).

Tall stubble (>15 inches) from wheat and other small grains is often characterized by rapid sprouting of volunteer annual grasses and forbs if not treated with herbicides, and the stubble, weeds, and missed crop can provide quality mid

Photo 6-4. This mixture of grasses and forbs serves as excellent brood cover for pheasants while also providing sufficient concealment for nesting. Insects for the diets of young chicks are plentiful in this type of cover. (AEG)

to late season brood habitat (Baxter and Wolfe 1973:32–33, Rodgers 2005). Post-harvest stubble from harvested wheat or other small grains in South Dakota is increasingly seeded with a cover crop such as peas, radish, or mustard to reduce weed growth and improve soil characteristics (Chapter 14). These cover crops along with the tall stubble can also provide late-season brood habitat along with good fall cover (Photos 6-5). A cover crop of mustard is especially attractive to pheasants from fall through early spring (Photo 6-6).

Photos 6-5. Use of radishes (top) and peas (bottom) as a cover crop on tall wheat stubble can improve this habitat for late broods and for fall and winter cover. These cover crops improve soils and reduce weed growth. (Courtesy of Jeff Hemenway)

Photo 6-6. This cover crop of mustard planted into wheat stubble during August at the Dakota Lakes Research Farm near Pierre attracts pheasants from late summer into spring. (LDF)

Older broods tend to spend an increasing amount of time in row crops such as grain sorghum, corn, and soybeans during the late summer when the plants provide overhead screening and escape cover; interspersed weedy cover in these crops or on the edges improves their value for pheasant broods (Baxter and Wolfe 1973:33). We have learned that it is next to impossible for a biologist with an antenna and radio receiver to approach and flush a radio-marked hen and her brood when they seek refuge in a green cornfield that is nearing maturity. Broods can move rapidly through the open understory of a cornfield and the overhead cover shields them nicely from aerial predators.

Despite their value as escape cover, cleanly farmed row crops have few weeds and are of little value as brood foraging areas. Consequently, interior portions of large fields are largely unsuitable for pheasant brood habitat unless embedded wetland or other patches of grass-forb cover can be found.

Weedy spots with an open understory and loose soil can be attractive as dusting and preening areas and for other loafing activities for broods during the day. Dusting and preening are used by pheasants and many other birds to remove parasites and maintain feather condition. Wild plum, chokecherry, or other shrubby cover can also provide shade and loafing areas for broods on hot days as can mixed stands of grasses and forbs. Larger deciduous trees in shelterbelts are of basically no value for pheasant broods (or for pheasant adults). After a few weeks of age, brood use of more open habitats for feeding such as harvested grain stubble or recently mowed alfalfa becomes important as long as escape cover is nearby (Photo 6-7). Broods also seek out open habitats near cover when the vegetation is wet with morning dew.

Photo 6-7. Pheasant hens and their broods become increasingly mobile as the birds mature beyond the first few weeks of life. These chicks are feeding on insects and will not venture far from protective cover at this young age of about 2 to 3 weeks. (CTS)

Brood size and overall pheasant production decline as the proportion of the landscape in row crops increases in intensively farmed areas. Large fields in corn, soybeans, or other row crops are very poor habitats for chicks, especially in their first few weeks of life when they need abundant insects. Thus, while agricultural crops and waste grains are an important and integral part of good pheasant habitat, intensive agriculture, clean farming, and lack of a diversity of habitats in an area leads to reduced production and recruitment of young pheasants into the fall population (Warner et al. 1984, Warner et al. 1999).

As was the case with nesting, federal land-retirement programs that provide permanent herbaceous cover can provide excellent brood habitat. Other U.S. Department of Agriculture (USDA) programs such as the Wetland Reserve and Grassland Reserve programs also provide valuable habitat for pheasant broods.

During dry years, wetlands can be an oasis of green vegetation and insects for hungry chicks. Natural wetlands, wetland edges, and wet drainages provide a variety of valuable brood habitats with abundant food sources and protective cover along their margins. A lack of moisture in the uplands causes green vegetation to go dormant, and when the grass and forbs turn brown they can no longer support the insects essential for feeding chicks. Wetland basins and wetland edges are often moist sites and become especially important when droughty conditions come to South Dakota.

Pheasants are not only affected directly by dry conditions but, in addition, a lack of livestock forage understandably leads farmers and ranchers to harvest more acres of hay than in wetter years, including areas that have been set aside for conservation. Problems with drought are most common in central South Dakota. Poor pheasant production resulting from low chick survival in drought years has been documented by the South Dakota Department of Game, Fish and Parks (SDGFP).

Like adult pheasants, chicks will drink from open water but these water sources are not essential to their welfare. Water in dew, insects, and succulent herbaceous vegetation is usually adequate for chicks.

Chick survival

Chicks are most vulnerable to mortality in their first few weeks of life when factors such as cold and wet exposure, predators, and mowing can be especially threatening. Unusually heavy rains and cool weather at peak hatch times can cause increased chick mortality. Mortality due to mowing of alfalfa and other haylands can be a problem if the chicks are in fields being mowed in the first weeks post hatch (Gates and Hale 1975:60). Brood hens may also be killed or injured during mowing.

A variety of mammalian and avian (hawks or owls) predators will prey on pheasant chicks, but predation is reduced when these chicks have easy access to good escape cover. Diverse landscapes with ample areas of permanent herbaceous cover provide habitats for other prey such as meadow voles, various frogs, grasshoppers, and a variety of other species. These other prey species can be considered "buffers" because they provide a smorgasbord for predators that, in good habitat, may lighten the predation rate on any single species such as pheasant chicks. If agriculture is too intensive, both alternate prey species (buffer prey) and diverse brood habitat are greatly reduced. Programs such as CRP greatly improve the availability of alternate prey and good habitat.

Aldrin and similar insecticides (chlorinated hydrocarbons) caused serious mortality in pheasant chicks in croplands before they were banned for most uses in North America (Labisky and Lutz 1967). Some insecticides such as dieldrin, now banned, may also cause behavioral changes in pheasant chicks produced by hens that have taken in this chemical in their food (Dahlgren and Linder 1974). Several currently applied insecticides may kill pheasant chicks but their effects during and after field application have not been adequately studied (Giudice and Ratti 2001). We caution that insecticide-related deaths of pheasants, especially young chicks, may be going undetected since treated fields are unsafe for researchers to enter and the carcasses of chicks rapidly decay or are scavenged by predators.

Insecticides often cause indirect problems due to reduction in insects that are important for maintaining chick body condition and growth (Messick et al. 1974). Herbicides also indirectly reduce insects (by killing herbaceous plants), reduce plant foods for pheasants, and cause a loss of protective cover (Blus and Henny 1997; Rodgers 2002, 2005).

Though losses of pheasant chicks from disease can be severe in captive reared birds under crowded conditions, this does not appear to be a problem in the wild.

Chick survival rates increase greatly by 4 weeks post hatching as they become more efficient at controlling body temperature and gain increased mobility. Improvements in flight and running abilities assist them in escaping predators and avoiding mowing equipment. By 4 weeks of age chicks have learned much about predators and other dangers. Yet, as a general rule, over half of the chicks die before they are nearing independence at around 10 weeks, mostly in the early weeks after hatch. Survival of over 50% of chicks to independence is unusually high (Photo 6-8).

A few examples of chick survival from research studies may be helpful. Brood hens and two or three chicks from each brood were captured and fitted with radio transmitters to determine survival rates in northern Iowa (Riley et al. 1998). The tiny radio transmitters on the chicks weighed only 0.04 ounce each and were surgically implanted underneath the skin between the wings with a small antenna projecting from the skin. The chicks were successfully returned to their radio-marked brood hen within an hour. Chick survival to 28 days averaged 46% in a landscape with 25% grassland while 37% survived beyond 28 days in a landscape with more cropland and just 11% grassland (Riley et al. 1998). Weasels, red fox, and mink were the primary predators of chicks.

Over an 8-year period, researchers in Wisconsin's best pheasant region compared estimates of chicks hatched based on nest searches and juveniles alive in early October and concluded that an average of 58% of chicks survived (Gates and Hale 1975:61).

Photo 6-8. By the time wild-reared chicks reach 6 to 8 weeks of age they have an excellent chance to survive into the fall. This older chick is still dependent on the hen. (Courtesy of Scott Weins)

Slightly over 80% of radio-transmittered hens that hatched clutches were able to successfully rear broods (one or more chicks still alive) to at least 8 weeks of age in high quality pheasant habitat near Huron (Leif 1994). Other brood survival rate estimates have ranged from just below 40% to over 90% (Giudice and Ratti 2001).

These studies represent chick and brood survival rates that one might expect to find in much of South Dakota's main pheasant range. Some broods are entirely lost to mortality as illustrated by Leif's 1994 study. Estimates of chick survival based on brood size changes can be misleading and biased higher than actual rates if total brood mortality is not considered. Brood combination or mixing also can reduce the accuracy of this type of survival estimation.

An example of brood survival estimates based on changes in brood size from hatching to 5 to 6 weeks of age is helpful here. In Illinois, chick survival to 5 to 6 weeks steadily declined from the early 1950s (78%) through the late 1970s (54%) as farming practices intensified and row crops on the landscape increased (Warner et al. 1984). The estimates from Illinois are higher than actual survival rates because loss of entire broods is not reflected in brood size changes. Nevertheless, the chick survival rates from Illinois were valuable in evaluating long-term changes in brood survival.

Long-term declines in brood survival observed in the Illinois study are related to declines in the quality and abundance of brood cover and food due to clean farming practices and lack of undisturbed cover appropriate for younger broods (Warner 1984, Warner et al. 1999). In a landscape heavily dominated by row crops, chicks have a difficult time locating sufficient numbers of insects to meet the demands of growth and development. Chicks that are below normal weight and in poor physical condition will generally have higher mortality rates than heavier, healthier chicks.

Chapter thoughts

Secure habitat for brood hens and chicks is one of the main keys for improving ring-necked pheasant populations on agricultural landscapes. If there are not adequate amounts of protective herbaceous cover with abundant insects for chicks in the first 4–6 weeks of life, pheasant populations will not thrive. Mixtures of forbs (such as alfalfa) and grasses provide more insect foods for chicks than cover dominated entirely by grass. Areas such as unmowed fields of grasses and forbs, wetland edges, ungrazed shelterbelts, unmowed roadsides, weedy field borders, wide fence rows, tall and weedy wheat stubble, and various odd field corners are all good brood habitats if left undisturbed. Diversity of herbaceous cover is almost always a positive. With that in mind, many volunteer herbaceous plants such as kochia (fireweed) and annual sunflower (excluding those identified as noxious weeds by the state) should be considered a valuable part of the habitat for improving brood survival.

CHAPTER 7
STAYING ALIVE — SURVIVAL AND MORTALITY

Many people have the perception that pheasants in the wild, particularly the hens, commonly live for several years. This is not the case. It is a rare pheasant, regardless of gender, that lives to see 3 years of age even in unhunted populations.

Estimates of survival rates in pheasants are usually made by monitoring birds that have been captured and fitted with radio transmitters. The weight and type of radio transmitter may reduce survival, as documented for backpack-mounted transmitters (Warner and Etter 1983, Marcstrom et al. 1989). For this reason, recent survival estimates (other than for chicks) have been based on transmitters mounted around the neck with a necklace or poncho and weighing less than 3% of the bird's weight. Survival estimates can also be made by other methods such as census comparisons and band recovery techniques.

We provide an overview in this chapter of survival in pheasants primarily after they reach the juvenile stage (10 weeks), an age at which their survival rates are similar to those of adults. Factors that can increase survival as well as the causes of mortality are discussed. Survival during the egg and chick stages has already been addressed in Chapters 5 and 6.

Roosters
Hunting mortality

As one would expect, hunting season is normally the period of highest mortality for cock pheasants. Biologists sometimes estimate percentage of cocks killed by hunters based on the change in the sex ratio from preseason to post season. Corrections need to be made to include the influence of some illegal hen kill on the post-season sex ratio. Illegal hen kill is generally around 10–13%

(Chesness and Nelson 1964). Hunting season mortality can also be estimated using roosters marked with leg bands or fitted with radio transmitters. Rooster mortality from hunting normally runs around 50 to 65% in South Dakota. Most estimates of annual survival (carryover) in roosters are at or below about 20% (Petersen et al. 1988).

The annual harvest rate (years grouped together) of radio-marked male pheasants near Huron during pheasant hunting seasons from 1997 through 2001 was 51% (Leif 2003). One-fourth of the season-long harvest occurred in the first 2 days of the hunting season and half of the total came in the first 9 days of the hunting season. A hunter-harvest survey indicated that 56% of pheasants shot in South Dakota were harvested in the first 11 days of the 2000 season (Gigliotti 2004). During the 2001 hunting season, hunters reported that 21% of their season-long harvest occurred on the opening weekend (Smith and Leif 2002). Weekly harvest rates in the remaining weeks after the first 9 days of the hunting season were estimated to be 4–5% of the male pheasant population (Leif 2003) (Photo 7-1).

Each rooster pheasant is highly capable of copulating with a large number of hens; in fact, a single rooster pheasant has been known to fertilize over 50 females in a captive situation. In the wild, the post-hunting season ratio of roosters to hens is seldom more skewed than one male per two or three hens in South Dakota. As noted in Chapter 5, infertility in wild pheasant hens has never been found to be a problem.

Photo 7-1. Mortality on cock pheasants during South Dakota's hunting season is normally 50 to 65%. (Courtesy of Doug Backlund)

Hunting season length

Long hunting seasons permit increased recreational opportunity and do not influence year-to-year populations of pheasants. If hens were hunted over a similar long season or if illegal hen kill became excessive, it could have a negative effect on the population. Fortunately, hunters are strongly supportive of the rooster-only harvest regulations; shooting hens is not only illegal, it is socially unacceptable. Most experienced hunters rarely make such a mistake.

Another factor of interest in evaluating long seasons is the reduction in hunters and hunting pressure after the first few weekends. Those who continue to hunt can have good success but the surviving roosters become increasingly adept at avoiding hunters as the season progresses.

In an interesting study, spring and summer roadside pheasant surveys were compared for the years 1964–1977 between the adjacent tiers of counties in southern Minnesota and northern Iowa (George et al. 1980). Agricultural landscapes in these bordering counties were quite similar. From 1964 to 1977, Iowa maintained a season averaging 55 days (51 to 58 days) with a bag limit of three in most years while Minnesota seasons averaged 23 days (0 to 38 days) with a bag limit of two in most years. After the harsh winter in 1968–1969, pheasants in both states suffered heavy winter losses of birds. Iowa maintained the same hunting season while Minnesota, under much public pressure, closed the pheasant season for 1969.

The 1969 closure of pheasant hunting in Minnesota received much public attention as did the notable increase in pheasants by 1970. Many viewed the 1970 increases as clear evidence that the closure had accomplished its purposes in increasing the pheasant population. However, across the border in Iowa, despite a long pheasant season with a bag limit of three roosters, the pheasant population also increased at the same rate as in Minnesota. These nearly identical rates of increase in adjacent counties of both states demonstrated that the pheasant season closure in Minnesota had been of no value as a method for increasing pheasant populations.

The closure of the Minnesota hunting season had resulted in the loss of pheasant hunting opportunities and a projected harvest of over 180,000 roosters. In other years throughout the 1964–1977 period, despite more conservative seasons and bag limits in Minnesota, the pheasant populations in both states followed remarkably similar patterns.

There have been other chances elsewhere to compare short versus long seasons and closed versus open seasons, and the same conclusions have been reached. Hunting season closures and restricted seasons have no obvious influence on year-to-year pheasant populations and annual population changes. Hunter harvest of roosters is not a factor influencing year-to-year reproduction by the pheasant population as a whole.

Annual hen survival rates

How long do hens live? Most estimates of annual survival of hens range between 20% and 50% according to reviews in Petersen et al. (1988) and Giudice and Ratti (2001). Annual hen survival rates in Illinois fell within the 30–35% range typical for the Midwest (Warner et al. 2000). In northeastern Colorado, during a year with mild weather patterns, 52% of radio-marked hens survived from spring to spring; higher losses occurred in years with more severe winter weather (Snyder 1985). In southwestern Minnesota, hen pheasants were estimated to have a carryover rate from year to year of 30–35% based on census data (Chesness and Nelson 1964). Radio-marked hens in eastern South Dakota (Beadle and Sanborn counties) had surprisingly high annual survival rates at 46% over a 3-year period with moderate winters (Leif 1996). Some studies have documented higher spring-summer survival rates in older, more experienced females than in younger (1-year-old) birds (Snyder 1985) (Photo 7-2).

Seasonal survival rates—emphasis on hens

Considerable seasonal variation in hen mortality can occur. Two seasonal periods of potentially high loss include spring and unusually severe winters. Hen mortality is generally low in South Dakota during winters unless conditions are unusually severe. Summer and fall feature abundant cover and food for hens and are generally periods with low mortality rates although some illegal kill of hens occurs in the hunting season. We emphasize hen survival in this section because of the importance of their survival to reproduction. However, male seasonal survival also can be influenced by some of the same factors.

Photo 7-2. Annual survival of hen pheasants is normally between 30 and 40%. (Courtesy of Doug Backlund)

Breeding season hen survival—early season cover and predation

Hen mortality through spring and summer has been estimated by several researchers. In this period hens are involved in prelaying, laying, incubation, and brood rearing, activities that can increase physiological stress on hens and vulnerability to predation and accidents (i.e., with farm equipment). Increased mortality and reduced survival due to predation have been observed mainly in April or early May when much of the herbaceous cover may be flattened (lodged) due to the winter snow pack and new growth remains minimal (Snyder 1985, Brittas et al. 1992, Leif 1996). As spring progresses, new grass and forb growth provides better concealment for pheasants. Some of the residual native grasses such as switchgrass and big bluestem tend to remain erect through winter and bounce back more readily after snow melt than common exotics (foreign introductions) like smooth brome; such plants provide important concealment cover in the spring and help improve hen survival (Photo 7-3).

The importance of concealment cover in spring was illustrated by a study in Colorado in an area of dryland farming (Snyder 1985). Survival of pheasants fitted with radio transmitters during the year was lowest in April due to lack of concealing cover and resultant vulnerability of hens to hawks (Cooper's hawks and prairie falcons) and great horned owls during this period. Growth of winter wheat provided protective cover for hens as the spring progressed and survival rates responded by increasing greatly. Similarly, in eastern South Dakota (Beadle

Photo 7-3. These hen pheasants are attempting to conceal themselves in residual and new growth spring cover but it is still marginal cover until further vegetation growth occurs. Marginal cover leaves hens more vulnerable to predators, especially raptors. (Courtesy of Doug Backlund)

and Sanborn counties), radio-marked hens had the highest mortality in April and May, mainly from predation by various hawks and great horned owls (Leif 1996). Survival increased later in the spring and summer as growing vegetation provided improved concealment (Photos 7-4)(Photos 7-5).

Photos 7-4. Prairie falcons are swift and beautiful raptors and are effective predators when prey, such as hen pheasants, come out into the open too far from taller, more erect, and protective cover. Predation by raptors is greatly reduced where pheasants are in or near protective escape cover. (Courtesy of Doug Backlund)

Photos 7-5. Residual cover from native tallgrass species generally remains at least partially erect through late winter and into the courtship and prenesting periods. This cover protects hen pheasants from raptors such as this great horned owl (inset) during the critical courtship and prenesting period. (LDF, inset courtesy of Scott Weins).

Hens still in harems or still depositing eggs (laying stage) appear to be more vulnerable to predation than hens that have started incubation (Leif 1996). Incubating females remain more concealed and are less easily spotted by raptors.

Researchers in Iowa observed 81% survival of hens from April 1 to June 3 and recommended increasing the size of permanent grass-forb cover patches as a means of increasing hen survival in the spring and early summer (Schmitz and Clark 1999). Of the 19% dying, two-thirds of the losses were due to mammalian predators, primarily red fox.

In all of these studies on spring survival, the recurring recommendation is to provide increased numbers of sites and acreage of concealment cover for hens during the prelaying and laying stages. Most of this cover would need to be standing residual herbaceous vegetation (including both grasses and volunteer weeds), patches of dense shrubs, or shelterbelts that include dense shrubby rows; these types of cover provide good concealment after snow melt and before sufficient new growth occurs. Native tallgrass prairie species such as switchgrass and big bluestem are much better at providing concealment for hens in spring than the widespread smooth brome that is more easily flattened by snow cover.

Hen survival in winter

Surprisingly, winters are often periods of time with high hen survival rates despite the cold, snow, and tendency of birds to concentrate. Near Huron, survival of pheasants was unusually high during three relatively mild winters 1990–1992 (Leif 1996). In fact, during November and January of those years, survival of radio-marked hens was 100%. Hen pheasants also had high survival rates in a mild winter in northeastern Colorado (Snyder 1985).

Winters with unusually severe conditions (extreme cold, ice, repeated blizzards, snow, and drifting) in the northern plains periodically lead to high pheasant mortality. In eastern South Dakota, 1996–1997 was one of the most severe winters of the century. Some drifts in the windward portion of shelterbelts were over 10 feet in height. Excellent winter cover in much of the area was mostly inundated with snow (Photo 7-6). Even extensive areas of tall and dense native grasses, dense cattail, sandbar willow stands, and common reed (more commonly

Photo 7-6. During harsh winter conditions, blowing snow will fill in much of the winter cover. A wide and dense shelterbelt will still provide protection on the leeward side. (CTS)

called phragmites) were mostly buried by drifting snow. Most pheasants were forced to move to the only available cover — dense shelterbelts that, because of their shape, width, and composition, provided some protection from wind and cold. Survival of radio-marked hens from December 1 to March 1 was dismal at only 3% (Gabbert et al. 1999). In the previous winter under more typical conditions survival had been much higher at 61%.

The necklace radio transmitters likely increased the stress on hens under these severe winter conditions and further reduced survival although other observations from the study area also confirmed that losses had been heavy on unmarked pheasants. August roadside counts in the region indicated that numbers of adult hens were reduced by 60% from the previous August, a serious reduction but not as severe as indicated by mortality of radio-marked birds.

Most deaths of hen pheasants in the eastern South Dakota study occurred during 4- to 5-day blizzard periods in December and January. Out of 41 deaths, 31 (76%) occurred during the blizzard periods (Gabbert et al. 1999). Fifteen of the hens were found intact with injuries and internal hemorrhaging, indicating they were killed by mammalian predators (D.H. Zeeman, Animal Disease Research and Diagnostics Laboratory, South Dakota State University, personal communication).

Under the severe winter of 1996–1997, pheasants were concentrated in the only remnant cover, usually the leeward side of multi-row shelterbelts, and in many cases appeared to be weakened and highly vulnerable to predation under blizzard and immediate post blizzard conditions (Gabbert et al. 1999). It was unusual that many hens were killed by mammalian predators but not consumed.

Observation by two of the authors of this book indicated hunters and hunting dogs did not hunt the study areas during the December blizzard periods; the season was not open during the January blizzard. Red fox, feral dogs, and a low population of coyotes all occurred on the study areas. Many of the hens appeared to have been nearly incapacitated by severe cold and snow when captured by predators and would likely have died of freezing or of eventual starvation if they had not been killed by predators (Gabbert et al. 1999).

Hen survival during unusually severe winters in southeastern North Dakota and north-central Iowa was also low and showed many similarities to the eastern South Dakota study (Perkins et al. 1997, Homan et al. 2000). In all of these studies, undisturbed herbaceous vegetation filled in first with snow, followed by smaller cattail wetlands. The last wetland habitats that fill with snow are larger wetlands with extensive cattail cover, phragmites stands, and sometimes larger stands of dense sandbar willow. Downwind portions of unusually large wetlands, 100 or more acres with extensive and nearly continuous stands of dense cattail, may retain sufficient cover on the leeward side to provide winter habitat even in the worst winters. Residual cover such as tall stubble, standing grasses and weeds, shelterbelts, or other vegetation that catches drifting snow upwind of wintering wetland cover can also reduce drifting into dense cattail habitat.

After most dense upland and wetland cover fills up with snow, pheasants are often forced to concentrate in woody habitats such as wide, dense shelterbelts to find protection from the wind (Kuehl and Flake 1998). Wide belts of woody cover planted around farmsteads to protect buildings, people, and livestock from wind are particularly valuable to pheasants. In many cases pheasants find shelter in dense shrubs, conifers, or other protective vegetation on the leeward side of tall drifts that have formed in the more windward portions of a wide shelterbelt (Photo 7-7). Nearby food sources such as corn food plots, unharvested corn, areas where cattle are fed, or windblown fields with abundant waste grains are also essential.

In areas without wetlands and dense cattails, pheasants are more dependent on multi-row shelterbelts with shrubs and evergreens for protection from the elements when most grass and forb cover fills up with snow. Most areas of the state have at least some dense upland cover (such as tall and dense switchgrass or stands of kochia), wetland winter habitat (cattails), and dense woody cover for wintering pheasants, but these types of cover are generally less abundant west of the Missouri River. Fortunately for wintering pheasants, areas west of the Missouri River, especially from Pierre through south-central South Dakota, tend to have less snow and warmer temperatures.

Lack of concealment cover and concentration of pheasants near shelterbelts containing tall trees (often plains cottonwoods) that may harbor great horned owls can contribute to increased predation losses in winter (Homan et al. 2000). Two other large raptors sometimes observed in eastern South Dakota in winter include northern goshawks and rough-legged hawks, but in general large hawks

Photo 7-7. The leeward side of dense shrubby cover provided attractive wintering habitat for these pheasants in central South Dakota. To function as high-quality winter cover, food sources should also be nearby. (CTS)

are much less abundant in winter than during spring and fall migration (L.D. Flake, personal observation; Gabbert and Schneider 1998). Lack of availability of alternate prey (buffer species) such as meadow voles and prairie voles (concealed by deep snow), may increase pressure on pheasants. Also, pheasants in poor physical condition suffering through unusually severe winter conditions can be especially vulnerable to predators.

What about reported winter deaths from starvation and suffocation? Starvation has been identified as a cause of pheasant death of both male and female pheasants during some severe winters. Birds found starving are extremely weak, may not be able to fly, and can often be caught by hand (McClure 1948, Nelson and Janson 1949). Starving pheasants also have razor thin breasts and retain little or no deposits of yellow fat (Photos 7-8).

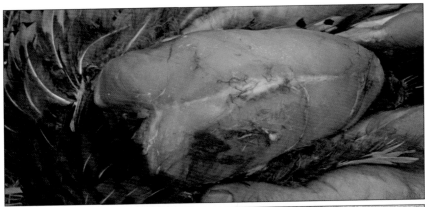

Photos 7-8. Good-condition pheasants have the full, rounded breast and a more pinkish color to the breast muscle as in this harvested male (top). Starving pheasants (hen and rooster) lack the fat deposits and become razor breasted with a dark red color to the breast muscle (bottom). (APL)

Hens are more susceptible to winter starvation than males because of their smaller body size; some have erroneously interpreted this to be a result of cocks suppressing hen survival through competition for resources (Photo 7-9). In recent studies in eastern South Dakota, some hens were in starving condition, but most pheasants were not emaciated to the extent described in some reports (Gabbert et al. 1999). Easily approachable pheasant hens in starving condition were observed in eastern South Dakota in the harsh winter of 2009–2010, as was also documented in Beadle County in the winter of 2000–2001 (C.T. Switzer and A.P. Leif, personal observation).

Pheasants in good condition and even with full crops will sometimes be found dead, with the mouth and beak iced up after a severe blizzard. Such birds are often caught in marginal cover without good protection from the wind and cold. Pheasants caught in this marginal cover face into the wind and bitter cold where first the nostrils and then the mouth freeze with layers or balls of ice. Most of 203 dead pheasants picked up after a severe storm in an Iowa study were judged to have died from freezing or suffocation (beak iced up) with little evidence of predation (Green 1938) (Photos 7-10).

A few hunters have shared stories of hunting dogs capturing and killing or injuring hens during a pheasant hunt, especially under conditions of deep snow and cold. Other hunters report rarely having dogs capture and kill or injure hens despite hunting pheasants throughout the season for several decades. With soft-mouthed dogs the hens can often be released unharmed, but in many of these cases the dogs crush the bird. Training your dog to make soft-mouthed retrieves while the dog is still very young could help alleviate these losses. The significance

Photo 7-9. There is no evidence that competition with cocks reduces the survival of hens during winter. However, it does appear that the smaller hens are more susceptible to winterkill than cocks in unusually severe winters. (Courtesy of Doug Backlund)

Photos 7-10. This male pheasant found near Miller suffered severe weight loss and apparently died of starvation in February after stress from multiple blizzards in 2010. The hen pheasant, found near Brookings after a mid season blizzard in the 1970s, had not lost weight and was apparently killed when ice formed over the nostrils and in the mouth, causing probable suffocation. (CTS, LDF)

of these losses of hens to hunting dogs on overall hen survival is thought to be small but such deaths have not been studied.

Coyote suppression of other predators—a help for pheasants

In recent years we have become increasingly aware that large predator species may influence the abundance of smaller predator species by killing or otherwise suppressing them. This phenomenon is called mesopredator suppression and has been most studied in relation to coyote suppression of smaller carnivores such as the red fox (Sovada et al. 1995, Mezquida et al. 2006). These studies have shown that intensive control of coyotes can lead to increases in populations of other smaller predators with negative consequences for nesting success.

Because of their influence in suppressing smaller predators, the presence of low to moderate coyote numbers can be a means for increasing nest success in waterfowl and other ground-nesting birds over broad areas of the northern plains (Sovada et al. 1995). Coyotes will, of course, prey on pheasants as well as pheasant eggs but they are not as proficient at nest and hen predation as the red fox. A few coyotes may be some of your best friends in terms of controlling predators like the red fox (Photo 7-11).

On the Fort Pierre National Grassland (FPNG), sharp-tailed grouse and greater prairie-chickens were found to have exceptionally high nest success (80% over a 3-year period) in years with adequate precipitation and herbaceous cover (Norton 2005). The presence of moderate numbers of coyotes on FPNG likely

Photo 7-11. Studies have shown that coyotes suppress some smaller predators such as red fox and, in this way, often have an overall positive influence on nesting success of ground-nesting birds such as pheasants and ducks. A moderate number of coyotes may result in more pheasants the next hunting season. (Courtesy of Doug Backlund)

suppresses red fox densities and perhaps those of other nest predators and, along with good nesting habitat, helps reduce nest predation.

The authors are supportive of normal hunting and trapping of coyotes as a means to manage coyote populations or to remove problem animals bothering livestock. Large-scale efforts to reduce or eradicate coyotes are not encouraged. Any type of predator removal will have other indirect influences that need to be considered when evaluating possible predator control efforts. Predator control is discussed in Chapter 11.

Accidents

Pheasant deaths from accidents have been recorded in virtually every study of pheasant survival (Photo 7-12). The highest losses of hens from accidents often occur during mowing of alfalfa or other hay during peak nesting or around peak hatch in mid to late June (Gates and Hale 1975:36, 60). Accidental deaths of chicks are discussed in Chapter 6.

Other than deaths of hens during hay mowing, accidents include various collisions with vehicles, power lines, or other structures. Road mortality can sometimes be at a peak during severe winters when birds gather along roadsides looking for food and grit. Pheasants killed along highways, especially territorial roosters during the spring, can be very evident to anyone driving in high-density pheasant areas. However, losses from automobiles are generally relatively minor in terms of total pheasant mortality.

Photo 7-12. First cuttings of alfalfa occur during or prior to peak hatch and can be a major cause of accidental death in pheasant hens, developing eggs, and newly hatched chicks during the nesting period. (CTS)

Deaths from power line collisions occasionally occur. In areas where pheasant population densities are unusually high, such accidents are more likely to occur when hundreds of birds are flushed toward power lines as hunters press through a field. In such cases, fields should be hunted in a way that pushes birds away from power lines if collisions have been a problem in the past.

Insecticides, fungicides, herbicides, and other toxins

Insecticides and herbicides can potentially influence juvenile and adult pheasants through direct death, reduced reproductive success, reduction in food sources, reduction in protective herbaceous cover (herbicides), and possibly even impaired behavior that renders birds more vulnerable to predation. Some of these threats apply to pheasant chicks and have been discussed in Chapter 6.

To our knowledge, agricultural insecticides currently in use in the United States have not been known to cause major die offs of juveniles or older pheasants when applied at recommended rates. Ring-necked pheasants can detect seeds treated with some insecticides and fungicides and will sometimes avoid eating these seeds if suitable alternative foods are available (Bennett and Prince 1981). Other researchers have found that, as is the case with treated seed corn, the fungicide or insecticide may not be distasteful enough to inhibit use of all or part of the seed by pheasants (West et al. 1969). However, we know of no evidence that treated seeds are killing pheasants.

Herbicides indirectly cause pheasant losses by reducing plant foods for pheasants, reducing insects (food for chicks) dependent on target plants, and causing losses of protective cover (Blus and Henny 1997; Rodgers 2002, 2005).

Polychlorinated biphenyls (PCBs), an industrial product widely found in the food chain, can have a depressive influence on pheasant egg production, hatchability, and survival of very young chicks through PCBs ingested by the hen. However, livers of pheasants collected in South Dakota indicated low levels of this contaminant that should not depress pheasant populations (Dahlgren and Linder 1971).

Diseases and parasites

Several diseases can infect pheasants, but problems with those diseases appear mainly in captive flocks where fowl cholera, Newcastle disease, tuberculosis, botulism, and several other diseases have been detected. Diseases in wild pheasants have not generally been found to be a major cause of mortality or population depression, although deaths from disease could easily go undetected if they occur only sporadically.

Antibodies from both eastern and western viral encephalitis have been detected in ring-necked pheasants in South Dakota (Dahlgren et al. 1974). These authors found a possible association of antibodies with the deaths of adult hens in spring and early summer, but the results were not conclusive.

As with all birds, one can expect a number of internal parasites and external parasites to be associated with pheasants. Ticks, lice, fleas, tapeworms, nematodes, and other parasites are common to pheasants but are not normally associated with die offs.

Chapter thoughts

Pheasants are short-lived birds with the ability to offset losses with prolific reproduction. Few pheasants live to reach 3 years of age even in unhunted areas. Hunting season length with harvest restricted to males has no influence on annual population trends as one might expect in a polygynous bird such as the ring-necked pheasant. While rooster mortality rates are highest during the fall hunting season, some of the lowest hen survival rates are normally during April and early May just after the snow melts and while the residual herbaceous cover is matted down or otherwise destroyed. Provision of standing residual grasses and weeds along with shrub cover can be especially important for protecting hens from raptor predation in the early spring after the hens have dispersed from wintering to nesting areas.

Woody cover (shelterbelts with dense shrub rows, shrub thickets, willow stands) and cattail stands (wetlands) benefit pheasant survival by providing concealment, escape cover, and protection from the elements, especially in winter and spring. Managers should focus on improving hen survival through the year to assure good reproduction — abundant habitat is the most easily manageable key to improved hen survival.

PART III: IMPROVING PHEASANT HABITAT

CHAPTER 8
EVALUATION AND TECHNOLOGY

Ring-necked pheasants require a variety of habitats and those requirements change with the seasons. Pheasant habitats must include space, protective cover, food, grit, loafing areas, and other needs.

Space provides a physical location to contain and arrange various habitat components, to allow for behavioral needs such as breeding territories for rooster pheasants and for appropriate dispersal to reduce predation. The placement of habitat components in relation to one another is sometimes referred to as habitat arrangement or juxtaposition. For example, placement of food plots near good winter cover, such as dense cattail stands and dense woody cover (shrub patches and shrub belts), represents appropriate arrangement or juxtaposition of two key habitat components needed by wintering pheasants (Larsen et al. 1994). Pheasants benefit by having habitat components arranged in close enough proximity so they can be easily accessed within their daily movements (home range). Home range areas can be less than 10 acres (Chapter 6) for a brood hen with young chicks or may exceed 100 acres for adults and older juveniles (Chapter 2).

In this chapter, we briefly review what pheasants need during the critical nesting, brood rearing, and wintering periods; address the process of "taking stock" of those critical pheasant habitats; and touch on some technologies that have had major effects on farming and pheasant management in recent years.

Pheasants and makeup of the landscape
Ratios of grassland to cropland

Regional pheasant abundance in South Dakota's pheasant range increases in relation to the amount of grassland on the landscape as long as adequate amounts of cropland are interspersed. Landscapes with a ratio of about 60% grassland habitat and the remaining 40% in other agricultural uses (cropland, shelterbelts, farmsteads, etc.) will consistently support some of the state's highest pheasant populations (unpublished data, U.S. Geological Survey National Center for Earth Resources, Sioux Falls) (Figure 8-1). In south-central Minnesota's cultivated landscape, the amount of Conservation Reserve Program (CRP) grasslands under USDA contracts in the early 2000s varied from a minimum of 0% to a high of 32%. Regional pheasant populations in these landscapes increased in direct relation to increasing acreages of CRP grasslands (Haroldson et al. 2006). Basically, the more grass-forb cover (CRP), the more pheasants.

South Dakota's lowest pheasant populations are generally found in intensively farmed regions with almost the entire landscape in row crops or in landscapes characterized by 80 to 90% (or more) native grassland with little to no cropland. The latter regions of native prairie (or mostly native prairie) are our premier habitats for prairie grouse and many other prairie-dependent wildlife species; we strongly recommend against conversion of remaining native prairies to croplands (Flake et al. 2010).

Pheasants clearly benefit from farming and resulting waste grain but are negatively affected when farming practices become so intensive that nesting, brood rearing, and wintering cover are greatly reduced. Enormous fields of single crops such as corn, soybeans, or sunflowers sometimes taking up an entire section or more replace valuable wildlife habitats and have an overall negative influence on pheasants.

Availability of winter cover

During severe winter weather, pheasants will sometimes travel 2 to 3 miles and occasionally more to locate adequate winter food and cover (Gabbert et al. 1999, Leif 2003). Thus, winter food and cover complexes are not required in every quarter section of land to sustain pheasant populations. In fact, one quality

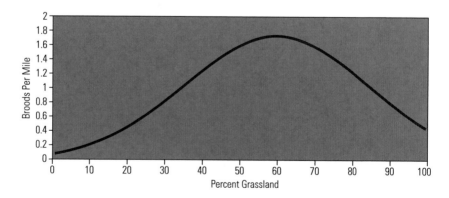

Figure 8-1. Broods per mile counts in relation to percent grassland on the landscape, South Dakota. (Courtesy of U.S. Geological Survey National Center for Earth Resources, Sioux Falls, S.D.)

winter food/cover complex per section of land is usually adequate to sustain a viable pheasant population in an area. However, if wintering areas are too far apart, losses to sudden blizzards will likely increase for birds unable to reach good cover. If you are interested in attracting and hunting pheasants, dense stands of cattails, kochia, or other winter cover (along with food sources) can be highly important in holding pheasants through the entire hunting season.

The availability of winter cover scattered across the landscape is critical to the success of ring-necked pheasants in much of the northern plains. During normal winters the most important wintering habitat is found in dense stands of cattails associated with wetlands (Chapter 7). Stands of phragmites and sand-bar willow associated with these wetlands can also be important. Larger glacial wetlands with dense cattails can harbor an abundance of wintering pheasants as long as adequate waste grain or food plots are nearby (Photo 8-1). The larger the area of wetland winter cover (primarily cattail), the less likely it is to fully drift in with snow in a severe winter.

In northern plains states such as South Dakota, dense shelterbelt plantings scattered over the agricultural landscape can play a critical role in the survival of ring-necked pheasants during periods of extreme cold, wind, and deep snow (Gabbert et al. 1999, Homan et al. 2000) (Chapter 7). Woody habitat may not be required each year and is of less importance to plains states south of South Dakota. However, dense patches of sandbar willow or wild plum and shelterbelts

Photo 8-1. Wetlands dominated by cattail and other dense vegetation provide protection from bone-chilling winds and are valuable for wintering pheasants. Waste grain in an adjacent harvested corn field provided food for these pheasants. (TRK)

with conifers and dense shrub rows are used by pheasants every winter if available. Dense woody cover is also important during the spring breeding period as part of male territories (Chapter 4) and may also provide escape or loafing cover at other times of the year (Photo 8-2).

Shelterbelts designed with shrubs and small brushy trees that provide thermal protection at the ground level yield a more suitable understory at maturity than those designed with deciduous trees that grow tall as they mature but provide minimal thermal protection or concealment at the ground. Shelterbelts with old, tall deciduous trees are also attractive to predators such as great horned owls and raccoons, making these shelterbelts of less value to pheasants.

Taking stock

Property owners with an interest in improving or maintaining healthy pheasant populations can develop appropriate management efforts on their land. The first critical step is to evaluate the potential of the farm or other property involved. This "taking stock" or evaluation exercise should be done regularly as habitat elements can change over time both on the property and adjacent lands.

A basic map is an invaluable tool. Aerial maps obtained through the Natural Resource Conservation Service are updated annually and should suffice for eval-

Photo 8-2. Protection from the wind on the leeward side of dense and wide shelterbelts can be critical to pheasant survival during severe winters in South Dakota. (Courtesy of Doug Backlund)

uating habitat availability and arrangement. Label grassland or grassland-forb nesting cover, grazed pasture, wetland winter cover, dense woody cover, alfalfa, row crops, and other cover types. If the mapping approach is too time consuming, you can still go through this habitat evaluation process in your mind as you travel about your farm or other property. However, keeping written records and actual maps can prove of long-term benefit in evaluating land-use practices and other changes that can influence pheasant habitat quantity and quality. Examples of changes through the years can include crop types; tillage practices (no-till, minimum till, etc.); wetland cover; shrub belt plantings; grazing, haying, and burning practices; amount of tall grain stubble with volunteer weeds or seeded to cover crop; available edges and odd areas with herbaceous cover; herbicide and insecticide use; and several other factors that can influence pheasant habitat and pheasants.

Photos and written habitat descriptions presented in this chapter and throughout the book can be used to rate wetlands, herbaceous cover, and other cover types in terms of their value as poor, adequate, or excellent for pheasant seasonal needs. If you are uncertain, your local conservation officer or regional private lands biologist with the SDGFP and local Pheasants Forever biologist could provide assistance (Photo 8-3).

Photo 8-3. In just the second year after planting, this seeding of tallgrass natives on the Bill Lee farm in southeastern South Dakota provides valuable habitat for pheasants through most of the year. Bill, Dawn Stephens, and their dog are shown in this late October scene. (LDF)

Be sure to consider mowing practices in alfalfa or hayland in your evaluation of pheasant habitat. Alfalfa attracts nesting pheasants but is normally poor nesting and early brood-rearing cover because the first mowing precedes peak hatch, which can destroy nests, kill or injure hens, and kill young chicks (Chapters 5 and 6). Second-growth alfalfa can be a valuable rearing area for middle age or older chicks but is still dangerous for late nests (renests) or late-hatched chicks. Grass hay that is not mowed until after July 15, preferably after August 1, provides valuable nesting cover, especially for renesting hens.

Row crops such as corn are of basically no value to nesting pheasants and broods in the first few weeks post hatch; the outer edges of these row crops are increasingly used by older broods, juveniles, and by adults as the summer progresses (Chapters 5 and 6). Winter wheat, because of early growth, can be quite valuable to nesting pheasants. Spring-planted small grains, including spring wheat, are of less value than winter wheat for nesting but are used by renesting pheasants later in the nesting season and can also be used by broods.

Small areas such as existing or restored shallow wetlands (temporary and seasonal wetlands) provide excellent habitat for nesting hens and pheasant broods and also support pheasants during much of the remainder of the year (Gates 1970). Grazing systems that leave adequate grass and forb cover in at least some pastures during the reproductive season can also boost pheasant production.

Many landowners make the mistake of trying to provide all the pheasant habitat requirements on their own property without ever looking across the fence. Property ownership has no meaning to pheasants.

If a large, dense, multi-row shelterbelt that provides good protection from wind and snow is located across the fence on a neighbor's land, it may have sufficient cover for wintering pheasants produced on your land. Perhaps the space on your land could be used for another complementary habitat component such as a food plot or nesting and brood-rearing cover that is lacking or limited.

If you have a strong interest in hunting you will want fall and winter cover that attracts and holds the birds on your own property even if it duplicates nearby cover on a neighbor's land. In the colder months, attractive winter habitats such as tall and dense switchgrass, volunteer stands of kochia and annual sunflowers, dense cattail wetlands, clumps of brushy sandbar willows near waterways, and dense rows of woody cover such as Amur maple and other shrubs on your land along with adequate food plots can attract pheasants from adjacent lands with less desirable winter cover. Even though you will be attracting birds and improving hunting on your own land, you will also be benefiting your neighbor's property by providing good pheasant habitat in the local area (Photo 8-4).

Technology influences on habitat management

Some crops fall into the rapidly expanding category of genetically modified organisms. The development of genetically modified crops such as Roundup Ready® corn and soybeans has changed the way public and private wildlife areas

Photo 8-4. Year after year the dense sandbar willow, cattails, and other vegetation in this drainage harbor high densities of pheasants, especially after snow begins to accumulate. The upland in the background is in native grass cover established through the Conservation Reserve Program. If you value pheasant hunting, be sure to keep such sites on the farm. (LDF)

are developed and managed. These crops were genetically engineered to provide resistance to nonselective herbicides. One negative effect of this type of farming operation is that the classic "weedy fence row" is practically nonexistent in South Dakota's farm belt. Furthermore, genetically modified crops have greatly increased the conversion of native grasslands, including those in marginal soil regions, into commodity croplands.

However, herbicides and herbicide-resistant crops can also be useful tools for killing undesirable grasses such as old stands of smooth brome and converting them into more desirable grasses or even into wildlife food plots. These herbicides have provided managers with a tool to reduce competing plants on a site by planting a resistant crop such as corn or soybeans prior to planting native grasses or other desirable grass and forb species. Additional herbicides have also been developed that do not harm some desirable native plants but kill or suppress undesirable plants, including some noxious weeds. These new herbicides can be an invaluable tool in managing pheasant reproductive cover (Photos 8-5).

Modern farming equipment has also forced changes in the design and layout of areas managed specifically for pheasants such as food plots or woody cover plantings. South Dakota has many nonfarming landowners that own properties specifically for recreational pheasant hunting. These landowners may contract with neighboring farmers to install wildlife food plots on their land. The size of the planting equipment used may dictate the size, shape, and placement of the food plots, woody cover plantings, contour grass strips, or other habitats being developed.

Photos 8-5. This seeded native prairie on the Bauer Waterfowl Production Area (WPA) in Beadle County is unusually diverse for seeded natives and was planted following a Roundup Ready® soybean rotation. Such areas along with untilled native grassland benefit native wildlife such as the grasshopper sparrow (inset) while also providing reproductive habitat for pheasants. (CTS; inset courtesy of Scott Weins)

Chapter thoughts

Ring-necked pheasants require a variety of habitat components that can be developed or improved by proper management. The spatial arrangement of these habitat components, such as placement of a food plot next to a dense cattail covered wetland (wintering), is also highly important. To enhance pheasant production, landowners should attempt to provide a variety of habitats that provide for the needs of pheasants throughout the year. Inventory of the available habitats, or "taking stock," is an important exercise to critically evaluate those habitats that are declining or missing on your property. Remember, pheasants often find needed seasonal cover by using adjacent habitats that may be found on two or more farms. What is important is that all the necessary habitat components are available on the landscape to support reproduction and survival. Specific habitats attractive to pheasants in fall and winter can also be used to attract and hold pheasants through the hunting season.

CHAPTER 9
CREATING AND REJUVENATING NESTING AND BROOD-REARING COVER

Planting grass and forb cover enhances ring-necked pheasant populations by providing security during the prenesting, nesting, and brood-rearing periods. If protected from annual mowing and grazing, herbaceous cover is also important to pheasants during other periods of the year, such as fall and early spring. The planting of grass-forb cover and rejuvenation of existing grasslands for pheasants also benefits upland nesting waterfowl, prairie grouse, and other ground-nesting birds.

Some management basics on nesting and brood-rearing cover

Basic nesting and brood-rearing cover has been discussed in Chapter 5 and Chapter 6. In general, nesting cover with adequate plant diversity will also provide interspersed brood-rearing areas; brood cover is characterized by a more open understory and abundant insects for food. Specific management techniques to improve brood-rearing habitat in existing grass or grass-forb plantings are presented later in this chapter.

Native warm- and cool-season plantings, native grasslands

Since the mid 1990s, state and federal wildlife agencies in South Dakota have favored the planting of warm-season native grasses, cool-season native grasses, or a mixture of both. Cool-season grasses have their best growth during the cooler periods of spring and fall. Examples of recommended cool-season native grasses for nesting and brooding cover include western wheatgrass, slender wheatgrass, and Canada wildrye. Warm-season grasses have their best growth during the heat of the summer, typically June to mid August. Some recommended native warm-season grasses include species such as Indiangrass, big bluestem, and switchgrass.

Warm-season native grasses have commonly been planted on CRP lands during this same period because this practice generally produced a high index score (environmental benefits) and was accepted into the highly competitive CRP (Photo 9-1).

Properly managed native tallgrass and mixed-grass prairie sites that have never been tilled have a much greater diversity of plants and are more valuable to native grassland birds than seeded native stands (Bakker and Higgins 2009). However, both native and planted prairies benefit many birds and both are valuable for nesting and brood-rearing pheasants. Additionally, the ability of native tallgrass species to remain erect in winter and recover to an upright position after snow melt is especially important for providing protective cover from hawks and owls in early spring (Leif 1996) (Chapter 7).

Dense nesting cover, smooth bromegrass, periodic rejuvenation

Dense nesting cover (DNC) is a term that can be used to describe a planted mixture of exotic and/or native cool-season grasses with legume components such as yellow sweet clover and alfalfa. Neither sweet clover nor alfalfa is native (indigenous) to North America. The term DNC was much more commonly used in the 1980s than in more recent years. Cool-season exotics used in these original DNC plantings were usually a combination of tall and intermediate wheatgrass or just smooth brome — both mixed with legumes. The definition of DNC today is somewhat ambiguous and not as commonly used, but it could fit any mixture of warm- or cool-season grasses, including natives, combined with a legume component.

Photo 9-1. Tallgrass natives such as this big bluestem are commonly established on portions of many Game Production Areas (GPAs). Other tallgrass species such as switchgrass and Indiangrass are often included in these plantings. (AEG)

Plantings of DNC were commonly used in the early 1980s in areas signed up in the state's Pheasant Restoration Program as well as on some public lands. Dense nesting cover (DNC) plantings were designed to emulate a "dirty" alfalfa field because alfalfa fields are known to have high pheasant nest and brood densities but also high nest, hen, and early brood losses during mowing (Keyser 1986). Thus, DNC plantings were established to provide undisturbed pheasant nesting and brood-rearing cover and attract pheasants away from production alfalfa fields. Research in eastern South Dakota has indicated this strategy may work, as both DNC and warm-season natives (tallgrass prairie species such as switchgrass and big bluestem) had higher pheasant nest densities than adjacent alfalfa fields (Rock 2006).

In the absence of any type of management such as periodic burning, grazing, or haying, classic DNC plantings using exotic cool-season grasses such as smooth bromegrass, intermediate wheatgrass, and tall wheatgrass often degrade to more monotypic (dominated by single species, low plant diversity) stands after 10 years or so. Smooth brome was commonly planted during the Soil Bank era and early years of the CRP because it provided quality livestock forage, the seed was inexpensive, and the stand was easy to establish. These initial smooth brome plantings became another source for the invasive problem we have with this species today in South Dakota and much of the northern plains (Photo 9-2). However, during the first decade after establishment, smooth brome does produce good numbers of pheasants. If interseeded with legumes, bromegrass increases in nesting value and improves as brood-rearing habitat as well.

Photo 9-2. The uplands on this Waterfowl Production Area (WPA) are dominated by invasive smooth brome and western snowberry and represent the type of area that should be rejuvenated or replanted. The dense, shrubby wetland on the right is attractive for wintering pheasants but the large trees should be removed to eliminate perching spots for raptors. (LDF)

Smooth brome can invade and completely take over a stand of native grasses. In fact, invasion of nonnative grasses (exotics) into native prairie sites and native grass plantings is a matter of great concern to land managers throughout the Midwest.

Stand establishment time

Sites planted to exotic cool-season grasses, such as tall wheatgrass, intermediate wheatgrass, or smooth brome, provide adequate nest concealment within 1 to 3 years after planting and may remain relatively valuable to nesting pheasants at least through 13 years (Eggebo et al. 2003). However, other research indicates that many cool-season grass stands begin to degenerate between 4 and 7 years of age (Higgins and Barker 1982, McCoy et al. 2001). Degeneration results from the loss of the legume component and subsequent reduction in value as nesting and brood-rearing habitat. Heavy accumulation of understory litter is often an indication of degeneration. Management of these degenerated grasslands with prescribed treatments such as haying and grazing along with interseeding of legumes is often needed to increase pheasant use and reproductive success. Treatments to rejuvenate exotic cool-season plantings should be conducted about every 4 to 7 years in the more moist eastern third of South Dakota; drier regions in central South Dakota need less frequent treatment (K.F. Higgins, South Dakota State University, personal communication).

Native tallgrass plantings (warm-season), characterized by plants such as switchgrass, big bluestem, and Indiangrass, often take 3 to 5 years to become well established. However, recently developed methods, seeding equipment, and seed quality can reduce the establishment period to 2 years in good soil with adequate and timely rainfall (Photo 9-3).

Photo 9-3. Switchgrass, a tallgrass native, can provide some good late winter and early spring habitat. This close-to-the-ground view is similar to what a pheasant would see. (CTS)

The addition of legumes and wildflowers to grasslands greatly enhances the quality of the grassland habitats for pheasant reproduction because these plants attract and support insects that are an important source of protein for both the hen and young chicks (Nelson et al. 1990, Leathers 2003, Rohlfing 2004). Pheasants will also include some leaves, flowers, and seeds from forbs in their diet. Maintaining desirable forbs in a stand of grass can be difficult where noxious weeds such as Canada thistle and leafy spurge are being sprayed or mowed to control them.

Both warm- and cool-season grasses can provide quality nesting and interspersed brood-rearing sites for pheasants, especially if the planting includes intermixed legumes and other forbs (Rohlfing 2004). Inclusion of legumes with grasses approximately doubled both nest abundance and nesting success in upland nesting waterfowl (Arnold et al. 2007); similar benefits can be expected for pheasants.

Seasonal values of warm- and cool-season plantings

Characteristics of nesting and brood-rearing cover can change during the growing season in both cool-season and warm-season stands. Standing residual grass (growth from previous year) and timing of new growth both influence the value of the stand for pheasants. Cool-season residual cover plus new growth, especially if the mixture includes legumes such as alfalfa, is more attractive to early nesting pheasants than warm-season natives that green up later. The value of cool-season grasses and intermixed legumes is especially important in dry springs (Rohlfing 2004). Warm-season grasses become more valuable to later nesting pheasants. Research in eastern South Dakota indicates similar nesting densities in warm-season and cool-season grasses, but higher nest success in mixed plantings (warm- and cool-season) or DNC (warm- or cool-season-plus legumes) than in pure warm-season stands (Rock 2006, Hankins 2007).

We recommend cool-season grasses or a mixture of cool- and warm-season grasses, both with the inclusion of forbs and legumes, for providing pheasant nesting cover along with interspersed areas of brood-rearing habitat.

Converting cropland to permanent herbaceous cover
Improving technology for native grass plantings

Many of the grassland plantings in South Dakota were developed via CRP conservation practices on tracts that had a crop history. In the mid 1980s, the success rate for native warm-season grass plantings was relatively low and it took several years for the plantings to mature. These early stands were often planted with poor quality seed using conventional drills that did not properly meter the fluffy seeds of some warm-season grasses; many seeds were also planted too deep to allow for proper germination and emergence. Competing annual grasses, particularly foxtail, robbed nutrients, sun, and moisture from planted seedlings. Mowing was the only feasible alternative to reduce the annual weed competition.

In fact, it was common for producers to mow the site multiple times the first growing season and at least once the second growing season to give the planted seedlings a chance at survival.

Since then, there have been improvements to planting equipment, seed propagation, and herbicides that have greatly increased the success of these types of plantings. Planting equipment was redesigned to handle the different seed types (Photo 9-4). Seed companies are producing clean, high quality, high germination seeds, and herbicide companies have developed products to reduce competition from undesirable plants. Today, the success rate of native grass plantings is nearly 100%, and a stand can often be well established by the second growing season with little or no mowing required.

Seedbed preparation

A critical and often overlooked component of any grass planting is seedbed preparation. Planting native grasses into soybean stubble in eastern South Dakota has produced the best results of any type of seedbed (Andy Gabbert, personal observation). Weed competition in soybeans and other row crops has already been suppressed. Soybean stubble provides a firm seedbed, leaves little residue behind after harvest, and usually has fewer soil ridges; seed-to-soil contact from the grass drill is improved by these characteristics. Soybeans also fix nitrogen for the subsequent crop. Fallow ground treated for weeds and stubble of other crops

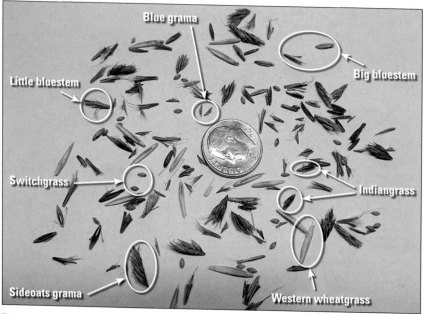

Photo 9-4. Native prairie grasses have a variety of seed shapes and sizes that can now be handled better with the appropriate planting equipment. (Courtesy of Jason Tronbak)

such as corn and wheat can also provide sites for planting native grasses, but in eastern South Dakota is not as desirable for planting native grasses as soybean stubble (Andy Gabbert, personal observation). Milo stubble can also provide a good seedbed for native grass seedings (Randy Rodgers, Kansas Wildlife and Parks [retired], personal communication).

Reducing weed competition

A combination of glyphosate (Roundup® or others) and imazapic (Plateau®) herbicides has been well documented for successful establishment of native grasses (Masters et al. 1996, Washburn and Barnes 2000, Bahm and Barnes 2011, Bahm et al. 2011). Applying these herbicides prior to planting provides excellent pre and post emergent weed suppression. The glyphosate kills most weeds and the imazapic will suppress many of the competing annual grasses, particularly foxtails, while allowing the planted seedlings to emerge. Rates applied are dependent on the amount of weed competition and knowledge of past weed problems. The imazapic herbicide will suppress some native forbs and some cool-season native grasses at higher application rates so refer to the imazapic label for guidance.

Applying herbicides properly and at the prescribed rate is the most critical step of a successful native grass seeding. Some mowing may be required in late summer if annual weeds such as ragweed, kochia, and annual sunflower look like they may be hindering (out-competing) the seeding or if noxious weeds have emerged. The native grasses will usually pull through and these annual weeds will decline in 2 to 3 years without any additional mowing. Many non-noxious weeds are valuable for pheasants and should be left if they are not competing strongly with seeded grasses and forbs for sunlight and moisture.

Mixing in some legumes and other forbs

If we add alfalfa or sweetclover along with other desirable forbs to native cool- or warm-season grass plantings we can improve their value for nesting and brood rearing (Photo 9-5). In recent years, exotic grasses used in the traditional dense nesting cover (DNC) of the 1980s have been de-emphasized in favor of native grasses in these grass-legume mixtures. The native forb component has also been improved. Alfalfa seeded into planted stands of warm-season native grasses is persistent and vigorous and will improve pheasant nesting, brood rearing, and other seasonal cover (Randy Rodgers, Kansas Department of Wildlife and Parks [retired], personal communication).

The current method for establishing grasslands with legume and other forb components involves use of a selective herbicide (imazapic; Plateau®) and is similar to the approach used in establishing warm- or cool-season native grasses. The imazapic herbicide, when used prior to planting, will injure or suppress the legume component and some species of cool-season native grasses. This negative effect can be countered in part by increasing the seeding rates for forbs and

Photo 9-5. A mixture of cool-season (photo) or warm-season grasses with legumes such as alfalfa provides excellent nesting and brood-rearing habitat. (AEG)

cool-season grasses, and/or decreasing application rate for imazapic herbicide (e.g., <2 ounces/acre). If only cool-season grasses are used in a DNC mixture, then imazapic herbicide is not recommended.

Be sure to check the label to find which species are suppressed and the specific tolerance levels. Imazapic herbicide is a selective herbicide that is relatively nontoxic to birds, mammals, and amphibians. It should be kept out of ponds or other water bodies. Equally or more suitable selective herbicides will likely be developed in the future.

High-quality seed and ecotypes

Grass and forb seed producers today do a good job of harvesting and cleaning the seed to prepare it for planting. There are also several varieties and ecotypes (adapted to specific soils, moisture, etc.) of seeds now available. When purchasing seed for a native grass and forb planting, be sure to select a variety and ecotype that is adapted to your locality. In general, the seed variety should be adapted to an area within a 200-mile radius of the area to be planted.

Sculptured versus shotgun seeding strategies

There are two basic strategies for placement of the seed in the field: sculptured (precision seeding) and the shotgun approach. Native prairie grasses have strong associations with different soil types or visually obvious topographic areas such as hills and draws within a field. For example, species that are more drought resistant may do better on the hilltops than others. Likewise, some species that tolerate more moist soil conditions will do better in wet zones within the field. Other grassland species may tolerate both dry and wet soil conditions.

In the sculptured approach, the native grass and forb species are matched to the soil conditions by planting the tops of all the hills with one mix, the wet zones with another mix, and the intermediate zones with yet a different mix of species. While this method is more time consuming, it does provide patches of varying habitat types within the field and adds to the diversity of the stand. In the shotgun approach, all the desired species are mixed and the entire field is planted at the same time. This method assumes that the native grasses will grow and thrive in those sites for which they are most adapted. The shotgun approach to seeding does work to establish nesting and brood-rearing cover but will not provide the same level of diversity as the sculptured seeding method.

Converting unproductive planted grassland to productive grassland

The conversion of one type of planted grassland to another type of grassland can be more difficult to accomplish than conversion of cropland to grassland. We do not advocate the conversion of native sod (e.g., land that has never been broken) as these habitats are becoming increasingly rare and could be improved via interseeding, prescribed burning, and haying and/or grazing. In some instances on unbroken sod, simply allowing an overgrazed pasture to rest for a growing season might be enough to allow native grasslands to flourish; resting the area can also help determine what type of management might be best to meet the management goal.

Land that has a previous farming history but was converted to grass may need to be renovated if the grassland is no longer productive for nesting and brood rearing. There are three basic strategies for converting unproductive grassland to productive grassland: farming strategy, fire plus herbicide, and haying plus herbicide.

Farming strategy

The farming strategy is to return the site to row-crop agriculture for a few years with the intention of planting the area back to productive grass and forb cover. This is the simplest and most reliable method but also takes the longest to accomplish. One scenario in this farming strategy approach is to hay the planted grassland, burn it down with a nonselective herbicide, and no-till plant a genetically modified row crop such as corn or soybeans for 2 to 3 years. We recommend planting the site to soybeans the year prior to establishing native grasses.

Fire plus herbicide

Under the fire plus herbicide strategy, burn the site with a prescribed fire in the spring and then follow up with a chemical burn (using nonselective herbicide) of the regrowth of existing plants. Then no-till the desired seed mix of grasses into the site. This method is less reliable than the farming strategy approach and is not recommended if forbs, including legumes, are planned for the seeding. This method may produce a flush of noxious weeds, particularly Canada thistle and musk thistle that will require control. Unfortunately, control methods for these noxious weeds negatively influence survival of planted forbs. Certain aminopyralid herbicides on the market are effective at controlling noxious thistles and have limited effects on some perennial forbs.

The residue of aminopyralid herbicide is long lasting and can accumulate in manure if livestock feed on vegetation from treated areas. This in turn has led to some crop damage where manure from cattle-fed forage was used as fertilizer. More effective herbicides toxic to specific noxious species and having minimal effects on desirable forbs will likely be developed in the future.

Haying plus herbicide

The haying plus herbicide method is very similar to the fire plus herbicide method with the same concerns for noxious weeds. The site is hayed (or grazed) in the fall or spring and a chemical burn is applied on the regrowth either in the fall or spring. The desired native grasses and forbs are usually no-till planted onto the site during spring (Photos 9-6). Nebraska Game and Parks Commission

Photos 9-6. Prescribed haying and herbicides were used on this Bitter Lake area (top) before reseeding with a mixture (bottom) of five species of warm- and three species of cool-season native grasses. Big bluestem, Indiangrass, and Canada wildrye had the best response. (AEG)

sometimes uses a post-frost herbicide treatment (glyphosate) in the fall to kill monotypic stands of smooth brome (for replanting with natives) on previously farmed land. The treatment can also be used to depress or kill invading smooth brome in seeded warm-season native grass. Post-frost treatment needs only half the herbicide (2% vs. 4% solution according to chemical label) required for the same results in the spring. This treatment requires that temperatures drop below 28 degrees Fahrenheit for at least 2 days prior to treatment. Temperatures during herbicide treatment must be well above freezing. The area to be treated must be hayed, burned, or grazed in the spring or summer to provide regrowth prior to spraying. Visual observations indicate the method can be effective in removing over 90% of the smooth brome. If the treated stand includes planted native grasses and forbs, the post-freezing herbicide treatment can kill most of the brome without killing the already dormant forbs and native warm-season grasses (Scott Luedtke, Nebraska Game and Parks Commission, personal communication). In contrast to these results, fall treatments with glyphosate proved ineffective for control of smooth brome in South Dakota, but there was no attempt at post-frost timing to increase vulnerability to the herbicide (Bahm 2009).

Use of glyphosate to control smooth brome on previously unplowed sod is not recommended due to damage to native cool-season components of the grassland. Managers should try less invasive methods (see following section) of restoration, such as burning or grazing, before applying a nonselective herbicide such as glyphosate.

Maintaining existing herbaceous cover for pheasant reproduction

The nesting potential of any grassland for pheasants is never static. It changes with stand age, species composition, and varying precipitation. The change in a grassland as it ages is sometimes called succession, a term widely used by biologists. Historically, native prairie grasslands were influenced by large herbivores (bison) and fires ignited by lightning or, in the past several thousand years, indigenous tribes. Indigenous peoples started fires to hunt bison that were attracted to the lush green forage that grew after the burn (Higgins 1986). These grazing and fire influences helped maintain native grasslands in a vigorous early successional stage.

Today, grasslands are susceptible to infestation by undesirable exotic grasses, invasive trees, and noxious weeds unless periodically subjected to disturbances such as fire, grazing, or haying. Invasive trees can include species such as eastern red cedar and the exotic Russian olive. Like native tallgrass or mixed-grass prairies, seeded stands of native grasses such as those planted for pheasant nesting cover thrive on being periodically rejuvenated by fire or grazing.

To maintain an optimal state for pheasants and other wildlife such as nesting mallards, all grasslands need to be managed. There are three basic types of grassland management: prescribed fire, grazing, and haying. Private lands enrolled in conservation programs may have restrictions on the type and timing of management that may be applied. Refer to the agency that purchased or is administering the conservation contract or easement before implementing any grassland management plan on your property.

Prescribed fire

Naturally occurring fires and accidental man-made fires are suppressed to reduce damage or injury to persons and property. However, prescribed burning (every 4 to 8 years) of most native prairie grasslands, particularly tallgrass prairie, increases plant vigor and density. Fire can also improve diversity of the grassland by promoting the growth of forbs and legumes that are attractive to wildlife (Higgins et al. 1989). Burning also removes the thatch layer (plant litter) that suppresses the growth of new grass tillers. The timing of a prescribed fire can also be used to alter the composition of the grass stand (Photos 9-7).

Early spring burns (April) generally favor cool-season grasses whereas late spring burns (May) generally favor warm-season grasses such as big bluestem. May is the most common month to conduct prescribed fires in South Dakota for suppression of invasive cool-season grasses such as smooth brome and Kentucky bluegrass; burning in May can also promote the growth of warm-season native grasses. Ironically, May is also a period of increasing nesting activity by ring-necked pheasants, waterfowl, and other ground-nesting birds. However, burning

Photos 9-7. Prescribed fire removes the thatch layer, kills invading trees, and enhances the vigor and density of stands containing native tallgrass prairie plants. Professional assistance in planning and carrying out prescribed burns should be sought to avoid possible fire escape from the target area. It is also essential that neighbors be informed of the planned burn. (Courtesy of Greg Wolbrink)

in May is sometimes needed to improve the grass stand and to increase nesting production in future years at the expense of reduced production the year of the burn.

Prescribed fire in the spring will destroy active nests of ring-necked pheasants and other birds unless some survive in patches skipped by the fire. It is still a worthwhile tradeoff. In nearly all cases, the nesting hen pheasant and nesting females of other bird species will escape the fire and renest in adjacent nesting cover. Therefore, it is extremely important to leave some grassland in the area for refuge and to provide an alternative nesting location when managing with fire. For example, you could use prescribed fire to rejuvenate half of a patch of cover in one year and the other half in the next year so that half of the nesting cover would still be available during each treatment year (Photo 9-8).

Mid to late summer burns, meant to imitate lightning caused fires, have been successfully used as a grassland treatment to increase growth of forbs (Engle et al. 1998; Randy Rodgers, Kansas Department of Wildlife and Parks [retired], personal communication). Late summer and fall burns cause some loss of fall and winter cover.

Fire is the preferred grassland management tool over grazing and haying for improving nesting cover for ring-necked pheasants on most state lands in eastern South Dakota (Andy Gabbert, personal observation). Although usually beneficial to nesting cover, it is also the most difficult management tool, particularly on private lands. Prescribed fire as a management tool has inherent liability risks and requires specialized training and equipment. Most private landowners do not have the fire management experience, manpower, or equipment needed to safely and effectively conduct a prescribed burn; therefore, fire as a grassland management tool is not common on private land in the upper Midwest.

Photo 9-8. Smooth brome and Kentucky bluegrass have invaded this seeded stand of tallgrass prairie on a Game Production Area (GPA). The area was scheduled for spring burning to reduce invading grasses and enhance the suppressed native species. (LDF)

If there is a strong interest, these potential hurdles should not discourage you from considering fire as a management tool. Contact SDGFP or U.S. Fish and Wildlife Service (USFWS) biologists at regional offices if you would like to learn more about prescribed fire, its implications for wildlife habitat, and required permits. There is a wealth of published information on the effects of fire on native flora and fauna. We recommend the five-part series "Wildland Fire in Ecosystems" (see Internet) published by the USDA (Brown and Smith 2000, Smith 2000, Zouhar et al. 2008) and the review in Higgins et al. (1989) for further reading.

Prescribed grazing

If prescribed fire cannot be applied as a grassland management tool, grazing on a prescribed basis is the next best option. Grazing treatments may have other influences on nesting birds by removing concealing cover and making birds more vulnerable to predation. In Wisconsin, intensive grazing by cattle led to trampling or predation of almost all artificial pheasant nests pre-placed in pastures (four eggs each) (Gates and Hale 1975). A similar study in the Texas Panhandle using artificial pheasant nests showed that cattle trampled 75% of nests in grazed pastures (Paine et al. 1996). However, by including both grazed and ungrazed cover types, less than 1% of the nests of prairie grouse, ducks, and pheasants are destroyed by livestock trampling in northern prairie landscapes (Ken Higgins, South Dakota State University, personal communication). Post-grazing responses of the herbaceous cover can be highly positive and can provide long-term benefits for pheasants and other wildlife. Like fire, grazing can influence the composition of the vegetation by adjusting the timing and intensity of the graze.

The use of grazing to promote nesting cover for pheasants can be divided into two categories, alteration grazing and maintenance grazing. Alteration grazing is prescribed in order to produce some type of change in the composition of the grassland community. For example, a manager may recommend a short-duration high-intensity graze during the month of May to suppress the growth of exotic cool-season grasses and promote the growth of native warm-season grasses and forbs. Grasses such as Kentucky bluegrass and smooth brome are particularly vulnerable at the time they are just developing seed heads. The basic idea is to injure or suppress the actively growing grasses to allow the release of the dormant grasses and forbs. Most often, the manager will need to apply the alteration grazing treatment for 2 or 3 consecutive years to achieve the desired results.

A maintenance graze may be used to restart succession. Maintenance grazing prescriptions are usually for longer periods and at lighter intensities than alteration grazing. As a general rule, maintenance grazing should be applied when the desired grasses are actively growing (Sedivic et al. 2007, Sedivic et al. 2009). Once the desired composition of the stand is achieved, maintenance grazing can be applied on a 3- to 5-year rotation to maintain the stand. Factors affecting the use of grazing may include adequate fencing, a source of livestock drinking water, and a willing cooperator in the neighborhood with sufficient numbers of livestock to apply the prescription (Photo 9-9).

Patch-burn grazing

Patch-burn grazing is the application of an old-school grassland management technique, but on a smaller scale. Native Americans used fire to attract bison to a particular area as they would be drawn in by succulent new growth following the burn. These burned areas would receive high intensity grazing whereas the adjacent unburned grasses would receive a lighter grazing intensity. Since bison were not restricted by fences and property ownership like today's livestock, this was an effective way to focus grazing intensity at a particular location.

Patch-burn grazing as a grassland management tool is gaining momentum in South Dakota. In essence, an area inside a fenced pasture is burned in the fall or early spring, and cattle are turned into the pasture. The cattle focus their foraging on the burned site but still continue to lightly graze outside the burn area. This has some advantages in that it concentrates the grazing without additional fencing, yet it produces varying plant height and plant diversity within the pasture or grazing paddock. Providing these grassland characteristics for wildlife is the principal reason patch-burn grazing is applied by some wildlife managers.

Prescribed haying

Where prescribed burning or grazing cannot be applied, haying or mowing is a better option than leaving land idle for too many years. For most landowners, haying is the easiest management practice to apply and has the greatest potential for treatment of grassland acres. Removal of residual vegetation and breaking up

Photo 9-9. Maintenance grazing with cattle can be periodically used to keep grassland cover healthy for pheasant nesting and brood rearing. This Game Production Area (GPA) is grazed at 3- to 5-year intervals to reduce litter accumulation (thatch) and stimulate the grassland plants. (AEG)

of the thatch layer in the spring will promote the growth of cool-season grasses. Similarly, summer haying of warm-season grasses will promote warm-season grass production later in the growing season (Photo 9-10).

Haying as a management option becomes progressively more difficult on grasslands that have not been managed for many years, as sapling trees begin to take hold and pocket gophers (plains and northern) and mammalian predators create holes and mounds, causing problems for the haying equipment and operators. Any initial hay cutting on old unmanaged stands will have virtually no value for livestock due to the high content of residual vegetation and low tonnage/acre. Raking the hay after cutting is important as this will break up and remove some of the thatch that suppresses plant growth.

Unfortunately, the mechanical action of haying equipment destroys pheasant nests and can also kill nesting hens and young chicks. Optimally, the treatment should be applied early enough to provide some late summer and fall cover and, more importantly, to provide concealing residual cover the following spring to enhance hen survival and provide early nesting cover. Since nesting normally starts in late April (peaks in early May) and peak hatching occurs between June 15 and June 30, any haying activity associated with grassland rejuvenation should attempt to avoid this period. Even July mowing will still cause losses of late nests (usually renests) and young chicks. However, waiting until late July or early August, while saving some additional nests and chicks, may not leave enough time for regrowth to provide sufficient residual cover for nesting pheasants the following spring, particularly in drier regions of the state.

Photo 9-10. This stand of warm-season native grasses on a Game Production Area (GPA) was hayed between July 15 and July 30. The photograph was taken mid September of the same year, demonstrating that native grasses will respond positively to an appropriately timed haying treatment. (AEG)

Even though the timing of these treatments may destroy some nests and chicks, the long-term benefits can be much improved nesting and brood-rearing cover and resultant recruitment of young pheasants. Other ground-nesting birds such as upland nesting ducks and prairie grouse will also receive long-term benefits from the improved cover. Cutting in the fall is an option for avoiding nesting birds but will temporarily reduce cover important for upland birds and upland bird hunting; it would also reduce capture of drifting snow for soil moisture recharge.

Ranching for livestock with secondary benefits for pheasants

Native grasslands and planted grasslands within the primary pheasant range managed by livestock producers can provide nesting and brood-rearing habitat and, at the same time, increase profitability of these working lands. Such management can also benefit many other upland nesting bird species such as mallards, blue-winged teal, sharp-tailed grouse, western meadowlarks, and upland sandpipers.

Biologists have studied grazing management techniques such as different grazing systems (i.e., continuous, rotational, short duration/high intensity, deferred), stocking rates, and timing of grazing during the year in relation to their influence on hiding cover (visual obstruction) for nesting birds (Naugle et al. 2000, Ignatiuk and Duncan 2001, Murphy et al. 2004). Studies of grazing lands in Montana and North Dakota indicated pheasant hens were selecting nesting sites in mixed-grass prairie in areas with vegetation that would obscure a nest, nesting hen, or other object on the ground to a height of about 10 inches or more (Fondell and Ball 2004, Geaumont 2009). For a livestock producer, that would be roughly cowboy boot high or, in many grasslands, equivalent to the "take half, leave half" concept.

Overall health of a grassland community can benefit from moderate grazing levels, as chronic overgrazing can reduce long-term forage production, alter plant communities, and reduce growth and survival of desirable plant species for both livestock and wildlife. Management practices that shift from continuous grazing to other grazing strategies that promote undisturbed cover or varying levels of residual cover will allow increased plant production and energy storage (Krausman et al. 2009), thus improving wildlife habitat and potentially providing greater income returns from livestock (Photo 9-11).

Financial returns on grazing management treatments vary amongst studies; however, some suggest that long-term treatments other than heavy continuous grazing practices appear more profitable and less risky during drought conditions, allowing the producer greater control over grassland conditions and movement of livestock (Holechek 1994, Holechek et al. 2000). Implementing prescribed grazing methods that improve the overall grassland health can greatly benefit landowners who have shared management goals of both livestock and wildlife production (Photo 9-12).

Photo 9-11. Big bluestem and sideoats grama planted in this grazing system provide excellent forage for cattle while simultaneously supporting a variety of ground-nesting birds. Pheasants nest, rear broods, and otherwise thrive with this kind of cover. (CTS)

Photo 9-12. White-tailed deer and many other wildlife species benefit from well-managed grasslands. This fawn remained still despite the approach of the photographer. (Courtesy of Keith Fisk)

Improving brood-rearing habitat

The ideal brood-rearing habitat has an ample amount of annual weeds or perennial forbs that attract insects important to young pheasant chicks. The understory of brood-rearing habitat is ideally not as dense as most planted cool- and warm-season grasslands (Photo 9-13).

Photo 9-13. This mix of Canada wildrye and various forbs will provide good brood-rearing habitat for pheasants and is also good nesting habitat. (AEG)

Brood-rearing habitats can be enhanced and developed in several ways. One approach is the addition of perennial forbs, including legumes, to the planting mix to provide abundant insects for young chicks and seeds and insects for older chicks. The grass-dominated overstory will provide adequate concealment from predators but, ideally, the understory should be more open for chick movement (Photo 9-14).

Another strategy is to plant grass-free blocks or strips of perennial forbs within the overall grassland patch. Equipment operators can more easily avoid spraying herbicides on nontarget brood-rearing habitats when planting in blocks or strips.

An approach used extensively in Nebraska and Kansas is to simply disk a small area within a patch or block of nesting cover multiple times to stimulate the growth of annual weeds. Although this method is very effective at producing brood-rearing habitat, it may create a noxious weed problem. We recommend initially disking a small area to evaluate the response of noxious weeds in the soil. Managers will often interseed desirable forbs and legumes into the disked area to suppress the growth of noxious weeds. In Kansas and Nebraska, sweet-clover, red clover, alfalfa, and increasingly, native forbs are often interseeded in

Photo 9-14. Perennial food plots make great cover for brood rearing and can provide food and cover through summer and fall for several years without replanting. A variety of forbs along with some grass is planted in these plots. The small yellow flowers are partridge pea. (AEG)

this situation (Randy Rodgers, Kansas Department of Wildlife and Parks [retired], personal communication; Mike Remund, Nebraska Game and Parks Commission, personal communication).

Lastly, whenever management (burning/haying/grazing) is applied to nesting cover, consider interseeding perennial forbs following the grassland management prescription. When the above-ground biomass is removed, it presents an excellent opportunity to add diversity to the site. Seeds can be no-till drilled or broadcast over the site following the management prescription. If using grazing as a management tool, we recommend broadcasting the seeds onto the area approximately 2 to 3 weeks before the cattle are removed. The hoof action of the cattle will, in essence, "plant" the seeds.

Volunteer patches of forbs mixed with grass, if they do not include noxious weeds, should be left for brood cover and may include forbs such as annual sunflower and kochia (fireweed). Weed patches can often be found along edges of fence lines, crop field edges or corners, wetland edges, roadsides, and other odd areas. These small weed patches and strips are important to broods. The value of voluntary or planted forbs in tall wheat stubble (>15 inches) as brood habitat is discussed in Chapters 6 and 14.

Other recommendations on reproductive cover treatments
Coordination—leaving nesting cover options for displaced hens

It is always a good idea to communicate your plans to your immediate neighbors to avoid large losses of nesting habitat in the same area in the same year if they are using the same management practices as you are. Grasslands next to alfalfa fields are extremely important to hens that may have lost their first nests in the alfalfa field. If no grassland acres with good nesting cover are kept for refuge, pheasants will often renest in the alfalfa field, only to have those nests destroyed at the next hay cutting. If, after scouting the area you find no other fields of herbaceous nesting cover nearby, then limiting grazing, fire, and other treatments to half or less of an existing field of nesting cover can be valuable for pheasants, particularly if severe drought were to slow recovery of the treated area.

Frequency of grassland prescriptions

There is no steadfast rule for the frequency or interval of grassland prescriptions that benefits pheasants. Most biologists recommend some type of grassland management every 4 to 7 years in the tallgrass prairie region in the eastern edge of South Dakota (Ken Higgins, South Dakota State University, personal communication). Longer intervals, as much as 10 years, are recommended in drier landscapes in central and western South Dakota. The amount of ground surface litter is probably the single best vegetation attribute that managers can use to determine when to apply treatments to their grasslands (Naugle et al. 2000). Unmanaged grasslands will have increased litter accumulations and reduced root biomass when compared to managed grasslands. As litter accumulates, the yield, vigor, density, diversity, and root biomass will decrease and the value of the stand will decline for both nesting and brood-rearing pheasants.

Control of invasive trees

Invasive trees can quickly reduce nesting space if left unchecked. Some primary invaders in South Dakota are eastern redcedar, Russian olive, Siberian elm, and common buckthorn. Russian olive, Siberian elm, and common buckthorn are exotic species that have spread much beyond the shelterbelt sites where they were originally planted. Eastern redcedar is indigenous to South Dakota and has been widely planted in shelterbelts. When in its proper place (shelterbelts), eastern redcedar provides good winter cover for pheasants, but it commonly invades grassland areas, reducing their quality as pheasant cover (Photo 9-15).

With the suppression of naturally occurring fires, woody invaders are now a source of concern in portions of eastern South Dakota. This may be so gradual that you do not notice that trees are replacing nesting and brood-rearing cover.

Early detection and action is imperative. Prescribed fire is an efficient and cost-effective tool to suppress and kill young woody invaders that are 6 feet or shorter in height. It is most effective when trees are young (<5 years) and there is sufficient fuel in the grassland to create a fire hot enough to kill them. As the

Photo 9-15. Eastern redcedar planted in multi-row shelterbelts can provide good winter cover for pheasants but, unfortunately, are highly invasive into surrounding grasslands. If you use juniper, Rocky Mountain juniper appears to be less invasive than eastern redcedar. (Courtesy of Matt Grunig)

trees become older and taller, fire is less effective and multiple prescribed burns may be needed. Mechanical removal coupled with herbicide applications is a viable alternative. Removal of invading trees is labor intensive and expensive. Hydraulically driven grinders/cutters can cut and grind a tree in the same motion by a single operator. This eliminates the additional steps of transporting to a central site and then burning or shredding the material.

Chapter thoughts

Establishing a mixture of cool- and warm-season grasses, exotic or native, can provide suitable pheasant nesting habitat as well as brood-rearing habitat for ring-necked pheasants. The addition of forbs, including legumes and various wildflowers, greatly enhances the quality of the grassland for reproduction because these plants attract insects that are an important source of protein for both the hen and young chicks. Nesting and brood-rearing cover can be established by converting former croplands to grasslands or rejuvenating existing poor quality grasslands to higher quality grasslands. Advances in new herbicides, seeding equipment, and seed propagation have greatly increased the success rate and shortened the time to maturity of newly established native grass stands. Grasslands dominated by native species thrive on being periodically renewed by fire and/or grazers. Nonnative grasslands (exotics) also require periodic renewal to remain productive as pheasant habitat. Grasslands can be rejuvenated and invading trees and exotic plants retarded using prescribed fire, grazing, or haying. Ranchers in pheasant country can use sound grassland management techniques that enhance profitability of livestock operations while simultaneously improving nesting and brood-rearing cover for pheasants and benefitting many other wildlife species.

CHAPTER 10
KEEPING AND ATTRACTING PHEASANTS DURING FALL AND WINTER

Landowners who maintain good nesting and brooding cover want their locally produced pheasants to remain close to home, especially during the hunting season. The key to keeping those birds around is to provide the appropriate seasonal habitat.

With highly attractive wintering habitat plus nearby food sources, landowners also can attract pheasants from adjacent lands where wintering habitat is limited or marginal in quality, thus improving their own hunting while providing secure winter habitat and enhancing survival and condition of wintering pheasants, especially hens. These surviving hens will be important in producing young on the home farm and on neighboring lands when spring and summer arrive.

In this chapter we focus on strategies to make your property attractive to pheasants during the fall and winter months and on improvements that will enhance hen survival and body condition from October through March.

Winter food plots and other food sources

By mid to late November, sometimes earlier, foods available for pheasants become less diverse and often more concentrated. With cold and often snowy conditions, high-energy seeds from harvested agricultural crops become increasingly critical as a primary food source (Chapter 3). In many years, waste grains and weed seeds provide adequate nutrition for wintering pheasants. However, some landowners also plant pheasant food plots near good winter cover to provide easily accessible food sources when snow covers waste grain.

Pheasant food plots may be planted separately in small blocks or simply created by leaving a few acres of unharvested crops. Corn is the staple food plot in South Dakota because it stands well during winters and is relatively easy to plant and maintain. Corn also provides partial concealment cover from raptors and wind protection cover while pheasants feed (Photo 10-1).

Corn usually remains erect after blizzards with the seed-bearing ears generally above the snowline in portions of the plot that have not drifted in. If the ears are too high for the pheasants to reach, marks in the snow indicate they use their legs and wings to launch upward to the ear to peck at the kernels or knock the ear down (L.D. Flake, personal observation). In one case, a wintering cock pheasant was observed flying into a row of corn in an apparent attempt to knock down stalks or ears of corn (A.E. Gabbert, personal observation). Pheasants have also been observed awkwardly clinging to the weight-bent tops of standing corn like chickadees while pecking at the kernels (George Vandel III, personal communication).

A popular strain of corn called CanaMaize® is increasingly used in pheasant food plots. CanaMaize® matures in only 65 days and reaches a height of only 4 or 5 feet. It produces abundant but small kernels of corn and provides a heavy canopy for birds. Because of its low stature, CanaMaize® is better for working hunting dogs and safer for pheasant hunters (Photo 10-2).

Tall varieties of forage sorghum along with interspersed rows of shorter grain-producing varieties can sometimes provide good winter cover along with food. In many cases these tall sorghum varieties will bend over due to blizzards

Photo 10-1. This large food plot (corn) of approximately 40 acres harbored hundreds of pheasants and numerous white-tailed deer in southern Spink County when snow had made finding food difficult. Dense cattails, shrub belt areas, and tallgrass cover (warm-season) on adjacent areas provided nearby winter cover. (CTS)

Photo 10-2. An early maturing, shorter strain of corn known as CanaMaize® has been developed for wildlife and for grazing. CanaMaize® is especially good for hunters and for working hunting dogs because of its low stature. (Courtesy of Jason Tronbak)

and heavy snows, forming natural roofs and wind-protected openings underneath for wintering pheasants. Short varieties of sorghum can also provide excellent food but not as much hiding cover and could be easily buried by snow (Photo 10-3). Corn works nicely with interspersed rows of grain sorghum; both are high-energy foods for wintering pheasants and have good digestibility (Bogenschutz et al. 1995).

Pheasants will commonly include soybeans in their fall and winter diet even where corn is available (L.D. Flake, personal observation). However, soybean stubble provides no concealment cover for feeding pheasants. Although pheasants can and do make it through the winter in areas where they are primarily feeding on soybeans, there is some evidence that soybeans are not as nutritionally valuable as corn for energy needs during cold periods. In that regard, soybeans are largely ignored in favor of waste corn by field-feeding sandhill cranes, northern pintails, snow geese, and greater white-fronted geese during migration in Nebraska (Krapu et al. 2004). Researchers found soybean energy content quite high but northern bobwhites (quail) were much less able to digest soybeans than sorghum seeds (Robel and Arruda 1986). Poor digestibility is apparently related to biochemicals that interfere with digestive enzymes (Bogenschutz et al. 1995).

Food plots vary in size but often run from an acre to 5 or even 10 acres. Larger block-shaped food plots are better than smaller ones because the drifting

Photo 10-3. Grain sorghum can provide excellent winter food sources for pheasants and is sometimes planted along with alternating rows of corn. (Courtesy of Roger Hill)

snow is generally caught in the windward rows. Don't expect a strip of corn or
sorghum planted for hunting to serve as a food plot during severe winters. Such
narrow strips of food and cover might better be described as pheasant hunting
habitat rather than general habitat even though the distinction can at times be
indistinct.

A Pheasants Forever informational release states that up to 50 rows of corn
on the windward side can be filled with snow after a severe blizzard in the northern plains. One useful technique is to plant several rows of corn on the windward
side followed by a gap for snow accumulation; the main part of the block-shaped
food plot is planted downwind of the snow accumulation area. Other types of
natural snow fences such as shrub belts on the upwind side of the food plot can
also reduce drifting into the food plot. Larger corn food plots on private land are
usually harvested in the spring to sell remaining grain and to reduce problems
with volunteer corn the next growing season.

Food plots can also be left standing for an additional growing season,
especially if they are larger and have not been depleted due to deer and pheasant use of grain during the previous year. If a food plot has ample amounts of
food left over, leaving the food plot for another growing season is an excellent
option that also saves time and money. Pheasant use of 2-year-old food plots in

eastern South Dakota was similar to use of first-year food plots (Larsen 1992). These second-year plots, on average, retained about one-third the amount of corn kernels on the plants at the start of winter as were present in new food plots. Weed cover within second-year food plots was three to four times greater than in first-year plots; thus, second-year food plots may provide pheasant loafing areas, nesting cover, and good brood-rearing habitat.

The degree of food plot use by pheasants is influenced by its proximity to winter cover, particularly cattail wetlands (Larsen et al. 1994). Food plot use is also related to winter severity. In a Wisconsin study, food plots and adjacent wetland cover (primarily dense brush) were preferred habitats for hen pheasants from October into April (Gatti et al. 1989). Placement of food plots near good wetland winter cover allowed hens to reduce their home range size and consequently improve survival (Photos 10-4).

One theory is that pheasants that utilize a concentrated food source near winter cover, (e.g., food plot next to a cattail wetland) will be in better physiological condition because of reduced energy expenditures from traveling, foraging, and avoiding predators than pheasants that lack these two habitat ingredients in close proximity. In a study designed to test this theory, researchers in eastern South Dakota found that food plot use had a positive effect on winter survival of hen pheasants, but home range size did not appear to influence winter survival during a typical winter (Gabbert et al. 2001). Pheasant hens collected from areas

Photos 10-4. The food plot (corn) on this Game Production Area (GPA) is flanked by a large cattail-choked wetland on private land that is used as winter cover. Inset: Pheasant tracks and use of corn kernels provide evidence of heavy use. (LDF, inset AEG)

of eastern South Dakota that were feeding on food plots of corn or sorghum had higher-quality diets and were in better physiological condition than hens collected from areas without access to food plots (Bogenschutz et al. 1995). This effect may be more pronounced during winters with deep snow and cold temperatures and may not be a factor during mild winter conditions (Purvis et al. 1999b).

High-energy seeds from food plots and unharvested corn adjacent to winter cover may be critical to the survival of pheasants in the northern plains during extreme winter conditions (Gabbert et al. 1999, Homan et al. 2000). Likewise, waste grains and soybeans in harvested fields as well as cattle feeding operations can provide needed food if the snow is not too deep and pheasants can get to the grains (Photo 10-5). Wind often blows the soil surface mostly free of snow in portions of harvested soybeans and other fields. These wind-blown areas can provide feeding areas that are at times used heavily by wintering pheasants (Photo 10-6).

One false rumor sometimes heard is that standing corn in food plots or unharvested fields will lead to massive suffocation of pheasants in winter. Not true! We have never observed a problem with radio-marked pheasants dying in corn food plots or unharvested corn. However, some deaths can occur in any kind of marginal cover, including small food plots, if pheasants are hit by an early blizzard and if there is no secure winter cover nearby.

Food plots should be placed adjacent to and preferably within a quarter mile of good wintering cover such as that found in dense stands of cattails in wetlands or near dense woody cover. Small food plots should be planted on the leeward side of winter cover so they will not be covered by snow drifts. Large food plots of over 10 acres (block-shaped) planted upwind of wintering areas can catch

Photo 10-5. Cattle feeding sites and undigested grain in cattle manure often provide food sources for pheasants in difficult winter situations. (Courtesy of Greg Wolbrink)

Photo 10-6. Waste grain in windblown crop fields is highly important in providing food for wintering pheasants. In fact, designated wildlife food plots only occur within the home range of a small percentage of South Dakota's wintering pheasants. (CTS)

drifting snow in the first 50 to 100 rows and help keep the downwind winter cover from filling with drifting snow.

The amounts of waste grain being left in harvested crop fields have been declining over the past few decades due to improvements in harvest equipment efficiency (Krapu et al. 2004). Unfortunately, reduction in waste grains available for pheasants and other wildlife could become a concern in the future.

Attracting and holding pheasants during the early hunting season

Pheasants usually face minimal stress in terms of available food and cover in October and often into at least mid November. Weather conditions tend to be mild and the birds have abundant food from seeds of agricultural crops, seeds of wild plants, leafy materials, various fruits (berries, etc.), and even grasshoppers. There is no immediate need for food plots at this time nor for heavy winter cover, but those needs may be only days or weeks away if an early blizzard hits.

Landowners and other land managers are often interested in attracting and holding pheasants on their land to improve hunting opportunities during this early part of the hunting season. This can be quite easily and effectively accomplished. If you want to make the cover attractive to fall birds simply follow the same suggestions we have provided earlier for producing good nesting and brood-rearing cover. An abundance of legumes and other forbs mixed with grasses as recommended for nesting and brooding cover is also what the juvenile and adult pheasants like in late summer and early fall. Intermixed weed patches or edges of sunflowers, kochia, or other weeds not classed in the noxious category are also nice additions to attract and hold fall pheasants (Photo 10-7). Fall pheasants are attracted to areas with mixed grasses and forbs in part because they often feed on the leaves, seeds, and fruits of a variety of wild plants (Chapter 3).

Photo 10-7. Weedy patches can be hot spots for holding pheasants from fall into spring. Old corn stalks and buffalo bur are visible. (CTS)

These areas also provide good loafing and night roosting sites. Likewise, the weedy edges of wetlands and vegetation growing in the basins of dry or moist wetlands are highly attractive to pheasants during the fall.

Croplands such as corn or sorghum within a half mile of permanent grass-forb cover are also important for early fall pheasants since the juveniles and adults are feeding heavily on seeds produced by these crops by late summer and fall. Seed-producing food plots can also enhance pheasant use of fall cover if planted nearby or embedded within patches of nesting and brood-rearing habitat. Most early season pheasant hunters with hunting dogs look for conceal-ing herbaceous cover (i.e., grasslands, wetlands, weed patches) with cropland nearby — a wise decision for finding pheasants. Dense shrubby cover can also be attractive fall habitat.

Late fall and winter cover

Primary winter protection for pheasants during the late fall and winter periods includes tall, dense grasslands such as switchgrass, dense wetland cover (cattails, phragmites, and sandbar willow), and wide and dense shelterbelts with dense ground-level woody cover. All wintering habitats need to be near adequate food sources, primarily waste grains, food plots, or unharvested crops. We now discuss cover needs from the mildest to the most severe winters (Photo 10-8).

Grasslands and weedy areas as cover in mild winters

During late fall or winter in years with little or no snow cover and mild temperatures, pheasants have a variety of sites in which they can loaf, roost (day and night roosts), or find escape cover. In these mild winters, grasslands and weedy patches can remain important to loafing and roosting pheasants for most or all of the late fall through winter. Pheasants also use cattails and dense woody cover in mild winters but they are not so dependent on these heavier types of cover as in colder and snowier winters.

As snow accumulates and drifts, grasslands fill in with snow and most no longer receive much use by pheasants. However, all grasslands are not equal in terms of their ability to withstand drifting snow. Smooth brome is poor cover because it is often flattened and covered by snow. Native warm-season grasses such as big bluestem, Indiangrass, and switchgrass maintain their vertical structure better than most exotic cool-season grasses as snow depths increase. Pheasants sometimes use snow tunnels formed in larger, robust fields of native warm-season grasses such as switchgrass even through fairly harsh winters. Because of their ability to remain erect or to spring back to an erect position, warm-season native grasses are also valuable as concealing cover to protect hens from raptors in the vulnerable prenesting period after snowmelt (Chapter 7) (Photo 10-9).

Slender wheatgrass, a native, and intermediate wheatgrass, introduced from Europe, are both cool-season grasses that are also relatively good at maintaining their vertical structure through winter although they are not usually dense enough to protect birds from blizzards. Grasslands upwind of wintering wetlands (cattail stands) or dense woody cover can serve another purpose by reducing the amount of snow that accumulates in these important winter habitats.

Kochia deserves special mention here. Stands of kochia can be dense and highly attractive to pheasants because they provide seeds for winter food, con-

Photo 10-8. During years with severe blizzards and persistent snow cover, winter habitat for pheasants can be scarce across some landscapes such as here in southeastern South Dakota. Wintering areas in this bleak landscape include blocks of warm-season natives (tallgrass species), a buffered area along a drainage, and farmstead shelterbelts. (AEG)

Photo 10-9. Residual warm-season natives and smooth brome (cool-season exotic) in winter. Residual smooth brome typically has a gray coloration and is easily flattened by a heavy blanket of snow. This area of CRP near the Sanborn-Beadle county line provided excellent pheasant habitat but has now been converted back to cropland. (CTS)

cealment, and wind protection. Many pheasant hunters have stepped into dense stands of kochia that literally exploded as pheasants took to the air. Kochia is a tall, rank plant that grows to unusual densities and heights in disturbed areas such as abandoned livestock corals enriched by manure. In dense stands, this plant is also wonderful for pheasants in winter (Photo 10-10).

Tall wheat stubble (>15 inches) where weeds or appropriate cover crops (green manure) have been allowed to grow is remarkably good pheasant cover unless it fills in with drifting snow (Rodgers 2002) (Chapter 14). Tall wheat stubble also keeps snow from drifting into adjacent wetlands and woody cover that is needed by pheasants in severe conditions.

Cattails as the winter gets tougher

Almost every hunter who has pursued late fall or winter pheasants in South Dakota has an appreciation for the value of dense cattails for wintering pheasants. These wetland wintering areas are also often enhanced by stands of tall and dense common reed grass or phragmites and by dense and shrubby sandbar willow stands (Sather-Blair and Linder 1980). These cattail wintering areas or wetland wintering areas are scattered over much of the pheasant range in South Dakota, although many have been lost or greatly altered due to drainage (Photo 10-11). As temperatures decrease and the water in wetlands begins to freeze, pheasants will increasingly move into dense stands of cattail as thermal and escape cover (Gates 1970). With increasing snow depth, pheasants are forced to use this heavier cover for their loafing, escape, and roosting sites, preferring it over dense shelterbelts and other upland woody cover (Gates and Hale 1974, Gabbert et al. 1999, Homan et al. 2000). Larger semi-permanent wetlands with extensive stands of dense cattail are some of the best habitats for wintering pheasants.

Photo 10-10. Wintering pheasants and deer (here, mule deer) are often attracted to dense stands of kochia as shown here in central South Dakota. These pheasants were likely feeding on grain sorghum and kochia seeds. (Courtesy of Doug Backlund)

Photo 10-11. A pattern of small scattered wetlands on private lands through much of the eastern half of South Dakota is extremely important for ring-necked pheasants. This wetland provides winter cover in the dense cattails along with nesting, brood rearing, and other seasonal cover in the grasses and forbs around the periphery. (Courtesy of Kent Jensen)

If you have good wetland wintering cover, all you need is a nearby source of cereal grains or other high-energy crop seeds to safely winter pheasants in most years. In addition to wintering pheasants produced on your own land, you will also attract additional pheasants that may lack good wintering habitat on neighboring lands.

We have observed large wetland wintering areas that supported hundreds, if not thousands, of wintering pheasants. Prior to the early 1980s, when Lake Thompson in Kingsbury County in eastern South Dakota was a large wetland dominated by cattails, river bulrush, and phragmites, it wintered several thousand pheasants each year and provided great cover even in the worst of winters.

Lake Thompson had many square miles of dense cattail and phragmites, and pheasants and white-tailed deer used the area heavily. Wetland emergent cover in Whitewood Lake and Lake Preston, also in Kingsbury County, provided similar though less extensive wintering cover. Areas near the wetland edges and close to harvested fields where food was available held the greatest densities of pheasants.

In the mid 1980s, Whitewood Lake and Lake Preston cycled back into large lakes during a prolonged wet period that has now extended over 25 years. Most of the wintering pheasant habitat has been flooded out. History indicates these lakes will cycle back into large, shallow wetlands that will again provide winter cover (dense cattails, etc.) for pheasants, white-tailed deer, and other wildlife. The characteristics of large wetlands such as Whitewood Lake and Lake Preston during wet cycles may also reflect increased runoff and flooding in the watershed due to drainage of many small wetlands that once held back flood waters (Photos 10-12).

We are confident that unusually large wintering areas positively influence the pheasant population within several miles of these marshes. There are several other large wetland areas with unusually extensive wintering cover in the state.

If you have a strong interest in pheasants you will also have an interest in keeping wetlands from being drained and farmed. Restoration of wetlands and

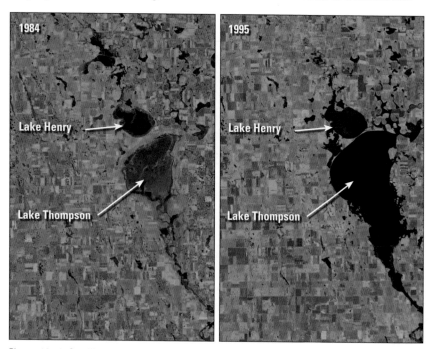

Photos 10-12. Satellite photos of Lake Thompson before flooding (1984) and again in 1995 show the cyclic changes that can occur in prairie wetlands. Before about 1985 Lake Thompson was a nearly dry wetland and provided prime wintering habitat for thousands of pheasants in the extensive stands of cattail and phragmites. (Photos Courtesy of U.S. Geological Survey National Center for Earth Resources, Sioux Falls, S.D.)

associated wetland cover is a positive move to help pheasant populations. Filling old drainage ditches or plugging a tile drainage is not an expensive process. Technical and financial assistance (up to 100% share) is available from agencies such as the Natural Resource Conservation Service (NRCS) (Wetland Reserve Program), U.S. Fish and Wildlife Service (wetland easements and Partners for Wildlife Program), or through the South Dakota Department of Game, Fish and Parks (Private Lands Habitat Program). Placing restored wetlands under a wetland easement or in the Wetland Reserve Program would be great for the pheasants and for family and friends that love to hunt pheasants.

Shelterbelts and farmstead areas

In most winters, wide and dense shelterbelts receive much less use by wintering pheasants than dense wetland cover in areas where both are available. However, in severe winters with deep snow, prolonged blizzard conditions, and extensive drifting, most of the dense cattail and phragmites stands (and other nonwoody cover) can be almost completely drifted in with snow (Photo 10-13). Pheasants are then often forced into their last option, dense woody cover in wide shelterbelts or around farmsteads (Kuehl and Flake 1998, Gabbert et al. 1999, Homan et al. 2000).

During such periods, tree roosting at night in dense shelterbelts in boxelder, wild plum, and spruce was observed in Iowa (Grondahl 1953). We have occasionally observed winter roosting at night in evergreen trees (usually pines or spruce) but have not seen roosting in deciduous trees except during daytime (Photo 10-14).

Photo 10-13. Much of the wintering habitat associated with dense cattails can be buried by drifting snow during the more severe winters. The protective cover associated with sandbar willow stands is still viable, but in the most severe cases even much of this woody cover is lost. (AEG)

Photo 10-14. Wintering pheasants will sometimes roost in trees during the day and occasionally in wind-protected tree sites at night. (Courtesy of Andy Lindbloom)

The actual influence of shelterbelts and other woody cover on pheasant survival rates was found to be questionable in research in central Illinois even though these habitats were thought to be important to pheasants for other reasons (Warner and David 1982). However, Illinois has considerably milder winters than found in the Dakotas. We consider wide shelterbelts that include dense rows of shrubs and other dense woody cover to be important winter habitat for pheasants in the Dakotas during unusually severe winters because they are often the only remaining cover above the drifting snow; in average or mild winters, they are much less important (Photo 10-15).

Shelterbelts, especially with large trees, attract mammalian and avian predators, so there is a tradeoff between needed winter habitat for pheasants and harboring of predators that can prey on birds or their eggs through the year. Shelterbelts that are installed to create winter habitat specifically for pheasants should include multiple rows of small and large shrubs (such as wild plum) along with conifers. During the extreme 1996–1997 winter in eastern South Dakota, all surviving radio-marked pheasant hens used shelterbelts at least eight rows wide with one or more rows of conifers (blue spruce, eastern redcedar, etc.). During this harsh winter, two radio-marked hens in Moody County abandoned a narrow shelterbelt and traveled 3 miles to larger, wider shelterbelts containing conifers (Andy Gabbert, unpublished data) (Photo 10-16).

Surveys of multiple sections of farmland for pheasants or pheasant tracks in eastern South Dakota during the severe winter of 1996–1997 supported results from radio-telemetry studies; virtually all pheasants were concentrated around dense shelterbelts and farmstead windbreaks after the abundant wetland cover had drifted in with snow (Kuehl and Flake 1998). Shelterbelts with a dense

Photo 10-15. Dense shelterbelts can provide good protection from snow and cold during severe winters. By watching areas regularly used by wintering pheasants seeking shelter, the birds can tell you what they need and what they will use. (Courtesy of Greg Wolbrink)

Photo 10-16. Shelterbelts with multiple rows of shrubs and conifers provide areas of winter cover on this Game Production Area (GPA) in southeastern South Dakota. Extensive corn food plots surround the shelterbelts, making this an ideal site for wintering pheasants. (LDF)

woody understory and with multiple rows of dense shrubs can be valuable for wintering pheasants. These shelterbelts should be ungrazed by livestock and preferably about 200 feet wide (or wider) (Trautman 1982:53). Food sources should be less than one-fourth mile from this winter cover.

Pheasants normally need protection from the elements beginning at the ground level or the level of the snow depth on the leeward side of the shelterbelt. When drifting snow accumulates in shelterbelts, pheasants will often find cover behind the limbs of conifers or other vegetation at the prevailing snow line or in pockets extending slightly below the snow line. In this case the snow level may be several feet above the ground.

Tall deciduous trees such as plains cottonwood, green ash, or Siberian elm provide perches for great horned owls and other raptors but provide little or no cover or other benefits to pheasants. When designing a shelterbelt for pheasants, consider a narrow spacing within each row of 4 feet apart for small shrubs and 6 feet apart for large shrubs. This will limit the crown height but provide a dense protective area at the ground level or at the level of the drifting snow.

Spacing between rows in shelterbelts designed for pheasants can range from 8 to 14 feet, depending on the method selected to suppress weed competition (mechanical cultivation or fabric). One problem with fabric is that it does not break down and can prevent suckering to form thickets for winter cover. If used, the fabric should be removed once the shrubs or other woody species are established.

County and state forestry, NRCS, local Conservation District, and SDGFP offices are excellent sources for help with designing a shelterbelt. There are numerous choices when it comes to species selection. However, wild plum, chokecherry, Rocky Mountain juniper, and Amur maple are all common selections that can provide habitat for pheasants during severe winters in eastern South Dakota. Rocky Mountain juniper is less invasive than is eastern redcedar (Gary Larson, South Dakota State University, personal communication). Silver buffalo-berry, caragana, northern hawthorne, hedge cotoneaster, common lilac, Hansen hedge rose, and Nanking cherry are common selections in the more arid central portions of South Dakota.

Although eastern redcedar and Russian olive continue to be planted for pheasant habitat, these invasive trees, as noted in Chapter 9, are also a growing concern in South Dakota and several other plains states. For this reason we do not list them. Realistically, these invasive species will continue to be used for shelterbelts in the immediate future.

Shelterbelts can be situated to help manage drifting snow. You may want to place shelterbelts in a location upwind of where you intend to maintain a food plot or even a combined food-winter cover plot such as tall forage sorghum interspersed with rows of corn or grain sorghum. Because South Dakota winters have northwesterly prevailing winds, it is recommended that shelterbelts be planted on the north or west side (or both) of the habitats you are trying to protect.

Rows of dense shrubs can be added to augment existing shelterbelts that lack the width and density needed to protect pheasants during severe winters. If space allows, upwind shrub rows or even rows of dense conifers with a downwind gap for snow to accumulate can be planted to reduce snow accumulation in winter-ing shelterbelts. The same approach can be used to reduce snow accumulation in food plots.

Wide and dense shelterbelts protecting farmsteads from severe winter weather often provide considerable wind and snow protection for pheasants. We have seen several situations where pheasants have survived the severest of conditions by moving into farmstead shelterbelts. These birds are usually feeding on spilled grain around cattle feeders. Existing farmstead windbreaks can be nicely augmented with additional shrub rows to protect pheasants during the unusually severe winters that can occasionally occur.

Landowners or managers should also consider how the placement of shelterbelts may affect grassland management options. For example, a shelterbelt surrounded by grasslands may cause additional problems when planning a graze rotation or a prescribed burn. Grazing can easily be destructive to shelterbelts, and it reduces the dense wintering cover needed by pheasants. Also, shelterbelts planted adjacent to croplands or wildlife food plots may be damaged by chemical drift. We recommend providing some type of buffer zone between newly planted shelterbelts and cropland areas. We strongly discourage planting shelterbelts in our dwindling native grasslands.

Winter cover and reproductive cover—placing them in perspective

Pheasants are highly visible while out scratching in snow-swept landscapes or looking for spilled grain along the roadsides during winter (Photo 10-17). Many of us understandably become concerned about the survival of these birds; those concerns are sometimes even expressed in newspaper articles and photos. However, under current habitat conditions pheasants generally have good survival during all but the most severe winters. Sometimes, survival in these unusually severe winters can be better than expected, as appeared to be the case in most areas of South Dakota following the severe winters of 2009–2010 and 2010–2011.

Lack of good nesting and brooding cover is not something that so easily pulls at the heart strings of the general public or that makes the newspapers.

Photo 10-17. Public concern is often voiced about the welfare of pheasants during winter because of their flocking tendencies and visibility to the public. Concerns about lack of or loss of nesting cover are seldom voiced by the public even though cover during the reproductive season is generally more critical for supporting good pheasant populations than winter cover. (Courtesy of Andy Lindbloom)

Everything seems to look green and lush during the reproductive season even in areas where most of the landscape is in row crops or other uses, largely unusable for nesting and early brood rearing. Although both reproductive and wintering cover are important, it is nesting and brooding cover that tends to determine the size of the pheasant population more than wintering cover. Even in the worst winters, enough pheasants survive for the population to recover fully within a couple of years if reproductive cover is available in sufficient quantity and quality. Providing safe winter cover is important but the biggest threat to maintaining strong pheasant populations continues to be the loss of undisturbed grass-forb cover needed during the reproductive period. Landowners, biologists, natural resource administrators, and others interested in pheasants should consider what the pheasants need most.

Chapter thoughts

Appropriate fall and winter habitat for pheasants is directly related to pheasant hunting opportunities, winter survival, and spring body condition. If both food and cover are available, pheasants will be attracted to an area, and overwinter survival of hens and unharvested roosters will generally be good. Pheasants remain in fairly light herbaceous cover through much of the fall. However, dense herbaceous cover (especially cattails) and dense woody cover in shelterbelts become increasingly important as winter arrives.

Public concern over winter losses and winter habitat seems to be greater than concern about pheasant nesting cover because wintering pheasants are easily visible as they search for food and grit in fields or along roads. However, the less visible hens during the reproductive period and the availability of good nesting cover are generally more critical in influencing South Dakota's pheasant populations than are winter cover and survival. Both should be considered in land management decisions made to maintain and improve pheasant populations.

PART IV: ARTIFICIAL AUGMENTATION, POPULATION MONITORING, AND HUNTING

CHAPTER 11
ATTEMPTS TO ARTIFICIALLY AUGMENT PHEASANT NUMBERS

No other game species in South Dakota captures the attention and interest of landowners, sportsmen, and the general public like the ring-necked pheasant, especially when they feel the pheasant population is under stress or in trouble. When pheasant numbers are low or declining, the response has often been to jump-start the population by releasing pheasants and/or controlling predators. During inclement winter conditions, concern that high numbers of pheasants will die due to starvation often spawns interest in winter feeding.

These efforts to augment the population do not provide long-term or broad-scale benefits. In fact, there may be unintended negative consequences to these management actions. In this chapter we will review the pros, cons, successes, failures, and the management considerations of releasing pheasants, winter feeding, and controlling predators.

Pheasant stocking

It can be a gratifying sense of accomplishment to open the door to a box of pen-reared pheasants and watch them fly off into a patch of habitat. That sense of accomplishment is sometimes affirmed when hunters go into areas near the release site the following October and shoot a limit of birds. But did the bagged birds originate from those that once lived in a pen or did they come from the wild birds already occupying that habitat?

While some pheasant managers are satisfied with their release programs and do not actually look at survival rates and returns of stocked birds, others want evidence that documents actual survival and harvest rates. Prudent pheasant managers seek confirmation by marking released pen-reared pheasants to assess the contribution of the releases to their overall management goals.

Pheasant stocking has been at times a contentious issue between state wildlife agencies, private pheasant managers, businesses that sell pen-reared pheasants, sportsmen's groups, and other organizations and individuals interested in pheasants. Some of the strife originates from the debate over the need to confirm perceived benefits of pheasant stocking programs and the validity of the information once it is collected.

Many different types and approaches to pheasant rearing and stocking have been evaluated in terms of survival of released birds, causes of mortality, hunting recoveries, and overall costs per bird in the hunter's bag. The evaluations of these releases have been critical in shaping our knowledge of this popular management practice. Releases of pen-reared pheasants where wild populations exist is also a concern because of the possible dilution of the genetics related to "wildness." Additionally, there is always the potential for pen-reared birds to introduce and spread diseases to wild populations of pheasants or other wild birds (Dahlgren 1967).

Summer releases of chicks and juveniles

Release of adolescent-aged (mostly 7–12 weeks of age) pheasants in the summer has been the most common artificial pheasant replenishment program and still remains popular with some pheasant enthusiasts. In South Dakota this release technique grew to its peak in the late 1970s through the early 1980s. Stocking pheasants was a component of a South Dakota Department of Game, Fish and Parks (SDGFP) pheasant management program called the Pheasant Restoration Program. Groups and individuals were paid a dollar per bird to raise and release 7-week-old pheasants. In addition to funding the release program, SDGFP also monitored the success of the program from leg bands returned to SDGFP from hunter-harvested birds.

Over 98,000 pheasant chicks were banded and released during the first 5 years (1977–1981) of the Pheasant Restoration Program (Solomon 1982). Thirty-five percent of the pheasants released were roosters and 65% were hens. As demonstrated by the predominance of hens in the release totals, the primary goal of the pheasant release component of the Pheasant Restoration Program was to enhance long-term pheasant populations through increased reproduction by hens that survived to the following breeding season.

The percentage of released male chicks harvested in the first hunting season following release and reported to SDGFP ranged from 3.7 to 6.6%. A questionnaire sent to cooperators indicated that only 43% of the banded pheasants that were bagged by hunters were reported to SDGFP. Consequently, the estimated harvest of released pheasants the first hunting season after release ranged from 8.6 to 15.3% and averaged 12 bagged roosters for every 100 male chicks released in the preceding summer (Photo 11-1).

Summer-released pheasant chicks must survive the winter and into the next reproductive season if they are to contribute to future pheasant populations.

Photo 11-1. Pheasant chicks must learn survival skills from a wild brood hen if they are to have a good chance to escape the many dangers encountered as a young bird. This chick was hatched in the wild and is being reared by a wild hen. (CTS)

Band recoveries indicated that less than 5% of the released male chicks survived into the following breeding season (Solomon 1982). No estimate of survival of female chicks was provided in the report.

South Dakota's experience with low band return rates on summer released pheasants has been repeated in many if not most pheasant states. In Iowa, release of pen-reared pheasants (both sexes) from 8 to 12 weeks of age resulted in very low band return rates from hunters. Those rates were often less than 2% with 10% the maximum (Farris et al. 1977:96). In some areas, no band returns resulted from summer released chicks, indicating low survival after release and/ or possibly low reporting rates by hunters. Since gender was not determined on released chicks, the band recovery rates for cocks would be approximately double the rates reported. As noted earlier, actual percentage of banded cocks harvested would be higher than recovery rates since all bands are not returned by hunters. Eight-week-old pen-reared pheasants fitted with radio transmitters released in Minnesota had mortality rates of around 74% in the first month after release, mostly due to predation losses (Hessler et al. 1970). However, a portion of this mortality could have been due to transmitter effects.

Release of male chicks from 5 to 10 weeks of age in Utah provided much better hunting season returns than observed in most other studies (Low 1954). Weekly releases of chicks from 5 through 10 weeks of age during summer over a 6-year period yielded band returns that generally averaged better than 20% and reached as high as 29% for 7 week-old birds and 31% for the 10-week-old birds (Low 1954). The Utah return rates on released pheasants were unusually high and further illustrate the importance of banding any released pheasants so that the recovery rates can be used to evaluate the management effort.

As described later in this chapter, there is a much more effective approach to release of pen-reared pheasants if the goal is to simply augment rooster shooting opportunities.

It is the hen portion of the pheasant population that is the most important element of future pheasant populations, since survival of adequate numbers of cocks for breeding has never been a factor limiting reproduction. In Wisconsin, female chicks were released during summers to enhance future reproduction (Besadny and Wagner 1963). Observations indicated low survival after release and no long-term effect of these chick releases on pheasant populations. A similar conclusion in South Dakota led to the discontinuation of any state-sponsored pheasant release programs by the late 1980s.

The newest method of releasing young birds in attempts to stimulate pheasant populations is through a device called a Surrogator®. This mechanism provides food, water, warmth, protection from the weather elements, and protection from predators until approximately 4 weeks of age, the time at which the birds are usually released. The Surrogator® is purported to acclimate young birds to their direct surroundings and imprint them to the area. There is little human contact, except for weekly maintenance.

Although a fairly new product, the Surrogator® has captured the attention of many landowners interested in bolstering their pheasant and quail populations. The Nebraska Game and Parks Commission evaluation of Surrogators® indicates that this release method is ineffective in building huntable populations of pheasants (Lusk et al. 2009). Results from this study indicated about a 12% survival rate of the 4-week-old pheasant chicks released from the Surragator® to the start of the pheasant season and less than a 1% annual survival rate. Only 6 of the 170 male pheasant chicks (3.5%) placed in Surrogators® were harvested.

Release of pen-reared hens in spring

With the growing acceptance of the futility of summer pheasant releases in the mid 1980s, groups and individuals intent on augmenting pheasant numbers through pheasant introductions shifted their efforts to releasing yearling hen pheasants in the spring. This approach was implemented under the presumption that population contributions would increase if overwinter mortality could be avoided. By the late 1980s, this management strategy was advocated by at least nine pheasant management groups in eastern South Dakota (Leif 1993).

Questions surrounding the contributions of spring-released hen pheasants to the population at large led SDGFP to initiate a scientific evaluation of the strategy in 1990 (Leif 1993, 1994). Over 3 years of study, 44 wild and 159 pen-reared hen pheasants were radio marked and followed on two study areas that had excellent pheasant habitat. Six-month survival (early April through early October) was 8% for pen-reared hens and 55% for wild hens. Predation was the only documented source of mortality for wild pheasants and the primary cause of pen-reared hen deaths. Additional pen-reared hen mortality resulted from collisions or other accidents with cars and farm equipment and from drowning in wetlands (Leif 1994).

As a result of the lower survival rates, a lower proportion (21%) of released pen-reared hens initiated incubation of a nest than their wild counterparts (68%). In addition, pen-reared hens that tried to nest were less successful (38%) than wild hens (63%), due again to higher rates of predation on pen-reared hens with active nests (Leif 1994). The 8% of released pen-reared hens that survived long enough to hatch a clutch also had lower (although not statistically different) rates of brood-rearing success (56%) than wild hens (83%) (Leif 1994). Pen-reared pheasants hatching clutches in England were much less successful in brood rearing (27% fledged at least one chick) than wild pheasants (81% fledged at least one chick) (Hill and Robertson 1988a). A chick was considered as fledged once it had reached 8 weeks of age.

In South Dakota, the resultant contribution of releasing hen pheasants in the spring was an additional 16 pheasants in the fall population for every 100 hens released. For every 100 wild hen pheasants on these same study areas, 169 pheasants were added to the fall population (Leif 1994). A similar lack of recruitment from pen-reared hens has been documented in England (Hill and Robertson 1988a), Sweden (Brittas et al. 1992), Oregon (Jarvis and Engbring 1976, Haensly et al. 1985), and Idaho (Musil and Connelly 2009) (Photo 11-2).

Photo 11-2. Because of their survival skills, wild hens captured in winter, radio marked and released, produced approximately ten times as many juvenile pheasants as did radio-marked, pen-reared hens released in the spring in the same central South Dakota habitats. (CTS)

Augmentation of pheasant populations with the release of hens in the spring is not a practical management option in South Dakota (Leif 1994). Pen-reared hens released in the wild suffer excessively high rates of predation because they are poorly adapted in terms of predator avoidance behaviors, such as seeking adequate concealment in available habitat. Furthermore, releases of pen-reared pheasants where wild pheasants are already established can attract predators to release locations, unintentionally increasing predation on wild pheasants (Leif 1994).

Autumn releases of cocks

Pheasant release programs were discontinued by the SDGFP in the early 1990s because of poor survival and low reproductive output of released birds. As of this printing, pheasant releases by private individuals and some civic groups continue in the state although the extent of those release programs is a small fraction of what it was in the twentieth century. With the growth in the shooting preserve industry in South Dakota, pheasant game farms have found a new market. It involves release of adult cock pheasants immediately before taking clients into the fields to harvest these birds (Photo 11-3).

Photo 11-3. Rearing of male pheasants until they obtain adult plumage (basic plumage) and subsequent release onto private fee hunting areas has proved to be an economically viable approach for improving pheasant hunting on commercial operations. This rooster was reared in the wild. (Courtesy of Doug Backlund)

Although many state wildlife agencies in North America have implemented "put-and-take" pheasant stocking programs, South Dakota has never implemented such a program. A number of evaluations of these programs have occurred over the years with the most current and definitive work on the topic conducted in Pennsylvania (Krauss et al. 1987, Diefenbach et al. 2000). Almost 8,000,000 pheasants had been released over 70 years by the Pennsylvania Game Commission when the study was conducted and almost all of the 217,000 pheasants shot in Pennsylvania in 1998 were released by the state (Diefenbach et al. 2000). Pheasant hunters shot 62% of cocks released on public land and 47% of cocks released on private land. Survival of released pheasants was very low (<6%) for the 30-day period following release due to both harvest and probable vulnerability to predators. The estimated cost of Pennsylvania's put-and-take release program was $33.82 (1998 dollars) per pheasant bagged (Diefenbach et al. 2000).

In South Dakota, private shooting preserve operators reported that they released 375,273 cock pheasants in the fall and shot 177,638 (47%) of them during the 2010–2011 preserve season (SDGFP, unpublished data). Growth in this industry over the past 2 decades (from 10 preserves in 1983 to 220 in 2010) is a good indication that successful business models can be and are developed for raising and releasing fully grown cock pheasants for shooting.

A put-and-take pheasant release program has never been implemented by SDGFP on a statewide basis because of the certainty that hunters would be unwilling to pay license fees that were comparable to the fees charged by preserve operators. More importantly, pheasant hunters in South Dakota enjoy the privilege and opportunity to shoot wild pheasants at levels unmatched anywhere in the world, an opportunity that is sustained without stocking of pen-reared pheasants.

Why were initial pheasant releases so successful in the early 1900s?

If stocking pen-reared birds does not increase pheasant populations, then why were the original releases in the early 1900s so successful in South Dakota? These releases of pheasants, both wild and pen reared, were into a landscape where these birds did not yet exist but where habitat was optimal. Surviving birds, even if initial mortality was high after release, provided the needed "seed stock" and exhibited an explosive increase as they filled this unoccupied and optimal habitat. It is doubtful that natural mortality factors such as predators or severe winters could have stopped this explosion under such ideal habitat conditions.

It is unlikely that we will ever again have a situation in South Dakota, North America, or elsewhere in the world where optimal pheasant habitat is unoccupied and simply waiting for the birds. The "seed stock" needed for population recovery is already present throughout South Dakota even after unusually poor years of pheasant reproduction or high mortality during a severe winter.

Trap and transfer of wild birds

Trapping and transplanting of wild pheasants was used by SDGFP in the 1920s to aid the rapid expansion of pheasants after initial releases in the prior decade (Leif 2007). In modern times, this practice has been used by SDGFP to jump-start populations that appear to be below the potential of available habitat. Biologists with the SDGFP also have assisted with attempts at establishment of wild pheasant populations by trapping wild birds and shipping them to Missouri (1990s) and Pennsylvania (2000s). The process of moving wild birds to a new release area is called translocation.

Survival of translocated hen pheasants is similar to that of resident wild hens (Wilson et al. 1992, Leif 1994). These studies also document that translocated hens settle in the general area and reproduce at levels comparable to resident wild pheasants. Consequently, releasing trapped pheasants is a viable management tool to facilitate range expansion into unoccupied habitat (Wilson et al. 1992) (Photos 11-4).

Trapping wild birds for transplanting is an effective management tool if, and only if, the appropriate habitat is present and it is empty of wild pheasants. As we have learned, pheasants are very prolific in South Dakota where habitat is sufficient. Transplanting wild pheasants will not increase the capacity of the habitat to support additional pheasants. If a base population of pheasants exists in an area, the best way to enhance numbers is through habitat development.

Photos 11-4. Biologists (Greg Wolbrink in photo) can use baited funnel traps (inset) to capture wild pheasants for trap and transfer or research purposes. (TRK)

Nevertheless, there are probably some situations where release of trapped pheasants (transplanting) may accelerate initial increases and spur long-term population growth. Trap-and-transfer projects of this nature were implemented in western South Dakota where pockets of predominantly unoccupied habitat created through irrigation projects were surrounded by large expanses of unsuitable habitat. Without a detailed evaluation of these programs, it is difficult to know whether these population augmentation efforts were successful or not.

Winter feeding
Keeping winter feeding in proper perspective

During harsh winters, especially when accumulations of snow make waste grain inaccessible, pheasants are frequently observed along roadsides looking for food and grit. During extreme or extended winter conditions, citizens often advocate that the state wildlife agency directly provide feed for pheasants or supply feed to landowners so they can feed pheasants. Even during normal or open winter conditions, some still feel it is necessary to feed pheasants.

Starvation can and does periodically occur in wintering pheasants. However, in all but the harshest of winters, pheasants are able to find adequate food sources (Chapter 7). The appropriate way to feed pheasants in severe winters is to plan ahead by providing winter food plots and closely associated winter cover (Chapter 10). Planning for food plots requires action in the previous spring and summer. Development of permanent winter cover such as dense rows of shrubs requires even longer-term planning (Photo 11-5).

Photo 11-5. Almost all of these tracks are from pheasants (a few deer) moving between heavy cattails, phragmites, and standing corn. The winter cover and food plot are less than 100 yards apart. (AEG)

Suggestions on winter feeding of pheasants with harvested grains

Although not a recommended management practice, we recognize that winter feeding using harvested grain may occur on many properties. Before implementing this practice, you should first consider some of its negative implications and shortfalls. First, if feeding does not occur in the proper location (e.g., in close proximity to quality winter cover), this effort may actually increase mortality as the birds are using additional energy to get to and from the food source and increasing their exposure to severe weather conditions and to predators. Second, even though pheasants are mobile and will move to food sources, grain placed in isolated areas or too far from winter habitat may not be discovered.

The following recommendations should be considered when feeding harvested grains. First, do not feed along roadsides as this will expose birds to traffic and potentially attract other wildlife, such as deer, increasing the chances of vehicle collisions. Second, supplemental food should be placed adjacent to or in close proximity to quality winter cover. Proper location of the feed will reduce exposure to weather elements and predation. Third, do not feed excessively as weather conditions can change and supplemental feed can be covered and not utilized. Piles of food and feeders may also attract unintended species (i.e., white-tailed deer, wild turkeys) that out-compete the pheasants for the food. Consider spreading the food over a larger surface area to help minimize the chances of feeding sites becoming focus points for predators. Fourth, if feeding begins, it must continue until sufficient areas of ground have been cleared of snow by melting or wind so other foods can be found.

Pheasants can become dependent on winter feeding once this concentrated food source is provided to them (Photo 11-6). Remember, even if temperatures remain near or below 0° Fahrenheit (-18° Celsius), feeding is not necessary if pheasants can get to waste corn, sorghum, or other crop seeds in areas of open ground or shallow snow. We emphasize again the greater importance of establishing quality wintering areas with sufficient winter cover and adequate nearby food plots in preference to winter feeding. Examples of quality wintering areas include wide and dense shelterbelts with shrubs and evergreens and wetlands with extensive stands of cattails, sandbar willows, and phragmites.

The cost of attempting to feed pheasants over several townships or throughout much of the pheasant range in South Dakota would be extremely expensive for a public wildlife agency and the benefits remain highly questionable.

Predator control

No matter what the current pheasant population level is or whether the trend shows an increasing or decreasing population, many people continue to advocate predator removal as a management tool to benefit pheasant populations. Red fox, skunks, raccoons, coyotes, various hawks, great horned owls, and sometimes American crows are the most common predators discussed. Reduction or elimination of mammalian predators and crows can often be a focus

Photo 11-6. This pile of grain has inadvertently attracted plenty of pheasants and white-tailed deer. If grain is intentionally set out for pheasants during a severe winter, be sure it is scattered near good winter cover and that food is kept there until snow melt allows birds access to waste grains in the field. (Courtesy of Michael Kavanagh)

point of private and sometimes public efforts to increase pheasant numbers (Riley and Schulz 2001).

Predator control is not new to pheasant management. Different approaches over more than 50 years have provided varying results in terms of their effects on pheasants.

Protected predators—raptors

Predation on pheasants by various raptors such as hawks and great horned owls has been discussed in Chapter 7 and, where related to pheasant reproduction, in Chapters 4, 5, and 6 (Photo 11-7). Because raptors are readily visible and are effective hunters, they are often blamed for reducing pheasant numbers. In particular, larger hawks and the great horned owl get blamed for pheasant mortality.

Unfortunately, most people make little or no effort to tell one species of hawk from another. Hawks that have minimal effects on prey as large as full-sized pheasants are sometimes improperly identified as causing major pheasant losses in spring and fall. While hunting pheasants, one of the authors observed an unusually high concentration of hawks soaring low over an expansive stand of tall and intermediate wheatgrass and occasionally diving into the cover to make or attempt a kill (L.D. Flake, personal observation). Two hunters that stopped to visit along the road had also observed these abundant hawks and made the statement that they must be killing large numbers of pheasants. However, the hawks

Photo 11-7. All raptors are protected by federal and state laws. This gyrfalcon, a rare winter visitor from the Arctic, is a remarkably beautiful and streamlined raptor capable of capturing larger prey. (Courtesy of Doug Backlund)

were northern harriers and, though they looked large because of their wingspan, are relatively small in body size and are not very effective at taking mature or nearly mature pheasants. In fact, these northern harriers were preying on the abundant voles that the hunters could easily observe scurrying about in the grass cover.

A few years ago, a cock pheasant was observed attacking and spurring a northern harrier that got too close (L.D. Flake, personal observation). As noted in Chapter 6, hen pheasants have been observed attacking northern harriers coming too close to their chicks. Yes, northern harriers can kill some chicks, but they are not very effective predators on full-sized pheasants.

All of the raptors that sometimes seem so common during spring and autumn migration take a variety of prey. In taking mice, ground squirrels, cottontails, and other species that can reach pest levels, they are serving an important function for landowners (Photo 11-8).

Unlike most mammalian predators, hawks and owls are federally protected and cannot be managed through shooting, trapping, or other means. Although some individuals may feel they are doing a service by illegally shooting and trapping hawks and owls, they are in direct violation of federal and state laws. The penalties for shooting or otherwise killing hawks, owls, and eagles are severe. Individuals killing hawks, owls, or eagles bring bad publicity to hunting and trapping in general.

Photo 11-8. Raptors are important in helping control rodents and other pests on farmland. This great horned owl is clutching an eastern cottontail. The light coloration, almost like a snowy owl, may indicate it has migrated to South Dakota from northern parts of the great horned owl range. (Courtesy of Scott Weins)

Mammalian predator and crow removal

Predators such as red fox, raccoon, opossum, coyote, skunk (both species), and badger can be legally trapped or otherwise killed throughout the year by resident landowners on their own land without a license; control on most other property is also legal throughout the year but requires a furbearer license. Crows can be shot during the lengthy spring and fall hunting seasons if you have any hunting license, predator varmint license, or furbearer license.

Studies have shown that intensive and continuous removal of mammalian predators and crows can increase both hen survival and nest success for upland nesting birds (Chesness et al. 1968) (Photo 11-9). Although intense predator control efforts may enhance production at local levels, it is essentially impossible to have the same effect at a landscape level. Results may also vary depending on which predators are removed. Between 1964 and 1971, a research study in South

Photo 11-9. Raccoons have increased in South Dakota in the past century largely due to the increase in denning sites (rock piles, old hollow trees, old buildings, etc.) and food (such as corn) associated with humans. They are effective predators on nests. (Courtesy of Scott Weins)

Dakota evaluated predator removal and the net effect on pheasant numbers. When red fox were removed, pheasant numbers increased by 19%; when red fox, raccoon, badger, and skunk were removed, pheasant numbers responded with a 132% average annual increase (Trautman et al. 1974). The response of pheasants to broad-scale predator reduction in this study was unusually strong.

Other studies have also shown that control of only a single predator species is often not successful in increasing nesting success. Nearly complete removal of striped skunks in North Dakota led to increases in nest success for waterfowl on some areas, but the gain was nullified on others because of predation by alternate predators such as red fox and Franklin's ground squirrel (Greenwood 1986) (Photos 11-10).

A 3-year study (2007–2009) was completed in South Dakota by South Dakota State University, SDGFP, and the Delta Waterfowl Association to evaluate pheasant and duck nest success in areas where most mammalian predators had been removed (trapped) versus areas with no removal effort (Docken 2011). Results showed an overall 15% nest success in control areas (untrapped) whereas the treatment areas (trapped) had 22% nest success rate. However, within the three treatment or trapped areas (each 36 square miles in size), nest success varied among years and in

Photos 11-10. Control of a variety of mammalian predators must be maintained over a broad area and on an annual basis to positively influence pheasant nesting success and chick survival. Striped skunks (bottom) are primarily nest predators while red fox (top) commonly take eggs, chicks, and even hens. (Courtesy of Scott Weins)

some cases pheasant nest success was lower in the trapped areas than in those without predator removal efforts. Mixed results suggest that the predator community makeup (types of predators) and abundance and distribution of pheasant habitat may play a more important role than actual predator removal efforts.

Other studies have provided important information on the influence of predator control and size of the control area on pheasant reproduction. Efforts to control red fox, striped skunks, and raccoons in northern and central Utah using professional trappers had no effect on fall pheasant numbers on 4-square-mile areas but appeared to have a positive influence on 16-square-mile areas. Apparently, predators from surrounding areas can easily replace the predator void in smaller control areas (Frey et al. 2003). Trapping must be conducted annually in the spring and summer to remain effective.

Intensive control of mammalian predators and American crows approximately doubled nest success and chick production of ring-necked pheasants in Minnesota during a study from 1960 through 1964 (Chesness et al.1968). In this study, intensive predator control using professional trappers, gassing of dens, and shooting of crows (a major nest predator in the study areas) was conducted annually during spring and early summer on an approximately 4,000-acre area. An equal sized area of similar habitat was left untrapped (control site) and used for comparison to the predator removal area (treatment site). The authors concluded that intensive control efforts would be required annually to benefit pheasant populations. The authors also noted that annual predator control was extremely expensive and may be cost prohibitive.

On the Pheasants Forever Inc. website is an excellent summary with recommendations on predator control for landowners interested in producing wild pheasants. Following are a few key points (paraphrased):

1. Excluding predators from small management areas with a predator-proof fence (electric predator fence) can be effective but requires a high level of maintenance. Materials for predator-proof fences and upkeep and annual removal of predators from within the protected area can consume a great deal of time and are prohibitively expensive.

2. If trapping will be part of a management practice, it must occur throughout the entire spring and summer period and should be conducted by a professional, full-time trapper to be as successful and productive as possible. Predators have large home ranges and will rapidly invade areas where predators have been removed.

3. To effectively negate predation on general landscape areas, the predator management efforts should focus on large contiguous areas. Research indicates a minimum area of about 16 square miles or larger is required (Frey et al. 2003).

4. The best way to reduce predation on pheasants and pheasant nests is to dilute predator influence by providing improved nesting and brood-rearing cover across the landscape.

Time and time again, predator removal is contemplated as the fix to increasing pheasant populations. Whether trapping at a local level, trapping to remove predators from larger township areas, or using electric anti-predator fencing to exclude predators from nesting and brooding cover, predator control is not going to have the landscape-level results or long-term results that pheasant enthusiasts expect or want.

A large-scale landscape approach to habitat improvement is ultimately needed to dilute the effects of predation and improve pheasant populations (Kuehl and Clark 2002). Predation on pheasant nests, hens, and broods can be reduced by adding large blocks of quality herbaceous cover over the landscape. This practice reduces predation effects on pheasants without the need for predator control. In addition to pheasants, upland nesting ducks as well as many other ground-nesting birds benefit from establishment of blocks of nesting and brood-rearing cover through increased female, egg, and hatchling survival.

Even when pheasant habitat is in relatively good condition and is abundant across the landscape, predation will always be a contributing factor to limiting pheasant production (Trautman 1982). Land managers wishing to use both quality habitat and predator control in tandem to increase pheasant reproduction and survival should be aware of the findings discussed above. Pheasant managers should also be aware of the value of coyotes in suppression of other predators such as red fox (Chapter 7) and also be aware that predator control programs may lead to increases in nest predation from species such as Franklin's ground squirrels and to increases in some other pest species as well.

Chapter thoughts

Practices discussed in this chapter are management options sometimes used in an attempt to help bolster pheasant numbers. Releases of pen-reared pheasants during spring (hens) or summer (adolescent birds 7 to 12 weeks of age) are not recommended as economically or biologically viable approaches to pheasant management. Release of fully sized cock pheasants in the fall or winter for short-term hunting opportunities can provide good returns. As pointed out by Pheasants Forever, rearing and release of pen-reared pheasants diverts needed funding from habitat improvement programs. Population enhancement through pheasant stocking is ineffective because pheasants that are raised in a pen are usually unable to learn the habitat utilization skills necessary to avert being killed by a predator. Predator avoidance is a learned behavior that wild pheasant chicks acquire from the hen.

In most winters pheasants can find adequate waste grains from harvested crops. We consider emergency winter feeding with harvested grains to be much less valuable than planning ahead and planting food plots near wintering areas.

Predator removal may provide a positive return if conducted annually prior to and during the breeding season by professional trappers over a large block of land that would include many farms. Effective predator control is extremely expensive. Dilution of predator influence on pheasants by improving the abundance of blocks (fields) of herbaceous nesting and brood-rearing cover on the landscape is the best method to reduce the effects of predators.

Stocking, winter feeding, or predator control should not be considered substitutes for proper habitat development and management. Priority efforts should focus on developing, improving, and maintaining the essential habitat components that will provide the best possible chance for pheasants to reproduce and survive.

CHAPTER 12
POPULATION MONITORING, HARVEST STATISTICS, AND SEASON STRUCTURE

In South Dakota three of the more common topics of daily conversation are the weather, prices of grain and livestock, and pheasants. It's interesting how pheasant populations, agricultural practices, and annual weather patterns are so closely connected. Agricultural practices and resulting landscapes on a long-term basis and weather conditions on a more short-term basis play a dominant role in influencing our pheasant populations.

Whether it is how successful hen pheasants were during the reproductive season or the survival of pheasants after an unusually cold and snowy South Dakota winter, pheasant enthusiasts want to know how the birds are doing in anticipation of the fall hunting season. Here we discuss what surveys used by the South Dakota Department of Game, Fish and Parks (SDGFP) reveal about pheasants, pheasant harvest, and hunters.

Surveys

Of all the wildlife and habitats that are monitored by SDGFP, no other species has such a notable compilation of survey data as the ring-necked pheasant. Long-term records of pheasant population trends and statistics are necessary to measure possible effects of various land-use changes, weather patterns, and other factors on their populations. Several survey methods have been used in South Dakota since 1946 when efforts to monitor pheasants became more extensive and standardized. Examples of now discontinued surveys were the cock crowing survey, spring and summer rural mail carrier survey, and the July roadside upland game survey (or roadside survey) (Trautman 1982:70–72). Currently, the three surveys used to collect population and harvest trend data are the pheasant brood survey, winter sex-ratio survey, and the hunter-harvest survey.

Brood survey

The pheasant brood survey has been conducted by SDGFP staff annually since 1949 to determine pheasant reproductive success, population trends, and relative densities of populations throughout the state. This information can be used to predict hunter success for specific geographic areas of the state for the upcoming fall hunting season. Other factors, such as status of the agricultural harvest, historical hunting success, and historical hunting pressure are also considered in making harvest predictions.

Survey indices are currently derived from 110 30-mile pheasant brood routes that are distributed across 57 counties in South Dakota where pheasants are found in sufficient numbers for surveying (Figure 12-1). Routes are surveyed from July 25 through August 15 each year using standardized methods on mornings when weather and dew conditions are optimal for observing pheasants. Weather and dew conditions that meet the survey protocol for "primary conditions" include vegetation that is thoroughly saturated from moderately heavy dew or rain during the previous overnight hours, sunshine with little cloud cover, and wind velocities that do not exceed 8 miles per hour (mph). Survey routes conducted when conditions are not optimal are considered secondary runs (Photo 12-1).

The combination of sun and dew entices pheasants to seek open sunny areas to escape the wet grass, thus making them easier to see and count. Light winds (0–8 mph) keep the dew-saturated grass from drying out while routes are being surveyed. These primary conditions are critical to getting a representative count of birds. On successive mornings, more than 20 broods have been observed on

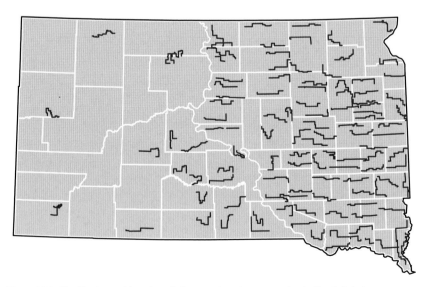

Figure 12-1. Distribution and location of pheasant brood survey routes in South Dakota.

Photo 12-1. For each established route, the number of roosters, hens, and broods is documented to calculate a pheasants-per-mile index. Chicks per brood are also counted where possible. (CTS)

a morning with primary conditions after observing less than five broods a day earlier in poor counting conditions (Chad Switzer, personal observation).

This combination of primary conditions is not present on most mornings. In the days before computers and internet weather websites, survey staff would have to set their alarm clocks early and step outside their homes well before sunrise to test the weather conditions before deciding to head out to the starting point of the survey route or go back to bed. Survey staff now have the luxury of checking the detailed weather forecast the night before and only need to set the alarm early when forecasted weather conditions are favorable.

Surveys begin at sunrise and conclude usually no later than 2 hours after sunrise. While traveling on the gravel roads at a speed of 15–20 mph, observers count all visible roosters, hens, and broods within ⅛th mile on either side of the road. Complete counts of pheasant broods observed on open areas such as roads or recently mowed areas are used to estimate average brood size. Counts of complete brood size are taken both on the established brood survey routes and opportunistically when complete broods are observed by biologists and wildlife managers at other times during the July 25–August 15 survey period.

The pheasant brood survey generates an annual index that varies in direct relationship to the actual numbers of birds in a region and is used to make comparisons of pheasant abundance among years. This index of abundance can be used to forecast what hunters might expect come fall. Varying weather and dew conditions and differing crop development and time of harvest (in particular, small grain) during the survey period can influence the results among years, but in general the brood survey has worked quite well as an index to annual reproductive success.

Pheasants per mile (PPM) indices are calculated by summing the product of the average brood sizes and total number of broods observed with numbers of cocks and hens observed on each route and dividing by miles on the route. For example, if a total of 15 broods (6.5 chicks per brood), 30 cocks, and 25 hens were observed on a 30-mile survey route the PPM index would be 5.1 pheasants per mile. Because of the multiplier effect of brood size and total brood count (brood size x total broods) in the PPM indices, brood data has a much greater influence on the index than numbers of hens or roosters observed. The status of the population in the current year is determined by comparing it with PPM estimates for the prior year and the average of the previous 10 years. As should be the case, nesting and brood-rearing habitat strongly influence the PPM index.

Attempting to interpret local pheasant populations by evaluating the results of one survey route by itself is an interpretation destined for inaccuracy. If a number of routes in a given area are all showing a similar trend, then a reasonable interpretation of a trend in the overall population can be made. Every year, the most anticipated number sought by the media in South Dakota is the statewide pheasant population trend. The population estimate is front-page headline news when released by the SDGFP, even if most hunters hunt localized areas that do not always match the state population trend. Before implementation of a localized population analysis in 1994, hunters were left to apply the statewide trend to their favorite hunting vicinity, an exercise that often resulted in frustration and consequently criticism of the SDGFP survey.

The 110 survey routes are regionally grouped into what are called local survey areas (mostly associated with city names), as this provides familiar places for hunters to reference. The 13 survey areas are then analyzed and compared with the previous year and the 10-year average PPM. Percentage change in PPM indices and statistical significance provide important information to wildlife managers and pheasant hunters. It is important to note, since pheasants per mile (PPM) estimates are relative density estimates, the comparisons are valid only between years within each local survey area.

The much anticipated pheasant brood survey report is completed before Labor Day (early September) each year and provides a summary of the survey results including the number of roosters, hens, and broods counted on the designated brood routes across the state. Most important to pheasant hunters, the PPM index is compared between the previous year and the 10-year average for the 13 survey areas. A detailed summary helps explain some of the factors that may have contributed to any increase or decrease of the PPM index in a particular area. Gain or loss of habitat or the influence of drought on nesting and brood-rearing cover or of a cold and wet June on brood survival are all examples of potential factors that can influence reproductive success.

Since initiation of the brood survey in 1949, the lowest statewide PPM index of 1.0 was recorded in 1976, a drought year and also a period when undisturbed nesting and brood-rearing habitat on the landscape was at an all-time low. In contrast to 1976, the highest statewide PPM of 11.4 was documented in 1961 during the peak of the Soil Bank era (Figure 12-2, Appendix 2). The 10-year average for the generally excellent pheasant hunting years from 2001–2010 was 6.0 PPM (Switzer 2010). During the past 60 years, the statewide PPM has responded positively to large-scale land-retirement programs such as during the Soil Bank and Conservation Reserve Program (CRP) eras and negatively to maximum crop production strategies as occurred in the mid 1970s (Chapter 1).

Average pheasant brood sizes have been documented since 1946, with the highest average of 7.9 recorded in 1952 and lowest average of 5.7 in 1959 (Appendix 2). The 10-year average for 2000–2010 was 6.5 chicks per brood (Switzer 2010). As noted in Chapters 5 and 6, poor reproduction is often associated with drought. However, droughts and drought severity often vary considerably across the state's primary pheasant range.

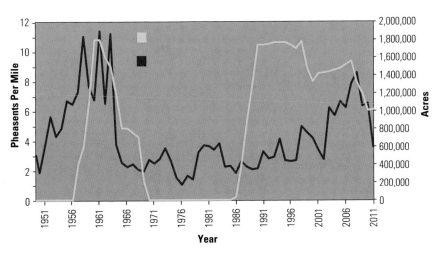

Figure 12-2. Statewide pheasants per mile (PPM) index, 1949–2011. Note that peak PPM indices values generally correspond with increased herbaceous cover on the landscape associated with the Soil Bank and Conservation Reserve Program eras. Data sources: U.S. Department of Agriculture Farm Service Agency (CRP acres) and Erickson and Wiebe (1973) (Soil Bank acres).

Winter sex-ratio survey

As pheasants congregate near limited winter habitat and food sources, SDGFP conducts counts of roosters and hens to estimate the post hunting season sex ratio (Photo 12-2). The winter sex-ratio survey is conducted annually from the end of the hunting season through March 31. The winter sex ratio serves two purposes: 1) to measure the overall effect of the pheasant season on the post hunt sex ratio of pheasants and 2) to provide an essential metric used in the calculation of a preseason population estimate (Appendix 3).

Conducted annually since 1947, the lowest statewide ratio of 21 cocks per 100 hens was recorded in 1980, 1981, and 1983. The highest statewide ratio of 63 roosters per 100 hens was recorded in 1950 (Appendix 2). The 10-year average sex ratio for 2000–2009 was 41 roosters per 100 hens. Plenty of roosters for breeding have remained even after the longest seasons (Trautman 1982:80).

Photo 12-2. The winter sex-ratio survey is conducted to estimate the level of harvest on roosters from the previous hunting season by comparing with the pre-hunting season sex ratio. Counts are only conducted with satisfactory snow coverage as shown here. (TRK)

Hunter-harvest survey

To obtain harvest-related statistics for pheasants, a hunter-harvest survey is conducted annually following the conclusion of the hunting season and includes number of resident and nonresident hunters (Figure 12-3), number of days hunted, number of pheasants harvested, and hunter satisfaction (Appendix 2).

Resident hunters are surveyed to obtain harvest statistics for the resident-only season, while both resident and nonresident hunters are surveyed for the youth and general pheasant season. For the regular pheasant season, surveys are randomly sent out to 8,000 resident and 8,000 nonresident hunters to ensure a statistically-sound sample based upon past survey return rates (Corey Huxoll, Hunter-Harvest Survey Coordinator, personal communication). Shooting preserve license holders are not surveyed for harvest statistics. Though the return of surveys is voluntary, approximately 75% of surveys come back. The cooperation from hunters in providing this information is valuable.

Preseason population estimates, hunter satisfaction

The pheasant brood survey, pheasant winter sex-ratio survey, and the hunter-harvest survey provide the information used for estimating the preseason population (Hickey 1955, Dahlgren 1963). The formula and an example showing how survey information is used for calculating the preseason pheasant population are presented in Appendix 3 (Paulik and Robson 1969).

Preseason population estimates since 1919 can be found in Chapter 1 (Figure 1-5) and in Appendix 2. Data collected from the surveys can be used to estimate average pheasant densities (Figure 12-4) and hunter densities by county. In addition, a measure of hunter satisfaction is obtained through the hunter-harvest survey using rankings ranging from 1 (least satisfied) through 7 (most satisfied). During the 10 years from 2000–2009, resident hunters reported an average sat-

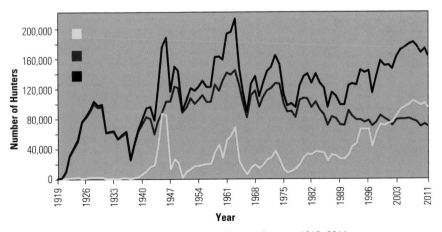

Figure 12-3. Numbers of resident and nonresident pheasant hunters, 1919–2011.

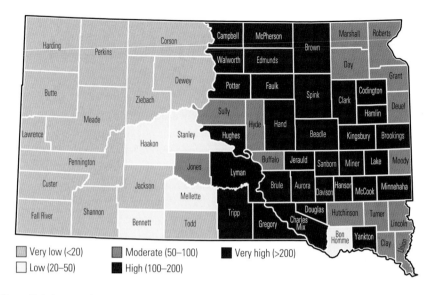

Figure 12-4. Average pheasant density (per mile²) estimates by county during 10 years from 2000 through 2009 when CRP acres were abundant.

isfaction of 4.9, with a low of 4.3 in 2002 and a high of 5.4 in 2007. Nonresident hunters reported an average satisfaction of 5.5, with a low of 5.0 in 2002 and a high of 6.0 in 2007. While hunter satisfaction is subjective in nature, it does provide a measurement of the overall experience of pheasant hunters.

Hunter and harvest statistics

For many pheasant hunters the opening weekend of the season is marked on their calendars early in the year. Pheasant hunting is a much anticipated event with family and friends often reuniting for this social gathering and small towns welcoming hunters and seeming to swell in size; "no vacancies" are common messages at most local motels.

The first pheasant season was in 1919 in Spink County, the site of some of the earliest successful pheasant introductions, where hunters harvested around 200 birds during the 1-day season (Switzer 2009). It took only 26 years from this first season in 1919 until hunters harvested a record 7.5 million pheasants in 1945 (Figure 12-5, Appendix 2). This is a great example of the reproductive potential of pheasants when provided quality habitat. Hunters harvested a record low 372,500 pheasants during the 1976 season, a period when the landscape was much less conducive for pheasants (Chapter 1). In the 10-year period from 2001–2010, average pheasant harvest was 1.7 million roosters, a number far in excess of any other state over this period.

An estimated 1,000 hunters participated in the inaugural season in 1919, with a record 212,000 hunters pursuing ringnecks during the high pheasant population year of 1963 (Figure 12-5, Appendix 2). During the generally excellent

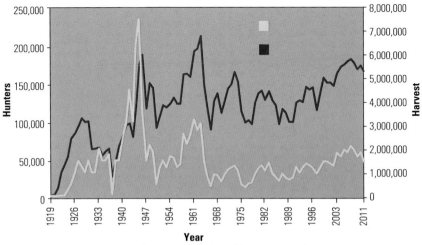

Figure 12-5. Statewide pheasant harvest and number of hunters, 1919–2011.

pheasant populations from 2001–2010, an average of 76,040 residents and 91,808 nonresidents took part in pheasant hunting seasons (Figure 12-3). Nonresident pheasant hunters have always been attracted to South Dakota for its great hunting opportunities, with numbers of nonresident hunters exceeding resident hunters since 2002 (Appendix 2).

The daily bag limit has been set at three roosters since 1979. Since that time, hunters have averaged 9.0 roosters per hunter for the season, with hunters bagging an average of 10.3 roosters for the season during the 10-year period from 2000–2009. On a historical note, hunters averaged a season bag of 54 pheasants back in 1944 when the preseason population was estimated at 15 million pheasants; during that year, hunters had a liberal daily bag limit of 10 pheasants, five of which could be hens (Appendix 2).

Season structure
General pheasant season

While the overall structure of past hunting seasons has varied greatly, the current season length and bag limit is one that is socially acceptable and provides abundant opportunities to pheasant hunters. During the past 90 years, pheasant hunting regulations have fluctuated considerably (Trautman 1982:81–82). During the first pheasant seasons held in South Dakota in 1919 and 1920, season length was held to 1 and 2 days respectively. From 1921 to the present, season length has varied from a remarkably long 163-day season in 1944 in one or more of the 11 units that year to a 4-day season in 1937 when pheasants were undergoing a precipitous decline (Trautman 1982:82) (Appendix 2). The highest daily bag limit was set in 1944 when hunters were allowed 10 pheasants; the lowest bag limits from 1921 to present (two cocks per day) occurred during the low pheasant years in the mid 1970s.

From 1919 until 1950, South Dakota pheasant seasons included an ever-changing management approach consisting of multiple units, specific season dates, and regional bag limits. For example, during the 1944–1945 pheasant season, the state established 11 regional management units that could be treated separately in terms of season length and bag limits. More recently, until 2006, the season was structured around two units. Since 2007, the state has been merged into a single pheasant hunting unit. Some changes in pheasant season structure may apply to specific areas such as Sand Lake National Wildlife Refuge and Lacreek National Wildlife Refuge. The start date for the regular pheasant opener is the third Saturday of October, a tradition going back to 1958.

Rooster-only hunting seasons have been authorized since 1947, but some hens were allowed in the bag in over half of the seasons from 1919 through 1946 (Trautman 1982:82) (Appendix 2). The daily bag limit of three roosters has been in effect since 1964, except for 1976–1978, when the daily bag limit was reduced to two roosters. A daily bag limit greater than three roosters could be implemented and would not hinder the pheasant population. However, the current limit is popular and distributes the harvest of vulnerable early season roosters to more hunters than if a higher limit was in place. Three cock pheasants along with a few hunting stories are considered an impressive take-home reward.

Early season shooting hours running from noon to sunset have been consistent since 1958. While many other states begin hunting at sunrise, the current shooting hour structure is socially accepted and an integral part of South Dakota's pheasant hunting tradition. Currently, shooting hours change from noon to sunset to 10:00 a.m. to sunset (Central Daylight Time) on the first Saturday after the general opener and for the remainder of the hunting season.

Special hunting seasons

In recent years the SDGFP Commission has established special hunting seasons that benefit youth and resident hunters. The most important additions have probably been the youth-only pheasant season for residents and nonresidents that began in 1999 and, more recently, the mentored hunting program for residents beginning in 2008.

The youth-only pheasant season is currently held statewide beginning the first Saturday in October and continues for 5 consecutive days. All youth (less than 18 years old) must be accompanied by an unarmed adult and must be safety certified (Photo 12-3).

The mentored hunting program is specifically for resident youth from 10 to 15 years of age. Participating youth do not need a hunting license to hunt pheasants or other upland game as long as the mentor has an appropriate hunting license. Youth in this age group must be accompanied by a safety-certified parent or other adult (with guardian's written permission) during the youth, resident-only, and regular season. The one-on-one interaction provided by the youth-only pheasant season and the mentored hunter program is intended to

Photo 12-3. These young men, mentored by their father, experienced a memorable day of pheasant hunting in central South Dakota. The two older Leif youth (the hunters) and their younger brother are, from left to right, Ethan (12), Elliot (7), and Drew (15). (APL)

teach hunter safety, hunter ethics, and respect for wildlife and their habitats (Photo 12-4).

According to the latest hunter-harvest survey, approximately 3,170 youth participated in the mentored hunting program during the 2010–2011 pheasant season, a number that has been increasing annually. Residents who take this opportunity to introduce an adolescent to the sport of pheasant hunting and the outdoors will likely find it a rewarding and memorable experience. We encourage resident hunters to participate in this program as a means to help recruit youth hunters.

To increase quality pheasant hunting opportunities for residents, a resident-only pheasant season was initiated statewide in 2001 on public lands and walk-in areas (WIAs). Walk-in areas are private land areas open to hunter access under lease agreement with the SDGFP. The resident-only season lasts for 3 consecutive days beginning on the second Saturday of October.

Photo 12-4. Youth hunters are critical to future conservation efforts for many wildlife species, including ring-necked pheasants. Mike Mueller and his son Carsten are enjoying a great hunt and an experience that will be remembered for the rest of their lives. (Courtesy of Chris Hull)

These recent youth and resident hunting options have been popular additions for the state's citizens. Specifics concerning the youth pheasant season, youth mentoring program, and the resident only pheasant season are presented in the current South Dakota Hunting and Trapping Handbook.

Linkage of surveys to global positioning and geographic information systems

Global positioning systems (GPS) are used to determine locations on earth, based on earth-orbiting satellites. Such systems are now commonly used by automobile drivers, hunters, fishermen, and many others to mark locations or navigate to specific sites and addresses. Use of GPS technology is broad and universal. Geographic information systems (GIS) are also widely known but not as commonly used by the public. GIS is used to develop and analyze computer-based maps using digital (latitude, longitude) data often gathered using GPS systems and satellite imagery. Today biologists are also using these powerful, satellite-based tools to study landscapes and habitats to assess their value for pheasants and other wildlife; any county in the state can be viewed with satellite imagery (maps) to determine the number of acres and the distribution of crops, pastures, shelterbelts, wetlands, undisturbed herbaceous cover, and other cover types.

Pheasant biologists and managers working with the SDGFP are now using these technologies to relate pheasant population data obtained from surveys to the habitat characteristics of the landscape in the survey areas. The GPS locations from survey data are used to link them to GIS maps of the landscape. Pheasant survey data that includes GPS locations can be said to be geo-referenced for use on GIS maps.

With the use of GPS and GIS technologies, pheasant biologists and managers develop computer-based habitat maps and then match up geo-referenced data from pheasant surveys to further examine the relationship of landscape composition (i.e., amount of grassland, cropland, wetland, etc.) to pheasant populations. These relationships between landscape composition and pheasant numbers are of particular interest to SDGFP personnel involved in pheasant management as well as the U.S. Department of Agriculture (Nielson et al. 2006). This information is also highly important to ongoing and future pheasant research and management (Chapter 15) and is important to thousands of hunters.

Chapter thoughts

A historic record of pheasant population trends and statistics is necessary to measure the effects of various land-use changes, weather patterns, harvest levels, and sociological changes on pheasant populations. Currently, three annual surveys are used to collect population and harvest trend data: the pheasant brood survey, winter sex-ratio survey, and the hunter-harvest survey. Using data collected from these three surveys, biologists are able to "back calculate" preseason populations, which is important in comparing population estimates to previous years and their relationship with habitat and weather conditions. Biologists for the SDGFP are beginning to create GIS databases and develop models to help predict pheasant response to land-use and habitat changes, along with relationships to the weather-related events that influence pheasant survival and reproduction. This information will not only assist biologists and landowners in managing pheasants but will also provide valuable information for pheasant hunters in predicting preseason populations.

CHAPTER 13
HUNTING PHEASANTS IN SOUTH DAKOTA

Ring-necked pheasants holding tight in a field of concealing grasses and forbs; colorful, cackling roosters rocketing upward out of cattails; or hens and roosters exploding from a snow-covered weed patch are all memories shared by many South Dakota pheasant hunters. So is the memory of hundreds of pheasants flying from the opposite end of a food plot or cattail wetland. For most avid pheasant hunters, memories of good flushing or pointing dogs are also part of those scenes. These experiences and recollections along with many friendships are important to thousands of resident and nonresident hunters that have pursued pheasants in South Dakota. For those who have hunted pheasants in South Dakota or those who hope to do so in the future, many rewarding moments await them in the coming seasons. From youngest hunters to those with decades of experience hunting pheasants, all know the anticipation and enjoyment of hunting these wary birds.

For hunters with minimal experience pursuing pheasants or who are new to hunting in South Dakota, we provide recommendations that should improve your chances for success and a memorable hunt. Others may want to see how our recommendations compare to their own. Our recommendations relate primarily to small groups hunting with dogs but can also be of value for hunters without dogs.

Miscellaneous preparations and considerations

South Dakota's general pheasant season has traditionally opened on the third Saturday in October, opening daily at noon for the first 1 to 2 weeks and at 10:00 a.m. (Central) thereafter; it closes for the day at sunset. In recent years the season has been extended and concludes at sunset on the first Sunday in January.

Resident or nonresident hunting licenses can be purchased over the Internet or at numerous outlets that carry sporting equipment throughout the state. Nonresident small-game licenses are valid for 10 days and are split into two consecutive 5-day periods that need not be continuous. Additional nonresident licenses can be purchased if desired (Photo 13-1).

We suggest you develop a regular exercise schedule to get in shape well before the pheasant season. Pheasant hunting will normally take you through a variety of habitats and over several miles each day. Pursuing birds through tall grass, weeds, and cattail cover to be in place for a shot when the dog is on birds takes plenty of exertion. Being in good physical condition will pay off!

Depending on the year and area, you may or may not need to contend with shallow water but in most cases it is good to have some knee-high boots available. Hip boots or waders may also help if you need to retrieve a pheasant from a marsh. Pheasants will commonly run out into shallow water or will use thin ice in emergent wetland cover as a type of refuge. It is not unusual for downed roosters to fall in areas of water or on thin ice where a dog or waders are needed to retrieve the bird. Most of the authors have broken through ice more than once while hunting in cattail-choked wetlands. A dry set of clothes and boots can come in handy.

Some areas of cover, particularly cattail stands, are quite dense and can be especially difficult walking. If snow is deeper than about 10 inches, you will likely find pheasants concentrated in cattails, some of it over ice, and will need to be in good condition to hunt very long during the day. Pheasants may also bunch up in plum thickets or other woody cover when snow arrives. Deep and drifting snow will greatly add to the challenge.

Photo 13-1. Extensive walk-in areas in central South Dakota have provided Budd Gould (Washington) and his son, Jeff (Idaho) several years of great pheasant hunting and quality family time. (Courtesy of Jeff Gould)

Even on the opener, be sure to bring layers of clothing so you can dress for weather ranging from uncomfortably hot to cold and snow (Photo 13-2). As on all hunts, avoid wearing new boots or at least bring the old boots along; it may also pay to bring moleskin, duct tape, or another type of tape in case you feel a blister coming on.

Hunting safety

Resident and nonresident hunters in South Dakota 16 years of age or younger are required to have taken a hunter safety course and to have a hunter safety certificate or card. Hunter safety certification from any state, province, or similar entity is valid. Much of the material discussed in this section is covered in these excellent courses. Mentored hunting, as a safety feature to help 10–15 year old hunters, is covered in Chapter 12.

The annual summary of hunting accidents in South Dakota is always sobering to read (Robertson 2010). Of 39 reported hunting incidents in 2010, 30 were related to upland game hunting, primarily pheasant hunting. Most shooting accidents while hunting pheasants are invariably linked to swinging the shotgun on pheasants with other hunters in the line of fire. (Swinging the shotgun refers to movement of the shotgun as the hunter attempts to hit a moving target.) Multiple hunters walking down the rows in row crops, like corn, sunflowers, or grain sorghum, toward multiple blockers on the other end ranks as the most common scenario for this type of shooting accident. Hunting standing crops with "walkers and blockers" can be a risky way to hunt pheasants.

Photo 13-2. Hunting pheasants in the late fall and winter over a hunting dog (German wirehaired pointer) is especially enjoyable and can be highly effective. Mary Clawson and her brother Mark Clawson are shown here on Mary's land north of Aberdeen. (Courtesy of Mary Clawson)

Other common accidents are due to carrying loaded (shell in chamber) firearms in vehicles, loading or unloading firearms, crossing fences with loaded firearms, and hunting dogs stepping on the triggers of loaded firearms on the ground. Although it is legal in South Dakota to carry a loaded shotgun, rifle, or other firearm in a vehicle, it is also careless and irresponsible! A loaded firearm in a vehicle has resulted in many tragic shooting injuries and fatalities, especially when the gun is being placed in or taken out of the vehicle. The state should not need to pass legislation for every aspect of safety in use of firearms.

To increase safety, make sure everyone in your party has a sufficient amount of fluorescent hunter-orange clothing that can be easily and quickly seen. Statistics from several states indicate that hunter orange greatly reduces the chances of being shot or of shooting in the direction of another hunter. Hunter orange is not required by law to hunt pheasants but you should wear it even when hunting alone because you will sometimes run into other hunters. It is doubly important to wear hunter orange when hunting pheasants during a rifle deer season (Photo 13-3).

Some hunters wisely bring extra hunter-orange caps for cases where a hunting companion has neglected to bring protective hunter-orange clothing. Even if you have a hunter-orange coat, shirt, or vest, we suggest that you always include a hunter-orange hat in your attire, especially if there is any chance that you will be hunting in tall cover such as dense cattails or tall weeds that obscure most of your body and clothing. The hat quickly stands out and it will help you to keep from getting shot and to avoid shooting a companion when a bird flushes. We urge you to always use hunter orange while hunting upland game and to shun hunting with anyone that refuses to wear these protective colors. Wearing only drab colors while hunting pheasants is a bad decision!

Photo 13-3. Hunter or blaze orange clothing improves safety by increasing the visibility of hunters as shown by two of the three hunters in this small family group. They are walking through a dense stand of phragmites. (LDF)

In tall, dense cover, don't think you will always know exactly where your hunting companion is in relation to a flushing rooster. Tall cover, wind, dogs following pheasants in various directions, pheasants flushing toward an unseen companion, and adrenaline can quickly lead you to make a dangerous shot. Most hunters have made a shot at a pheasant and then realized an unseen companion could have moved into a danger zone. Try to keep in regular contact by sight or by making sounds that can be heard by the other hunter or hunters in a small group. Stealth can be helpful in getting closer to pheasants before they run or fly but, if you cannot see a nearby hunting companion, safety should trump stealth every time. A good tip to follow when hunting in tall cover is to never shoot until you see sky between the bird and cover.

If you choose to hunt in a "walker and blocker" type situation with a group, we encourage you to be extra careful and to strictly avoid shooting at low flying birds that might be in line with another hunter. Shooting at or near ground level at a crippled pheasant can also be dangerous for other hunters and to hunting dogs. A good jingle to recite on the trip out to the field is: "If it's low, let it go. Bird up high, shoot it on the fly."

Be careful out there and choose your hunting companions wisely. Shooting injuries and even life threatening accidents can and will be avoided if you take the extra time to mentally prepare and follow the simple rules of hunting safety. You will greatly reduce the risk of an accident by careful use of firearms, choosing your hunting companions wisely, wearing hunter orange, and hunting in smaller groups.

We would also recommend protective eyewear while hunting, even if hunting alone. Appropriate eyewear can help protect your eyes from stray pellets and from sharp vegetation such as dead limbs or cattail spikes.

Shooting has caused serious hearing damage for many hunters. One of the authors hears a constant ringing (tinnitus) in the left ear due to years of shotgunning; proper use of hearing protection could have avoided or greatly reduced this hearing damage. Protective ear plugs that at least dampen the sound of the shot are recommended. Hindsight is easy for those that have suffered damage; we urge you to heed this recommendation and to save your hearing.

Where to hunt

The first and most important item about where to hunt is the South Dakota Hunting Atlas. The South Dakota Hunting Atlas is free and can be picked up at most places that sell licenses. It can also be ordered over the Internet on the SDGFP web site at no cost or viewed, printed, or downloaded on your GPS unit (gfp.sd.gov). The Hunting Atlas does an excellent job of mapping public lands as well as private lands leased for public hunting by the SDGFP. Public and private lands open to free access (walking) are color coded and detailed enough to locate sections (1 square mile) and quarter sections.

Private lands leased by the SDGFP for public hunting (walking) include primarily walk-in areas (WIAs) and Conservation Reserve Enhancement Program

(CREP) lands; further information on CREP lands is presented in Chapter 15. Controlled hunting areas are also leased (SDGFP) private land areas but require checking in with the landowner or at a self-check-in site; only a limited number of hunters are allowed access and the land may have other restrictions. Hunting access is free on private lands leased for hunting access by the SDGFP (Photos 13-4, 13-5).

Photo 13-4. This large walk-in area in central South Dakota east of Pierre provided extensive herbaceous cover along with adjacent fields of harvested corn (cropland not shown). Pheasant hunting was remarkable on this area in 2009 and hunters were also likely to flush greater prairie-chickens. (LDF)

Photo 13-5. Good grass cover, a corn food plot, and moist lowland areas all indicate substantial pheasant numbers on this walk-in area near Onida. By mid season, these areas are often uncrowded and yet still offer productive pheasant hunting. (LDF)

The SDGFP website has a helpful section on hunting areas with information on hunting on WIAs, CREP lands, controlled hunting areas, public lands, and private lands. Private land access, other than WIAs or other publicly leased hunting areas, is by permission only or in some cases, on a fee basis. Many of the fee areas provide lodging, hunting dogs, and guides. Additional discussion on hunting on private lands is included in Chapter 15.

If part of a WIA or other land leased for hunting access by the SDGFP appears to be grazed, tilled, or otherwise of low value to pheasants, remember that some landowners generously place many additional acres of their land into the program at little or no cost. Portions of WIAs that lack much cover may also be valuable for field hunting waterfowl, deer, or other game and may have been valuable to pheasants earlier in the season. It is a great program for hunter access!

Public areas (excluding WIAs and other private lands leased for public hunting) that have pheasant hunting include South Dakota Game Production Areas (GPAs), U.S. Fish and Wildlife Service Waterfowl Production Areas (WPAs), some federal refuges such as Sand Lake National Wildlife Refuge (December opener), State School and Public Lands, some SDGFP Parks and Recreation Lands (check Hunting Handbook for restrictions), Bureau of Land Management lands, national grasslands (U.S. Forest Service jurisdiction), Bureau of Reclamation lands, and Corp of Engineers lands (Photo 13-6). Hunters can also hunt pheasants on a public road right-of-way as long as they are not hunting within 660 feet of farm homes, other regularly occupied buildings, or livestock.

Additional electronic maps allowing hunters to locate public lands in South Dakota are available through the Wildlife Inventory and Land Management Application site (WILMA) on the SDGFP website; maps can be viewed as three types: satellite, road, and topographic maps. Each map has zoom-in features for closer examination. The website includes a help section for learning how to use the zoom and other map features.

Photo 13-6. Numerous Game Production Areas (GPAs) are managed by the South Dakota Department of Game, Fish and Parks for wildlife habitat and are open to public hunting. (LDF)

South Dakota also has excellent pheasant hunting on tribal lands. Hunters desiring to hunt on tribal lands should contact tribal wildlife agencies regarding seasons, license fees, and hunting opportunities. Indian reservations such as Standing Rock, Cheyenne River, and Lower Brule all offer outstanding pheasant and prairie grouse hunting opportunities.

A map showing average pheasant harvest per county is included in Chapter 1 (Figure 1-9). Areas with the highest densities of pheasants and highest harvest will likely be the most crowded with hunters early in the season. Experienced hunters, especially locals, know that areas of the state with lower overall densities of pheasants can often provide excellent hunting on local hot spots.

Areas with adequate cover within a half mile or less of agricultural fields such as corn, sorghum, or wheat usually hold good numbers of pheasants — the closer to cropland the better. Many good hunting spots on public areas may not get much pressure because they do not look that good from the road and may require walking a half mile or more. Even places like the Fort Pierre National Grassland, better known for prairie grouse hunting, have pheasant hot spots.

The regions with the highest densities of pheasants are generally the most difficult for obtaining permission on private land. In most parts of the state, many landowners will allow free access but the opening weekend may not be the best time for asking. Later in the season, permission is more likely to be granted. Hunter-landowner relationships are discussed more fully in Chapter 15.

When to hunt

The long pheasant season in South Dakota gives hunters the opportunity to hunt under a variety of conditions in terms of weather, harvest of standing crops, density of hunters, and degree to which the pheasants are "educated." Season, time of day, crop harvest, and snow cover are all factors we discuss in this section.

Early season—escaping the crowds

Most pheasant hunters eagerly look forward to the opening day, weekend, or week of the hunting season, as evidenced by the heavy turnout on some public areas (Photos 13-7, 13-8). On some of the larger Game Production Areas in prime pheasant counties, parking areas may be overflowing on the opening weekend well before the daily noon opening. If you are hunting on public areas or WIAs on the opener it might be advantageous to hunt in counties less well known for pheasant hunting where the public areas are relatively uncrowded. Pheasant hunting can still be good.

Late afternoon is a great time to avoid competition on the opener and throughout the early portion of the season. By 4:00 p.m., most pheasant hunters that had eagerly awaited the noon opening on public land have left because they tired of walking or have shot their limit of birds. This is also the time when many pheasants start moving back into the public areas from adjacent private lands where they have spent much of the day feeding and loafing in corn fields or

Dense wetland cover   **Planted tallgrass prairie**

Photo 13-7. Most Game Production Areas (GPAs) offer a variety of cover for pheasants and pheasant hunters. This GPA (Reynold's Slough) provides extensive upland herbaceous cover, wetland winter cover, wide and dense shelterbelts (with shrubs and conifers), and scattered food plots. (LDF)

Photo 13-8. Even on opening day, cock pheasants are notorious for running. Experienced hunters often work their dogs toward heavy cover, edges, or corners where the birds will be more likely to hold. (Courtesy of Doug Backlund)

other feeding sites. The values of late afternoon hunting have been observed and practiced by each of the authors for many years.

It can often pay dividends to take it easy during the heat of the day in early season, saving more energy for the last few hours. Experienced local hunters very often focus on the last one or two hours before sunset early in the season because that is when the birds are most likely to move from standing crops into the grass to roost. Hunting late in the day is especially effective on dark, cloudy days because birds head to roost much earlier (Photo 13-9).

Follow the crop harvest

Waiting until the corn is or has recently been harvested in late October or early November can be a terrific approach for finding great pheasant hunting with low competition. Hunting on both private and public land improves and the conditions for hunting dogs are usually good. As you drive to hunting spots be aware of specific areas where the corn, sunflowers, or other grain crops are being cut or have been recently harvested. After the harvest is complete, numerous pheasants that had used these grain crops for loafing and feeding will spend much more time in the undisturbed cover on public or private lands. Many of these birds have seen little or no hunting pressure.

Photo 13-9. Grass or grass-forb fields (like this stand of switchgrass) next to standing corn can be excellent sites to hunt toward evening when the pheasants head for roosting cover, especially if the adjacent corn is unhunted and on private land. (LDF)

Annual precipitation declines from east to west while crop harvest normally progresses from west to east in South Dakota's pheasant country. Hunters can use this pattern to find regions where harvest is underway or has been completed. For nonresidents, crop harvest reports from the U.S. Department of Agriculture can be of value in planning a pheasant hunting trip to South Dakota. If you know people in the state or have established friendships from previous South Dakota hunts, you can also just call them for local crop harvest reports.

In areas with unharvested crops, it can pay to work cover along the edge of these croplands even at midday. Pheasants will sometimes loaf in this cover during the day and these edges can be good hunting. If you do hunt cover on the edge of standing crops, an especially quiet approach is suggested so that pheasants do not run back into the standing cropland as you work the cover (Photo 13-10).

When it snows: mid to late season

Experienced pheasant hunters know that the first appreciable snowfall can provide some of the year's best pheasant hunting. Pheasants seem to be a bit surprised by the first snowfall and hold more tightly for hunting dogs, at least in the first few days. A nice snow of 4 to 6 inches without high winds can make for

Photo 13-10. Close flushes of roosters usually await hunters and hunting dogs every day of South Dakota's long season. (Courtesy of Scott Weins)

a perfect day (Photo 13-11). Pheasant tracks are readily visible so you can learn much about the birds. The birds often start moving into dense cattails or other heavy cover at this time. However, many are also still in herbaceous uplands, providing the upland cover has not been overly filled and flattened by the snow. Native tallgrass species such as switchgrass and big bluestem and weeds such as kochia tend to remain more erect than does the exotic smooth bromegrass under the weight of snow and may hold birds late in the season. In some cases, tall upland vegetation such as dense switchgrass will also form protected pockets or tunnels (tent-like areas under bent grass) under the snow where pheasants can find protection under surprisingly harsh winter conditions.

Stands of cattails, phragmites, and sandbar willow associated with wetlands are particularly good places to find pheasants as the snow and cold arrive (Photo 13-12). On a cold, windy, late fall or winter day, kneel down in thick cattails and you can quickly see how valuable this habitat is for pheasants and white-tailed deer in providing protection from wind chill. Patches of dense shrubs such as wild plum, chokecherry, or other dense shrubs can also be good at this time. Pheasant tracks and hunting dogs will verify what the birds consider as winter cover. Pheasants in this cover are normally close to a food source such as a harvested corn field or a standing food plot.

Photo 13-11. Pheasants can bunch up and become flighty later in the season, especially when hunting in areas with large numbers of birds. Hunters will still get a few roosters to hold tight in heavy cover. (CTS)

Photo 13-12. No wonder South Dakota is such a magnet for pheasant hunters when you often see pheasants like this around beautiful spots of winter cover. Hunting late in the year, with snow, can be an exceptional experience, but you need to be in shape! (CTS)

There is nothing more classic in pheasant hunting than to have dogs working or pointing hot scent and then to have a rooster pheasant burst through the snow and vegetation just a few yards in front of you. Often in mid to late season, you need to give the dogs extra time in working a small area to find pheasants holding tightly under the cover and snow.

Moderate snow cover in mid to late season can be the best of all times to hunt pheasants. Crowds are gone, the roosters are fully colored, and pheasants are concentrated in heavier cover. It is also a good time to visit with landowners because the crop harvest is finished and fewer hunters are afield.

Hunters planning to visit the state should be aware that during occasional severe winters, deep snow and drifting can make it unbelievably difficult to hunt pheasants. In some cases snowshoes can help but they can also be unwieldy when trying to walk through cattails or other tall dense cover. Walking through deep snow to get to pheasant cover in large cattail marshes makes for an exhausting hunt. If you hunt in these conditions, you need to be in great physical shape and have a strong heart! From experience we can tell you that a deer trail pounded out through the cattails looks wonderful when you find one; unfortunately, these trails do not usually go where you want to go and will not get you back to your vehicle. Drifting snow can also make road access to hunting areas difficult or impossible on many county roads unless they have been recently plowed.

Severe winter conditions are usually regional within the state and hunters can normally find parts of the state where snow is not as deep and where hunting conditions are less difficult. The winters of 2009–2010 and 2010–2011 were unusual in that regard in that most of the state's primary pheasant range was inundated by 12 inches or more of snow for much of the last month of the hunting season. Still, snow melted more rapidly in the central and south-central portions of the state's pheasant range than in the eastern and northeastern portions, allowing hunters more reasonable access to birds in these normally warmer portions of the state. Pheasants receive almost no hunting pressure in areas where snow is deep and has drifted because the birds are so difficult to access.

In most years, late season hunting, even on public areas, is some of the best and least crowded hunting available (Photos 13-13, 13-14). You are more likely to see larger flocks of pheasants as they group up late in the season. Some of these flocks will have hundreds of pheasants. However, there are that many more wary eyes and ears to make your approach more challenging. If you have the will and determination to walk through the snow to these wintering areas, chances are you will have a rooster or two in hand and a great story when you return home.

Ways to hunt: hunting dogs, other approaches

In general, the most experienced and dedicated pheasant hunters are typically accompanied by hunting dogs (Photo 13-15). Either flushing or pointing dogs can be highly effective. All of the authors have long hunted with a hunting dog or dogs and prefer to hunt alone or with one or two other hunters.

Photo 13-13. Some of the best and least crowded hunting is available in mid to late season when birds have moved into winter cover. Cock pheasants are extra wild and wily by mid season but hunting can still be terrific. We recommend layers of clothing and boots made to handle snow so you can adapt to the weather conditions. (Coutesy of Doug Backlund)

Photo 13-14. Pheasants will concentrate in this type of wetland thermal cover (mostly cattails) during winter if located near harvested croplands or food plots. Hunters should be careful about thin ice but in most cases the water is less than 1 to 2 feet deep below the dense emergent cover. (CTS)

Photo 13-15. Dense cattail cover edged by a broad strip of weedy cover (annual sunflowers, kochia, ragweed, etc.) and close to harvested grain or food plots is a great recipe for success when hunting pheasants. Ron Fesler from Brookings and his yellow lab are getting ready to walk this private land site. (LDF)

An especially enjoyable and effective way to hunt is with one or, at the most, two other hunters, each person with his own dog, all hunting in the same general area and direction but often hundreds or more yards apart. This approach provides the safety of having others know where you are while allowing much individual freedom in working your dog. The hunters keep contact by sight and sound at regular intervals. This type of hunting allows working the cover in the direction the scent takes the dog without concern about staying in a line, working a specific area of cover, or competition between dogs. This method works best with hunters that have traditionally hunted together. It is a highly successful approach.

A few hunters are able to successfully hunt pheasants alone and without a bird dog. One trick is stealth and knowing the behavior of pheasants in terms of the habitats they use. The method works best with some snow cover. By walking slowly and being quiet, you are able to surprise the birds, causing them to flush at close range. Hunters that have quietly and slowly walked cover for white-tailed deer know that surprising pheasants at close range is not uncommon. You need the patience to walk slowly and stop in likely spots; sometimes a little squeaking, clicking, or other noise mouthed when birds are near can help make the birds nervous and get them to flush. If you use this method you also need to be a good shot and be within close enough range to make an instant kill; without a dog you are unlikely to retrieve many crippled birds.

Some pheasant hunters will line up near corn fields, sorghum, or sunflowers to pass shoot pheasants flying into roosting cover from corn fields or other cropland surrounding public hunting areas. Hunters will also sometimes just watch public hunting areas from the road or field site for cocks to fly into evening roosting cover and then quickly move over to that spot to attempt to flush the bird. Both methods can be used by hunters without dogs, but it is still preferable to have a hunting dog with you, especially if it is necessary to retrieve a running bird. Shooting birds as they head for roosting cover works especially well on dark cloudy days when pheasants go to roost earlier in the evening.

Pheasant hunters in large parties often hunt pheasants by walking abreast through a food plot or crop such as grain sorghum or corn and pushing towards blockers posted at the other end of the field. Regulations allow for a maximum of 20 guns in these group hunts. These hunts are traditional for many South Dakota hunters and can be effective. The "walkers" or "drivers" need to remain in a relatively straight line because persons out of position are in greater danger of coming into the line of fire when a bird or birds flush. For those without bird dogs this is one of the options that will produce birds but, if good hunting dogs are not used, it can also produce excessive crippling losses.

We primarily address pheasant hunting with bird dogs. Hunting with a good dog or dogs brings about increased success and greatly reduces losses of downed birds, especially those that run after being downed. We believe it is the most enjoyable and rewarding way to hunt pheasants. Much of the enjoyment is in watching a hunting dog or dogs work pheasants. The dogs need not be trained by professionals to be highly effective on pheasants, especially if you hunt the dog regularly. In our experience, most hunting dogs learn on the job and flush or point pheasants by 6 months of age. They also make great family pets (Photos 13-16, 13-17).

Photo 13-16. These boys know firsthand how important hunting dogs are in locating, flushing, and retrieving pheasants. From left to right the boys are Joshua and Justin Gabbert and Phillip Novak; Andy Gabbert from Brandon was their mentor. (AEG)

Photo 13-17. Two family pets, a German shorthair and a Brittany, on point in pheasant country. These dogs love the hunt and never seem to want the day to end. (Courtesy of Jack Connelly)

Shooting distances: reducing crippling and loss of downed birds

Rooster pheasants are notorious for running after being knocked down by shot and can be difficult to find even with a bird dog. They may also be hit by shot and die later without the hunter even knowing the bird was hit. For this reason, we urge hunters to avoid long shots that are less likely to produce a clean kill or may leave birds carrying lethal shot. It is one of the most discouraging feelings to drop a pheasant and not be able to find it or to know you have left a bird wounded.

Both steel and lead shot are effective at taking pheasants. Hunters using steel shot should use shot with slightly larger pellet sizes (2 or 3 shot) to increase killing power at longer distances. One good reason to use steel shot is so that you can hunt on Game Production Areas, Waterfowl Production Areas, and any other public lands where steel or other nontoxic shot is required and still have the ability to move back and forth between private and public lands. Four of the five authors of this book completely switched to steel shot several years ago and the other shoots mostly steel. All of us have been well satisfied with steel shot in terms of lethality to pheasants and keeping crippling loss at a minimum.

Hunters can greatly reduce the chances of wounding and losing pheasants by shooting at closer distances. For the authors and most experienced hunters, that distance is usually less than 30 yards and often no more than 25 yards using an open or modified choke. To improve your effectiveness and avoid crippling birds we suggest you pace out distances in the field to get a feeling for where 20 or 30 yards would be. Most of your good shots at pheasants are available within 30 yards or less (Photo 13-18). Hunters shooting at pheasants over about 45 yards away are bound to hit some birds, perhaps knocking down a few, and leaving others with embedded shot that may later be fatal to the bird. While a few hunters are effective at killing pheasants at 40 or 45 yards out, most should not even be firing at birds at those distances as they do not have the shooting skills or killing power (if they hit the bird) to kill cleanly. The best policy is to be conservative on your shots.

Hunting dog safety

Heat stroke

The biggest threat to hunting dogs, especially during the early part of the pheasant season, is heat. High temperatures on the opening day of pheasant season have often exceeded 80 degrees Fahrenheit. Over 100 hunting dogs died of heat stroke in the state on the opening weekend for pheasants in 2003. Take plenty of water for the dogs while in the field and consider avoiding the hottest hours of the day. If your dog is in poor shape or getting older the chances of heat stroke increase dramatically. Watch your dog for evidence of hyperventilating as the dog attempts to cool an overheated body. Extreme salivation, stumbling, and glossed over eyes (anybody home in there?) are all signs to watch. Some hunters take their dog's temperature during normal periods and then check the dog for increased body temperature in the field to detect overheating and possible heat stroke (Photo 13-19).

If the dog appears to be in trouble, get out of the heat and be sure the dog has water. Placing ice on the dog's belly, rubbing with cool water, getting the dog into the shade, or even putting the dog in a vehicle with air conditioning can

Photo 13-18. It is quite an adrenalin rush when those big cackling roosters jump up almost in your face. These hunters are holding off shooting until the bird is a little farther out so the meat will not be ruined. (Courtesy of Chris Hull)

Photo 13-19. Labrador retrievers make excellent hunting companions and are particularly adept at finding and retrieving downed birds. Be aware of potential heat stress on hunting dogs if you hunt early season pheasants. (CTS)

help. You should read up about heat stroke in dogs by checking Internet articles on that topic or visiting with your veterinarian. Knowledge gained could save you from the loss of your family pet, a valuable dog, and a hunting companion.

Snares or traps set for furbearers

It is a good idea to ask landowners if they know of any steel traps (leg-hold or Conibear®), or snares that have been set on their property. We suggest a few precautions for hunters with dogs.

Hunting dogs can and do get into snares set for raccoons or other furbearers. Many dogs will calmly sit still until they can be released from the snare. However, if they struggle the snare will tighten and can choke and kill the dog. We suggest you learn how to release a snare before the hunt in case your dog does get entangled; you may want to purchase a snare and practice setting and releasing it. It is wise to carry a multitool pliers on your belt for such situations.

Dogs will occasionally get caught in leg-hold traps but most are not dangerous. Release the dog by simply stepping down on the spring or springs on the side or sides of the pan. You should probably cover the dog's head with your coat or shirt or other item to calm the dog and reduce the chances that it might reflexively bite you during the release effort.

If your hunting dog gets its head caught in a Conibear® trap it will likely be killed almost instantly or, if not, will soon be dead if you cannot release the trap. The powerful Conibear® trap closes instantly over the head of the dog as it sticks its head into the opening to investigate the smell of the bait. A friend lost a springer spaniel to a Conibear® trap in South Dakota while hunting pheasants and has had three other instances (over 30 years) where he found his dog close to a wooden box containing a Conibear® set for raccoons (Spencer Vaa, personal communication). If you have not checked on how to release a dog from a Conibear® trap we suggest you check those procedures on the Internet or, preferably, on an actual trap. Without prior preparation you will probably not be able to open a Conibear® trap in time to save your dog if it is still alive. Just search the Internet for "hunting dogs and Conibear® traps" to find release procedures.

Overall, the chance of your hunting dog getting into some kind of a snare, leg-hold trap, or Conibear® trap is small, but it can happen. You should be aware of this danger and prepare yourself to properly react if your dog gets caught in a snare or trap.

Rattlesnakes, cactus, and blue-green algae

Hunters can encounter prairie rattlesnakes while hunting in the river breaks along the Missouri River or in any areas west of the Missouri River in South Dakota (Photo 13-20). This is of particular concern for dogs that have not received snake avoidance training. Keep away from black-tailed prairie dog towns because prairie rattlesnakes concentrate on these areas and use prairie dog burrows for winter denning (hibernacula). They also sometimes like areas

Photo 13-20. Prairie rattlesnakes can occur in pheasant country near or west of the Missouri River. Be careful to keep your dog away from cover too close to prairie dog towns where rattlesnakes tend to concentrate in the fall. (Courtesy of Doug Backlund)

near water because of the rodents. Preseason vaccinations to reduce the effects of rattlesnake bites are available. If you suspect or know your dog has been bitten by a rattlesnake, get the dog to a veterinarian as soon as possible.

Three species of prickly pear cactus occur in the state but are not usually abundant in the heavier herbaceous cover preferred by pheasants. Although you will run into cactus while hunting pheasants in some central and western portions of the state, it is more of a problem in native mixed-grass prairie areas where you are likely to find sharp-tailed grouse and/or greater prairie-chickens (Flake et al. 2010). We recommend that you carry pliers or a multitool to remove cactus from your dog if hunting in areas that may have cactus.

During the early, warm portions of the season, hunters should be aware that dogs have at times died after drinking stagnant water from stock ponds or shallow natural wetlands. The poisoning is due to a scum of blue-green algae that has caused the water to become toxic. Poisoning from blue-green algae is much more likely to occur earlier in the year during the start of grouse season but we felt this danger should be mentioned.

Chapter thoughts

In most years, pheasant hunting in South Dakota is the best in the world. Public access hunting areas in South Dakota are abundant and are clearly shown on the annually printed South Dakota Hunting Atlas (also on the Internet). Permission must be obtained to hunt on private lands (excluding WIAs) but many landowners, especially later in the season or outside of the highest density pheasant areas, will allow hunting access. Hunting access is greatly influenced by hunter behavior — please be courteous and thoughtful! Numbers of hunters decline after the first few weekends of the season but hunting opportunities remain excellent. Crop harvest can greatly improve hunting in late October or early November, and snow and cold concentrate pheasants in heavy cover and improve hunting later in the season.

A hunting dog or dogs greatly improve hunting success and reduce losses of downed birds. Dog owners should be aware of dangers to dogs, particularly from heat stroke. Hunting corn fields using "walkers and blockers" without dogs is a traditional and successful means for hunting pheasants, but the loss of downed birds can be high and it is the most risky method of hunting in terms of shooting accidents. All hunters can reduce loss and crippling of pheasants by being selective and avoiding long shots. We urge hunters to wear hunter orange to reduce chances of a hunting accident and to be cautious in handling, transporting, and shooting their firearms.

PART V: FROM THE PRESENT INTO THE FUTURE

CHAPTER 14
PHEASANTS IN AN EVER-CHANGING LANDSCAPE

In the future as in the past, populations of ring-necked pheasants will fluctuate from year to year based on weather factors that directly influence both the habitat and reproductive success. Less commonly, unusually high losses of hens in severe winters can influence populations in the following year or two. It is the quantity and quality of habitat on the landscape that will determine long-term trends in pheasant abundance. Whether statewide populations fluctuate around 8 million or more pheasants as in the most recent 2000s or around 2–3 million pheasants as in the mid 1970s will depend on the quality, quantity, and arrangement of habitat on the landscape.

If the landscape has the appropriate habitat composition (grassland, wetland, cropland, etc.) and habitat quality, pheasants normally bounce back rapidly after years with poor reproductive conditions or after unusually severe winters. However, reductions in the amount and quality of nesting cover, winter cover, and other habitat requirements on a more permanent basis will result in long-term declines in pheasant populations.

Over 95% of the land in South Dakota's primary pheasant range is privately owned and is critical to ring-necked pheasant populations. The abundance of pheasant habitat and pheasants is closely tied to the agricultural economy, agricultural practices, and conservation programs. It is also related to landowners' interest in pheasants, their knowledge about pheasant habitat needs, and their commitment to maintaining key habitats.

This chapter will help readers to be aware of several challenges and opportunities related to maintaining our pheasant habitats and populations. This awareness can help in preserving South Dakota's pheasant hunting heritage.

Ring-necked pheasant management plan for South Dakota

It is essential that management agencies like the South Dakota Department of Game, Fish and Parks (SDGFP) have clearly stated goals and objectives for wildlife management in the form of management plans.

To provide strategic guidance for the management of pheasants in the future, the SDGFP developed the Ring-necked Pheasant Management Plan for South Dakota (2009–2014) (Switzer 2010). This plan provides direction with detailed goals, objectives, and strategies to help maintain South Dakota as a showcase for pheasant management and as the premier destination for pheasant hunters across North America. The plan includes the following five goals: 1) to partner with private landowners to conserve, restore, and manage habitats critical for pheasants and other wildlife species; 2) to conserve, restore, manage, and preserve habitats critical for pheasants and other upland nesting birds through fee title purchases, management agreements, and partnerships with other agencies and managers of public land; 3) to continue to monitor populations and habitat trends and conduct research as needed to address population and habitat-related questions; 4) to provide the public with access to quality pheasant habitat on private and public land; and 5) to inform and educate the public about pheasant ecology, management, and research.

The management plan is for all South Dakotans interested in pheasant hunting and the conservation of pheasant habitat (Photo 14-1). As with any plan, adapting to new and unforeseen circumstances is critical for successful implementation and achieving desired outcomes. The current management plan and all future revisions can be found on the SDGFP website (gfp.sd.gov).

Habitat quality: an important key to pheasant abundance

We have discussed habitat quality in several chapters. For example, grasslands with an abundance of interspersed legumes and other forbs are more valuable for pheasants than a low-diversity grassland lacking forbs and dominated by a single species such as smooth brome. The importance of habitat quality was evident in studies in Brookings County in eastern South Dakota (Vandel and Linder 1981). Researchers found no change in cover-type acreages (alfalfa, small grain, etc.) from 1958–1959 to 1977–1978 even though pheasants (brood counts and crowing counts) had declined at least 90%. They concluded that changes in cover quality, such as earlier mowing of roadsides, earlier mowing of alfalfa, and reduction of forbs in remaining grassland cover could be just as important as changes in acreage of cover types.

In South Dakota's primary pheasant range, grasslands, roadsides, and odd areas with sufficient concealment for nesting and brood-rearing hens are more valuable if they have an appropriate mixture of legumes and other forbs along with grasses (Photo 14-2). Such areas are more diverse and of better quality than, for example, aging stands of pure brome grass. Indiscriminate use of herbicides to kill broadleaved weeds will limit plant diversity in pheasant nesting and

Photo 14-1. An important goal of the South Dakota Pheasant Management Plan is to provide hunters with access to quality pheasant habitat and hunting on both private and public lands. (TRK)

Photo 14-2. Alfalfa and yellow sweetclover mix with smooth brome on this diverse roadside. This type of roadside can be valuable for nesting and brood rearing if left unmowed until at least mid July. (AEG)

brood-rearing areas and will inhibit pheasant production. These herbicide treatments suppress the insect abundance that is so important to chicks in the first several weeks after hatch. Unfortunately, pheasants need weedy areas, and such areas do not fit very well with today's clean farming.

Ongoing and future agricultural changes could also bring some much needed good news in terms of diversity and resultant quality of the habitat for pheasants. We discuss some of those agronomic changes later in this chapter.

Pheasants will always need undisturbed grass and forb cover

We have previously documented how amounts of permanent herbaceous cover on the landscape and long-term trends in pheasant populations have fluctuated in relation to the Great Depression, World War II, and, since the late 1950s, the Soil Bank and Conservation Reserve Program (CRP) (Chapter 1). Trends in pheasant populations will undoubtedly continue to follow changes in the amounts of permanent herbaceous cover on the landscape, particularly nesting and brood-rearing cover. As hundreds of thousands of acres of CRP grassland are converted to cropland, we can expect to see pheasant populations decline in proportion to these losses of habitat — history will be repeating itself (Chapter 1). Declines in pheasant numbers with loss of CRP grasslands can be expected to be most severe in heavily tilled landscapes dominated by row-crop monocultures that will provide minimal amounts of nesting and brood-rearing cover without a land-retirement program (Riley 1995, Nusser et al. 2004).

Some of the CRP losses are being offset by new enrollments into CRP or other long-term land-retirement programs (Chapter 15), but the new enrollments are currently dwarfed by loss from expiring contracts in most parts of the state. Pheasant enthusiasts can bemoan the loss of federal land-retirement acreage, but the fact is these land-retirement programs have never been perpetual. In the future, federal land-retirement programs will probably continue to periodically provide abundant herbaceous habitat followed by years of poorer habitat as funding and contracts expire and as commodity markets influence land management decisions (Photo 14-3).

Keys to the future may include more limited but long-term conservation easements to develop and protect pheasant habitat. More diverse and sustainable agriculture, with inclusion of crops like winter wheat that can provide nesting, brood-rearing, and seasonal habitat (tall stubble), could become an important stabilizing force in maintaining pheasant populations.

Ethanol production and pheasants

Use of corn-based ethanol as a fuel additive has spurred the conversion of grasslands to corn in eastern South Dakota and, unfortunately, has led to increasing losses of large blocks of herbaceous cover and of overall habitat diversity im-

Photo 14-3. To maintain strong pheasant populations, South Dakota's agricultural landscapes must include interspersed fields and odd areas of herbaceous cover (grasses and forbs) of adequate height and density for pheasant hens to have a good chance to reproduce successfully. (Courtesy of Scott Weins)

portant to pheasants and many other wildlife species (Government Accountability Office 2007, Fargione et al. 2009, Brooke et al. 2010). The feasibility of other sources of vegetation for ethanol production, such as switchgrass or other grasses or grasslike plants, is currently being studied and could preserve and enhance wildlife habitat (Bies 2006, Tilman et al. 2006). Permanent cover from perennial grass crops would also conserve soil and water resources; allow more limited use of fertilizers, herbicides, fungicides, and insecticides; improve carbon sequestering (removal of carbon dioxide from the air by plants); and provide additional nesting, brood rearing, and other seasonal cover for pheasants (Altieri 2009). Timing of harvest of perennial grass or grasslike biofuels, as with alfalfa mowing, would remain critical to nesting success of pheasants, upland nesting ducks, and other ground-nesting birds.

Research on the use of algae to generate biofuels is being conducted by several universities, commercial companies, and even military interests in the United States as well as in several other countries. Development of commercial production facilities for algae-generated biofuels is underway and could help diversify biofuel production so it is more economically independent (without government subsidies) and not so dependent on a single agricultural crop such as corn. Use of algae for biofuel production also provides carbon sequestering benefits.

Diversification of biofuel production will likely have many impacts on the environment—hopefully the positive influences on pheasants and other wildlife will outweigh the negatives.

Wetland cover—a great place for pheasants

Everyone in South Dakota should be asking a very simple question: Why have we experienced three major flooding events in a 15-year period (1996–2011) that are only predicted by climatologists to occur every 100 years? While a part of the answer lies in a likely shift in climate, the primary reason is because of the reduced ability of landscapes to hold extensive spring runoff and precipitation. Water that no longer is retained in wetlands has to go somewhere and that somewhere is down the watershed (drainage region). These same wetlands are also very important to many species of wildlife.

If you want pheasants on your land, protect existing wetlands from being drained or altered and restore wetlands that have been drained. From shallow wetlands that dry up in several weeks to larger, deeper wetlands with dense cattail patches, they are all valuable for pheasants and other wildlife species. As discussed throughout the book, pheasants are attracted to and benefit from lush wetland cover both in the wetland and on its periphery for many reasons. Wetlands also make great places for pheasant hunting with your bird dog.

Many shallow wetlands with important pheasant habitat are being drained each year, most commonly using advanced tile drainage technology. Tile drainage operations are becoming increasingly common in eastern South Dakota. Shallow wetlands, often called ephemeral, temporary, or seasonal wetlands by biologists, usually hold water only during a few weeks or months each year but the vegetation associated with them is used regularly by pheasants. Many of these small, shallow wetlands lack federal protection (wetland easements) from drainage. In addition to further loss of wetlands, increased flow to remaining larger wetlands from drain tile often floods emergent vegetation, reducing the value of these wetlands to wildlife (Photo 14-4).

Some of the remaining deeper and often larger wetlands that commonly support dense cattails, phragmites, and dense stands of sandbar willow are being converted to cropland if not protected by federal wetland easements; these represent areas of critical wintering habitat for pheasants. Both landowners and hunters have commented to the authors that loss of wetland habitat in the eastern third of South Dakota is more intense as of 2010–2012 than they can ever recall. We are especially appreciative of those farmers that recognize the value of these wetlands (wildlife, water storage, flood control, forage, etc.) and who have attempted to protect them from drainage. Wetlands hold considerable value to the human and wildlife populations that inhabit the associated watersheds (Photo 14-5).

Photo 14-4. Unfortunately, tile drainage is eliminating many shallow wetlands in eastern South Dakota and the valuable herbaceous cover they provide for pheasants. (Courtesy of Matt Grunig)

Photo 14-5. Pheasant droppings and tracks verify the importance of this wetland thermal cover to pheasants. When wetlands are drained and converted to cropland, associated pheasant populations decline. (AEG)

No-till, winter wheat, and tall stubble—projected effects on pheasants

No-till farming is an increasing agricultural practice that can and will influence farming rotations, conservation, and even wildlife populations. Winter wheat planting in South Dakota is directly related to the use of no-till farming as discussed in the following subsection. In portions of the Midwest, winter wheat and tall, weedy wheat stubble have been driving forces at least as important as or more important than federal land-retirement systems such as the Conservation Reserve Program in supporting good pheasant populations (Rodgers 2002, 2005). Kansas, Nebraska, and eastern Colorado are all areas where pheasants have especially benefited from winter wheat and tall wheat stubble.

No-till

No-till agriculture has become a prominent practice in many counties in South Dakota, particularly in the central portion of the state east of the Missouri River. In some counties such as Potter and Walworth, over 90% of the cropland is no-till. Several other counties in central South Dakota show similar trends, with no-till on over 60% of the existing cropland (Natural Resource Conservation Service, Pierre, unpublished map).

Benefits of diverse, appropriately applied, no-till agriculture after a few years of implementation include much improved soil structure, improved soil nutrient levels, remarkably improved earthworm numbers (and other soil organisms), improved water infiltration of the soil, and reduced wind and water erosion (Dwayne Beck, Dakota Lakes Research Farm and South Dakota State University, personal communication). Diversity refers to the numbers of different crop types in the rotation, crop sequence, planting and harvest time variation, and several other aspects related to no-till operations. The reduction in siltation of lakes, wetlands, and rivers is another important byproduct of no-till agriculture. These are all positives for watershed ecosystems and for farmland.

Diverse no-till agriculture can be sustainable and highly profitable and for this reason will likely continue to increase in the future. The positives and negatives of no-till for pheasant populations are not entirely clear but bear careful watching. For pheasants, the most desirable crop in no-till rotations at this point is winter wheat since it can have considerable values for nesting, brood rearing, and fall-to-spring habitat (Rodgers 2002, 2005).

No-till is making it practical to grow winter wheat in northern portions of the Interior Plains and Great Plains, even into the southern half of Canada's Prairie Provinces. In South Dakota, winter wheat is often damaged by winterkill when the seedlings are exposed to intermittent warming spells that initiate premature growth followed by extreme cold. No-till leaves post-harvest plant stubble and residue that collect drifting snow, forming a protective and insulative blanket that reduces soil and ground level temperature fluctuations; these reductions in temperature fluctuations protect winter wheat from winterkill. Even stubble without snow cover helps moderate soil temperatures.

Negative influences on pheasants may occur with no-till agriculture that lacks diversity and makes heavy use of herbicides. No-till winter wheat-row crop rotations in Kansas were initially devastating to pheasants because they involved heavy use of herbicides that destroyed the broadleaved weeds that were so important to pheasant use of wheat stubble through most of the year (Rodgers 2002, 2005).

No-till can involve simple soybean-corn rotations that provide little nesting or brood-rearing habitat compared to more diverse systems that may have value for pheasants. In several counties in central South Dakota such as Potter and Sully, tilled wheat-summer fallow rotation has been largely replaced with no-till winter wheat rotated with a diversity of crops such as spring wheat, corn, sorghum, sunflowers, flax, millet, canola, or other crops. Agronomists in the northern plains are attempting to develop a broadleaved crop (canola is a possibility) that could be planted directly into no-till stubble in the fall and that would produce a crop the following summer (Dwayne Beck, Dakota Lakes Research Farm, personal communication). This fall-planted broadleaved crop, if harvested after mid July or later, could be valuable as nesting and brood-rearing habitat since it would be undisturbed by spring planting.

Researchers on no-till agriculture are developing methods such as planting of cover crops to reduce use of herbicides since herbicides represent a considerable cost to farmers and can be damaging to pheasant habitat. We are hopeful that appropriately diverse no-till rotations along with reduced herbicide use will have multiple habitat values for pheasants. More diverse no-till rotations are already becoming more prevalent in the Midwest.

While pheasants are currently abundant in counties like Potter (>90% no-till), Sully (>61% no-till), and McPherson (>52% no-till), diverse no-till farming is only one part of the landscape equation. The percentages of grassland to cropland on the landscape in counties with over 50% no-till are at levels that have been found to be associated with the state's more abundant pheasant populations (Figure 8-1). If interspersed grassland habitat (herbaceous cover) within the state's prime pheasant range is greatly reduced and replaced by cropland, we would expect pheasant populations to decline regardless of the relative prevalence of no-till and conventional till practices.

Winter wheat

The best news for pheasant enthusiasts would be the development of crops and cropping practices that are profitable for landowners and that provide safe cover for pheasants, especially during the nesting and brood-rearing seasons. Winter wheat fits this description (Chapters 5 and 6). Winter wheat currently makes up just over half of South Dakota's approximately 3–3.5 million acres (2008–2010) of wheat—the remainder is spring wheat. If no-till continues to increase in use in South Dakota, we would expect an increase in acreage of winter wheat as it is incorporated into the crop rotation.

Two things make winter wheat more valuable than spring wheat for nesting pheasants: 1) overwintering roots and tillers allow more rapid development of green nesting cover in the spring even if the winter wheat is grazed in the fall, and 2) by planting in the fall, farmers avoid destruction (during planting) of early spring nests in residual cover such as tall stubble (Photo 14-6). Timing of harvest in winter wheat is critical. If winter wheat is harvested before mid July, many pheasant nests can be destroyed (Dave Dahlgren, Kansas Department of Wildlife and Parks, personal communication). Harvest after August 1 is preferable for protecting nesting pheasants.

The potential value of winter wheat for nesting in comparison to spring wheat is illustrated by recent Ducks Unlimited studies. In North Dakota and Canada, ducks nested at 10 times the density in new growth winter wheat as they did in spring wheat; the winter wheat produced 24 times as many ducklings as an equal area of spring wheat (Ducks Unlimited, Bismarck Area Office, unpublished data) (Photo 14-7).

We again caution against replacement of grassland, particularly native grassland, with winter wheat or any other cropland type. Grassland losses are associated with excessive erosion and losses of habitat for a wide variety of wildlife, including pheasants.

Photo 14-6. Planting winter wheat (left) avoids spring disturbance of stubble and develops much earlier cover for pheasants, waterfowl, and other ground-nesting birds than spring-planted varieties (right). Harvest of winter wheat in South Dakota is generally a little over 2 weeks after peak pheasant hatch. (Courtesy of Ducks Unlimited, Bismarck Office)

Photo 14-7. This hen is holding tight on her nest in winter wheat in central South Dakota. The radio-marked bird wears a whip antenna. The necklace-mounted transmitter is not visible. (Courtesy of Josh Jensen)

Tall stubble

Fortunately for pheasant populations, agricultural practices are increasingly leaving taller stubble (>15 inches) when harvesting a variety of small grains, canola, flax, and other crops. Tall stubble and no-till can pay financial dividends on crops planted into the rotation in the following spring because of improved soil structure, increased soil moisture, reduced wind erosion, and a generally more wind-protected and favorable ground level environment for seedlings.

Volunteer weed growth in tall wheat stubble greatly enhances the value of this habitat for pheasants throughout the year (Rodgers 2002, 2005). Studies on wheat-fallow rotation in Nebraska and Kansas have shown that farmers delaying post-harvest use of herbicides or tillage until the following spring and summer had a much higher net financial return on their wheat crop than those using herbicides or tillage during the fall (Alan Schlegel, Kansas State University, Western Kansas Agricultural Research Center, Tribune, personal communication; Grier 2003). Unless noxious weeds are a problem, it seems logical to reduce or eliminate the costs of herbicides in post-harvest small grain stubble until spring. Fewer herbicides, more profit, and more pheasants—sounds like a great idea!

We have already pointed out the values of post-harvest tall wheat stubble for pheasants, especially when accompanied by volunteer weed growth or appropriate cover crops (Chapter 6). In Kansas, wheat stubble taller than 16 inches harbored an average of nine times more pheasants during winter than stubble shorter than 9 inches (Rodgers 2002). If volunteer broadleaved weeds such as kochia and annual sunflowers are allowed to grow in the post-harvest period without herbicide treatment, they will allow increased pheasant use and help support (buttress) even the tallest wheat stubble and keep it from flattening out during winter storms (Rodgers 2002). "Green manure" cover crops seeded into wheat stubble can serve a similar function (see Photo 6-5).

If wheat stubble will have no support from volunteer weeds or cover crops, then flattening (lodging) under winter storms becomes a much greater problem. Randy Rodgers (Kansas Department of Wildlife and Parks [retired]) suggests that stripper headers be used to maintain a greater height on wheat if preharvest height is 20 inches or shorter. If over 24 inches tall at preharvest the wheat should probably be harvested by using a conventional sickle bar header set relatively high. Wheat between 20 and 24 inches falls into a "toss-up" category as to which harvest method would leave the most optimal height stubble for avoiding lodging (Rodgers 2002). If volunteer weed growth is allowed or if stubble will be seeded with appropriate cover crops, stubble will be better buttressed against winter flattening, and stripper headers are probably the best bet for maintaining good pheasant habitat even if the preharvest wheat is over 24 inches (Photo 14-8).

Interestingly, much of the private land leased for public hunting of pheasants (and other game) in Nebraska is located in fields of tall stubble from winter wheat (Grier 2003). Even in South Dakota's winters, tall wheat stubble indirectly

Photo 14-8. Stripper headers leave tall wheat stubble that can moderate soil temperatures, conserve moisture, and provide important habitat for pheasants in no-till farming operations. (Courtesy of Ducks Unlimited, Bismarck Office)

enhances winter cover by reducing downwind drifting into more secure winter habitats such as dense shrub patches or wetlands with extensive stands of cattail. If winter wheat is drilled into tall stubble, the stubble can also provide residual nesting cover along with the new growing winter wheat.

Long-term drought and climate change

History tells us that South Dakota can expect periodic droughts that may last a year, a few years, or even over a decade. When droughts occur they are usually hard on ranchers, farmers, and pheasants. We do know that pheasants thrived during drought in the 1930s, a period when much land was left weedy and unplanted due to the Great Depression. In general, however, drought brings on much competition for limited livestock forage and leaves little cover for nesting and brood-rearing pheasants. In addition, grasslands in federal land-retirement programs (such as CRP) are often made available for emergency grazing and haying in counties designated as disaster areas. When drought conditions create these situations for livestock producers, forage provided by CRP contracts is an understandable use. However, pheasant reproduction on these hayed land-retirement areas, if cut before mid July, will be reduced and can be very poor.

Severe drought in one summer can even influence reproductive success of hens in the following year if little residual cover is available early in the following nesting season (Martinson and Grondahl 1966). Sparse vegetation is also unable to support the insects needed by pheasant chicks in the first few weeks post hatch. One thing is certain, we will have future droughts and they will affect pheasant populations.

The authors of this book are biologists and do not claim proficiency in climatology but we should mention the subject of global climate change. Most climatologists predict that global warming and global climate extremes are increasing due to the effects of increasing carbon dioxide and other greenhouse gases in the atmosphere. If these predictions concerning global warming due to the greenhouse effect (increasing carbon dioxide in the atmosphere) are correct, both droughts and wet cycles will increase in intensity in the Midwest in the future. During the drought cycles, pheasants would be negatively influenced by the reduction in herbaceous plant growth they are dependent on throughout the year; this would include increased drought influences on the many prairie wetlands so important to pheasants (Johnson et al. 2010). Like most farm crops, pheasants are better adapted to moderate weather patterns than to more extreme cycles of droughts and deluges.

Chapter thoughts

History has shown the critical importance of permanent herbaceous cover and land-retirement programs to pheasant populations. Long-term trends in pheasant populations will continue to reflect the abundance of suitable cover on the landscape, particularly for nesting and brood rearing.

We have many challenges facing us in maintaining pheasant populations. At the same time, opportunities to improve pheasant habitat will likely continue through future federal and state conservation programs and through agronomic changes that favor more diversification and sustainability and less dependence on chemicals. Each new day the future becomes the present — for pheasants and everything else in life. We are always better off when we meet those days with optimism.

CHAPTER 15
CONTINUING A REMARKABLE JOURNEY

It has been a most remarkable journey since South Dakota's first pheasant season in Spink County in 1919. If you love to hunt pheasants and have been part of this journey, you should count yourself as fortunate. There is no place on earth like South Dakota, where ring-necked pheasants have been so abundant for most of the past century and where opportunities to hunt these magnificent birds are so readily available.

In this chapter we touch on a few aspects related to habitat conservation programs, pheasant hunting, and the future.

Habitat conservation programs

Opportunities and incentives remain available for private landowners to enroll in federal and state conservation programs that benefit wildlife, soil, and water resources. These programs are "moving targets" in terms of annually changing enrollment options through the years. Various agencies involved in these programs, including South Dakota Department of Game, Fish and Parks (SDGFP); the Natural Resource Conservation Service (NRCS); the Farm Service Agency (FSA); and the U.S. Fish and Wildlife Service (USFWS), have staff that are informed on these programs and are willing to assist landowners.

Federal and state conservation programs available at the time this book was written are examples of programs that can be used to increase and improve pheasant habitat (Photo 15-1). National Farm Bill programs and other conservation programs will change with time, with some programs likely ending within a decade or less after this book is published. Still, these land-retirement programs and other habitat programs provide examples that have worked and can continue to work in improving pheasant populations.

Photo 15-1. Habitat programs lead to greater reproductive success, improved hen survival, and better pheasant populations. These pheasant chicks will quickly disappear into the adjacent cover if a predator approaches. (Courtesy of Scott Weins)

Federal land-retirement programs

Federal programs for retiring croplands into permanent herbaceous cover are likely to remain available in some form in future years because of their broad values in conserving soil, water, and wildlife. The current trend to sign up fewer but more environmentally sensitive acres and to renew those contracts on a continuous basis may be one of the future trends. An example of this approach is the current sign-up of 10- to 40-acre CRP contracts on areas that protect wetlands. The ratio of uplands to wetlands in the program can be as high as 4:1. In addition, the USDA accepted 120,000 acres in general sign-up in South Dakota in the spring of 2010 and 47,000 acres in general sign-up in the spring of 2011. These sign-ups are generally offered in smaller acreage enrollments than in earlier CRP years.

An intriguing option is the Conservation Reserve Enhancement Program (CREP), which includes USDA funding along with partial matching of funds from the SDGFP. The program improves soil and water management and wildlife habitat by establishing up to 100,000 acres of undisturbed grassland in the James River watershed. These acres will include expiring CRP contracts and can include mixes of both introduced (exotic) and native plant species. Rental rates are the same as for CRP contracts; however, an incentive has been added to the base rental rate as an attractant to enroll in the program. The incentive payment and all other eligible establishment costs are paid by the SDGFP. In all, SDGFP is providing 20% of the total CREP payments. A major component of the CREP program is that all enrolled properties are open to public hunting and fishing (Photo 15-2).

Photo 15-2. Up to 100,000 acres of land will be enrolled in the Conservation Reserve Enhancement Program (CREP) in the James River Valley. Hunters are allowed walk-in access to all CREP lands. (CTS)

Unfortunately, federal land-retirement programs such as the Soil Bank and CRP remain short-term solutions for maintaining pheasant habitat. For the benefit of pheasants and other wildlife habitat, landowners and hunters must inform decision makers on the importance of such land programs in future agricultural policies and federal farm bills.

Wetland and grassland easements

We have placed USFWS wetland and grassland easements together here because grassland easements are not accepted without also placing the embedded wetlands under easement. While wetlands can be accepted separately, grasslands without embedded natural wetlands would not qualify for the easement program. Because of their popularity with many landowners, there are more requests for these voluntary perpetual easements than available funding can support. Wetland and grassland easements within the state's primary pheasant range protect important pheasant habitats for wintering (cattails), nesting, brood rearing, and other habitat needs.

Permanent easements are available on qualified wetlands and grassland/wetland complexes by contacting the nearest regional office of the USFWS. Landowners receive a substantial one-time payment in exchange for protecting the wetlands. Landowners can still farm, graze, or hay these wetlands as long as the wetland basins are not filled (soil, subsoil, rocks, logs, etc.), drained, burned, or leveled. The easement remains with the land even if sold, so this program provides long-term protection (Photos 15-3).

Photos 15-3. In addition to benefiting pheasants, wetland easements provide essential habitat for many other wildlife species. Two such species include the great blue heron and the secretive Virginia rail (inset). (Courtesy of Scott Weins)

Wetland Reserve Program

The Wetland Reserve Program is a USDA program for private landowners who plan to restore wetland habitats to full function. Technical assistance is available through the NRCS and non-government organizations such as Ducks Unlimited. The program can be set up in perpetuity or in contracts lasting up to 30 but no less than 10 years. Wetland Reserve lands often provide key winter cover.

If a wetland has been converted to cropland or used as pasture land, it has a good chance of qualifying for the Wetland Reserve Program. Almost 40,000 acres of private wetlands in South Dakota are under the Wetland Reserve Program. This popular program has been around for over 20 years and will hopefully continue to be a part of the federal farm bill in future decades (Photo 15-4).

Other programs

In addition to their own private lands programs, the SDGFP is involved in efforts to provide habitat for pheasants and other wildlife through cooperative efforts with federal agencies such as the NRCS and the USFWS; they are also involved in cooperative efforts with private organizations such as Pheasants Forever and Ducks Unlimited. Habitat biologists with the SDGFP can be valuable in advising and assisting landowners on federal, state, and private conservation programs that will benefit pheasants (Photo 15-5).

Photo 15-4. The abundant pheasant tracks in this photo tell an important story: maintaining and restoring wetlands is an important component of pheasant habitat management. (AEG)

Photo 15-5. This private land in Clark County was converted from cropland to a stand of big bluestem for late summer grazing and wildlife with assistance from the SDGFP and the Natural Resource Conservation Service. The unusually successful results of this native grass seeding provided excellent grazing plus good pheasant habitat less than 5 months after seeding. (CTS).

Direct assistance to private landowners who wish to improve pheasant habitat on their land is provided by the SDGFP. In these programs the SDGFP assists with technical expertise and costs in establishment of herbaceous nesting cover, dense woody plantings for wintering pheasants, food plots, fencing of valuable habitat to exclude grazing, wetland restorations, and other projects that will benefit pheasants and other wildlife. Landowners who are interested in pheasants and other wildlife habitat are encouraged to visit the private lands link on the SDGFP website. Pheasant habitat programs can be integrated nicely into the farm system, making the area better for both wildlife and people (Photos 15-6).

Photos 15-6. The South Dakota Department of Game, Fish and Parks can assist with technical expertise and financial costs in establishing good pheasant habitat. These pheasants attest to the value of these wetland and shrubland habitats! (CTS)

Future hunting opportunities

A deep tradition has been built around pheasants and pheasant hunting, not only for many South Dakotans but also for those who visit our state each fall. Numerous pheasant hunting opportunities are found across South Dakota's diverse landscape (Chapter 13). The following topics need to be considered to assure that South Dakota's remarkable pheasant hunting continues into the future.

The role of hunters

Hunters play a crucial role in the management of pheasants and other wildlife species. Hunting license sales revenue and federal excise taxes on sporting goods (Wildlife Restoration Fund) are critical sources of revenue for SDGFP to purchase qualified land from willing sellers, lease private land from cooperating landowners for public hunting access, and establish and manage habitat on private and public land.

Federal funding comes from the Wildlife Restoration Fund that is derived from a sportsmen-supported federal tax on arms, ammunition, and archery equipment. This fund resulted from passage of the Federal Aid in Wildlife Restoration Act (or Pittman-Robertson Act 1937). These funds are apportioned to state wildlife agencies for wildlife management purposes based on the number of hunting licenses sold and land area. The original sponsors of this act wisely included a provision that states are ineligible for these funds if hunting license fees are diverted for purposes unrelated to wildlife management such as road building. This approach has been highly successful in making sure hunters' license fees are directed toward the management and restoration of wildlife.

The Wildlife Restoration Fund is valuable for the conservation of a broad array of wildlife including ring-necked pheasants. Despite the trend of declining hunter numbers in many states, resident pheasant hunter numbers in South Dakota have remained relatively steady and nonresident hunters have increased over past years (Figure 12-3). However, South Dakota is not immune to this national trend, and SDGFP has implemented programs and seasons to retain current hunters and recruit new hunters to the sport of pheasant hunting (Chapter 12) (Photo 15-7).

Hunter-landowner relationships and access to private lands

South Dakota's rich pheasant hunting traditions involve strong friendships developed between pheasant hunters and private landowners and their families. With approximately 95% of the land base within South Dakota's main pheasant range privately owned, it is imperative for pheasant hunters to establish connections with farmers and ranchers.

Nonresidents, particularly those new to hunting in South Dakota, may have no friendships or contacts with private landowners in the state and often feel intimidated by the thought of asking permission to hunt. South Dakota's

Photo 15-7. Josh Switzer of Pierre loves to follow his father (Chad) on short outings and even carries a pop gun. Josh learns about pheasants, pheasant habitat, and other wildlife and gets to chat with his father on these outings. The blaze orange hat indicates he is also learning hunting safety. (CTS)

population continues to shift from a rural to urban setting. Unlike those residents who were fortunate enough to either grow up on a farm or have rural family or friends, fewer urban residents have the benefit of these connections. This demographic change has made it somewhat challenging for many of the state's urban residents. Urban residents and nonresidents must do some extra work to contact rural landowners if they want to find places to hunt pheasants on private land.

The fear of being "turned down" for permission to hunt should not discourage those without rural contacts from driving into farmsteads to meet landowners. While farmers and ranchers often have traditional groups of family and friends visiting to hunt during the early portion of the pheasant season, many are willing to provide access later in the hunting season.

If granted permission to hunt, be careful to treat the property of landowners as if it were your own. Hunting only those areas designated by the landowner, shutting gates (if you open them), avoiding livestock, removing trash, and picking up spent shells will go a long way toward developing and preserving friendships and future hunting opportunities. Hunters who show common courtesy and respect will usually be welcomed back. Additionally, make sure you do not bring a crowd of hunters. Those you bring should respect the permission you have obtained and not return on their own, bringing additional hunters.

Hunters can become involved and more closely attached to the land by helping landowners with various projects on the farm such as fencing work or planting of habitat. Some hunters provide seed for winter food plots or for herbaceous cover plantings. Other ways of developing long-lasting contacts might include inviting landowners and their families to dinner, taking them to a landowner-appreciation banquet, bringing them a pheasant cleaned and skinned or plucked after the hunt, or just sending a thank you note. These small acts will go far toward establishing lasting connections with landowners. Many of you have already developed cherished and long-term friendships with landowners and their families. Such positive relationships often become an important fabric of our lives. Those relationships will also help assure pheasant hunting opportunities in the future (Photo 15-8).

Public access

The continued availability of quality pheasant hunting areas open to public access is an important matter for most resident and nonresident pheasant hunters and is a top priority for the SDGFP. Types of land hunted can be categorized as non-fee private land, private land requiring an access fee, shooting preserves, public land, road rights-of-way, and walk-in areas (WIAs). Implemented in 1988 as a component of the Pheasants for Everyone Program, South Dakota's WIA Program has been used as a model by many other states to improve public hunting access opportunities. Private landowners who are willing to enroll their property in the WIA Program are the key to its success.

Photo 15-8. Hunters who show common courtesy and respect for people and property are often welcomed back by private landowners. Holly Lindbloom is from Pierre. (Courtesy of Andy Lindbloom)

Results of hunter surveys indicate that resident pheasant hunters spent 68% of their pheasant hunting time and nonresidents 43% of their time hunting pheasants on private land without paying a fee to the landowner (Gigliotti 2004). Residents spent 16% of their pheasant hunting time and nonresidents 13% of their time on public areas (excluding road rights-of-way) or WIAs. Surprisingly, residents spent 12% of their hunting hours hunting road rights-of-way while nonresidents hunted these areas 6% of their hunting time. We encourage pheasant hunters that hunt road rights-of-way to park and walk the ditches—you will have greater success and a more enjoyable hunt.

The voluntary WIA Program provides annual payments derived from hunting license revenue and federal Wildlife Restoration Funds to participating landowners in return for providing public walk-in hunting (Photo 15-9). To accommodate landowner interest, meet the needs and desire of pheasant hunters,

Photo 15-9. This Brittany, belonging to Dale Gates of Pierre, had several great points and retrieves on pheasants on this walk-in area in central South Dakota. (LDF)

and to increase the quality and dispersion of public access throughout the state, the WIA Program has remained adaptive throughout the years. To increase acres available for pheasant hunters, habitat retention payments are included in WIA contracts on CRP to give landowners an incentive to keep their marginal cropland acres in CRP and to provide quality hunting habitat.

Walk-in-area (WIA) options currently available to cooperating landowners include a season-long contract, a delayed opening start contract that gives family and friends exclusive hunting opportunities during the first 2 weeks of the season before the area is open to the public, and a controlled hunting contract where the landowner indicates the number of hunters per day and other special provisions on the land. These options and the entire program will continue to evolve with time.

Since the inception of the WIA Program, enrollment in the state has grown from 26 cooperators and 23,161 acres in 1988 to 1,300 cooperators and 1.3 million acres in 2011. These figures include many extensive contracts on ranches that are outside the primary pheasant range but are often excellent for big game and prairie grouse hunting. Within the main pheasant range, there were 868 contracts and 324,378 acres of WIA in 2010 for an average of 374 acres/contract. Contracts for WIAs east of the Missouri River averaged 320 acres (Mark Norton, unpublished data).

Many WIAs within the primary pheasant range are lands also enrolled in the Conservation Reserve Program (CRP). Losses of CRP acres will have an influence on the future success of the WIA Program. In an effort to provide additional public access and create or maintain existing CRP contracts, SDGFP has partnered with the USDA to implement the James River Watershed Conservation Reserve Enhancement Program (CREP) as described earlier under the section on federal land-retirement programs.

In addition, the acquisition and management of public land has been a cornerstone for enhancing public hunting opportunities. The most notable public lands providing pheasant hunting in South Dakota include Game Production Areas acquired and managed by the SDGFP and Waterfowl Production Areas acquired and managed by the USFWS. Other public lands that support pheasants and pheasant hunting are discussed in Chapter 13. The dispersion of quality pheasant habitat and provision of public hunting access throughout South Dakota's pheasant range are key components in ensuring future hunting opportunities for pheasant hunters.

Fee hunting: licensed pheasant preserves and fee access areas

Fee hunting for pheasants can take place on fee-access areas open during the regular season and licensed shooting preserves open for a more extended season (September through March). Licensed shooting preserves are clearly defined as commercial hunting operations while fee-access areas, to a lesser degree and varying extent, are also a type of commercial hunting operation.

A variety of fee-access areas (excluding licensed preserves) exists, ranging from charging by the day (per hunter) to fully guided service with lodging. In many instances, fee-access areas allow hunting by permission for no fee during part of the pheasant season and may be open to friends most of the season. Fee hunting on licensed preserves generally provides the primary source of income for the owner or owners. Fee hunting on private lands open by fee access generally provides a supplemental source of income.

Fee hunting benefits a segment of pheasant hunters. In the early 2000s, residents spent 12% and nonresidents 36% of their pheasant hunting time on private fee-access areas (excludes licensed shooting preserves). Resident and nonresident pheasant hunters spent 2% or less of their hunting time on licensed shooting preserves (Gigliotti 2004).

Shooting preserves provide extra hunting opportunities because they have an extended season from September 1 through the following March. Most fee hunting operations provide pheasant habitat and often benefit other wildlife species. However, some pheasant hunters are concerned that fee hunting operations reduce the available free access on private lands. Fee hunting has and will continue to have direct and indirect effects, both positive and negative, on pheasant populations, wildlife habitat, and public access opportunities. Pheasant management and hunting opportunities will be more successful in South Dakota if there is regular communication and cooperation among commercial hunting operations, pheasant hunters, and SDGFP.

Economic values of pheasant hunting

According to a survey of resident and nonresident hunters by Gigliotti (2004), hunters reported that "time spent with friends and family and the overall outdoor experience" were the top two reasons why they enjoyed pheasant hunting in South Dakota. Whatever their reasons might be, the activities and expenditures associated with pheasant hunting have a significant influence on local economies across the state (Erickson and Wiebe 1973).

For motels, restaurants, convenience stores, and other service-related businesses, the annual pheasant season has a profound influence on the economics of local communities all across South Dakota. Using survey statistics from the 2006 National Survey of Fishing, Hunting and Wildlife-Associated Recreation (U.S. Department of Interior 2006) and an inflation rate of 3%, the estimated economic boost attributed to pheasant hunting was $231 million in 2010. The previous 10-year average for total pheasant hunting related expenditures was $163 million (Switzer 2010). It is important to note that these are estimates of dollars spent by pheasant hunters. Economists typically use a "multiplier" to calculate a higher total economic impact (Photo 15-10).

In general, higher preseason pheasant counts translate into more pheasant hunters. Other factors, such as the previous year's hunting success, gasoline prices, or economic conditions, can also influence hunter numbers. More pheasant hunters translate into more license sales as well as increased support through the federal Wildlife Restoration Fund. These hunting license sales as well as Wildlife Restoration Funds support a budget that allows SDGFP to invest in habitat and public access for pheasant hunters and to meet the goals of other conservation efforts. Habitat development for pheasants supports a variety of other species of wildlife and has indirect benefits, such as expanded opportunities for other types of hunting, reduction in flooding, improved water quality, and reduced soil erosion. For pheasant hunting to continue to have a strong positive influence on the state's economy, future farm bills and agriculture policies must include financially attractive options for landowners to incorporate conservation programs into their land management decisions.

Photo 15-10. Pheasant hunting provides an economic boost for many businesses in South Dakota. This enormous pheasant statue is found on the eastern edge of Huron along Highway 14. (Courtesy of Travis Runia)

The annual Governor's Pheasant Hunt markets the quality of life and economic opportunities available in South Dakota to business leaders from across the nation. There are not many places where the pursuit and hunting of an upland game bird creates such excitement every fall and also contributes so greatly to the economy of local communities (Photo 15-11).

Research needs

After the first successful introductions of pheasants in South Dakota early in the 20th century, it was the goal of wildlife managers and interested landowners to expand pheasant populations into all areas of the state containing suitable pheasant habitat. To learn more about this exotic game bird, scientific research on pheasants in South Dakota began in the 1940s and 1950s and continues today; the topics and results of most of these research studies are evident in this book. Wildlife researchers and managers have learned much about ring-necked pheasant biology and habitat requirements throughout their range. Many interesting books and hundreds of research publications attest to the wealth of

Photo 15-11. Pheasants annually attract well over 100,000 pheasant hunters who provide an important boost to the state's economy, especially for motels, grocery stores, restaurants, and other services in many small communities. (Courtesy of Doug Backlund)

information available on ring-necked pheasants. In South Dakota, considerable research and management information has been published in journals or is available in various SDGFP reports or other sources such as university theses. Citations in this book attest to the contributions of Carl Trautman, Bob Dahlgren, and others to our knowledge of pheasants in South Dakota.

Changing agricultural practices, growing human populations, energy development (ethanol industry), evolving federal and state conservation programs, and other factors have created new questions that need addressing.

Improved research technologies and methods have also created new opportunities for wildlife researchers to address research questions concerning pheasants and their habitats. For example, technologies such as computer software programs, satellite imagery, geographic information systems (GIS), and global positioning systems provide research and management tools unavailable to earlier researchers and managers (Chapter 12).

The South Dakota Department of Game, Fish and Parks (SDGFP) and South Dakota State University are currently conducting a research project to predict (model) regional pheasant abundance based on the overall landscape by measuring proportions of cropland, grassland, wetlands, and other land-use types. Satellite imagery, USDA Farm Services data (croplands, CRP), and SDGFP pheasant survey information (geo-referenced) are all critical ingredients needed to develop a model of this type.

As current and future research results are obtained and interpreted, SDGFP will continue to build upon GIS databases and develop models to help predict pheasant population response to land use and habitat changes. This information will assist biologists and landowners in prioritizing habitat development efforts, and will provide valuable information for pheasant hunters in predicting pre-season populations and potential or expected hunting success.

Research results will need to be shared with the public, conservation partners, and private landowners. Pheasant management based on sound, scientific data becomes increasingly important in the face of massive landscape changes and increased farming intensity (Photo 15-12).

Researchers also need to evaluate potentially positive changes such as increases in winter wheat acreage (on existing cropland), tall stubble, post-harvest cover crops, and increased crop diversity associated with the expanding trend toward no-till farming in major portions of South Dakota's prime pheasant range.

Photo 15-12. Pheasant research will continue to benefit pheasants, pheasant habitats, and human users. This hen is being fitted with a necklace radio transmitter that will allow researchers to monitor her activities and survival. (TRK)

Studies on winter wheat use by nesting pheasants are underway at this time. The SDGFP, private landowners, hunters, and federal agencies (especially through federal conservation programs) play key roles in implementing important research findings that can help determine the future of South Dakota's pheasant populations (Photo 15-13).

Chapter thoughts

Continuation of federal and state conservation programs and the reproductive and wintering habitats they protect and provide are critical if South Dakota is to remain a mecca for pheasants and pheasant hunters. Access to pheasant habitat and pheasants on public lands, private lands (by permission), and WIAs will remain highly important in attracting both resident and nonresident hunters. New programs to involve youth in pheasant hunting are critical to ensure hunter participation and involvement in hunting and conservation programs in the future. Pheasants are important to hunters but hunters also represent an important economic stimulus for the state, especially for many service-related businesses. We must continue to work together to ensure that conservation programs valuable to soil, water, and wildlife are made available to landowners in future farm bills.

Photo 15-13. Warm- and cool-season grasses (background) planted on this experimental grass farm near Colman are harvested as hay every third year and are also used for cattle grazing. This field (round bales) and adjacent fields planted into switchgrass (harvested for seed) also produce important cover for pheasants and other wildlife. The pheasant hunters are Carter Johnson (left) from Brookings and Leigh Fredrickson from Missouri. (LDF)

Past, present, and future—an overview

South Dakota's fertile soil, climate, and landscape featuring a diversity of crops, intermixed grasslands, and wetlands on small farms provided an optimal setting for the release and establishment of ring-necked pheasants in the early 20th century. Through prolific reproduction, natural dispersal, and trap-and-transfer, pheasants spread rapidly from the James River Valley through most of the state's available habitat. The success of ring-necked pheasants was beyond the imagination of pheasant management pioneers; hundreds of thousands of pheasant hunters have harvested over a hundred million cock pheasants in South Dakota since the first pheasant season in 1919.

Long-term trends in pheasant abundance have followed a pattern directly linked to habitat available for nesting, brood rearing, and other needs. The Great Depression, World War II, and long-term land-retirement programs have all influenced the quantity and quality of pheasant cover and resulting numbers of pheasants on the landscape. Substantial increases in amounts of protective and concealing herbaceous cover across the state, as in the peak of the Soil Bank and Conservation Reserve Program, have been closely associated with major increases in the pheasant population. Loss of permanent herbaceous cover and intensive fence line to fence line (or roadside to roadside) farming for row crop monocultures, in contrast, have been directly and consistently associated with declines in pheasant abundance.

Pheasants will always fluctuate somewhat with annual weather conditions and, occasionally, will even be set back due to heavy losses of hens during extremely cold and snowy winters. However, if adequate amounts of herbaceous nesting and brood-rearing habitat along with winter cover are interspersed with cropland across the landscape, pheasants will recover rapidly from years with poor reproduction or unusually high winterkill. Fortunately, pheasants are highly productive and are persistent in their nesting efforts. Given reasonably good habitat, that persistence pays off in good reproduction and recruitment of young in most years (Photo 15-14).

Practices such as releasing pen-reared chicks and juveniles in the summer or adult hens in the spring will provide little benefit to pheasant populations. Control of an array of mammalian predators is expensive but can be somewhat effective as supplementary management if essential pheasant habitats are present. The best way to manage predators is to reduce their effectiveness by increasing the amounts of nesting, brood rearing, and other seasonal cover on the landscape.

Management practices to improve, maintain, or create cover for pheasants are readily available for landowners. Biologists with conservation agencies such as the South Dakota Department of Game, Fish and Parks, U.S. Fish and Wildlife Service, and the Natural Resource Conservation Service are available to provide planning assistance. State and federal agency biologists can also provide specific information on conservation programs that can provide economic incentives.

Photo 15-14. When habitat is abundant across the landscape the pheasant numbers in South Dakota can be difficult to believe. This wintering concentration in woody cover illustrates the point. (Courtesy of John Knight)

Each landowner or land manager makes a difference. Even just protecting small wetlands, roadside cover, woody cover, and unfarmed corners and strips can have a positive influence on pheasants and other wildlife.

Agricultural practices will continue to evolve and have a major influence on pheasant populations in the years and decades to come. Development of economically viable cropping systems that conserve soil and water, reduce use of herbicides and pesticides, and that include crops (or crop stubble) to provide nesting, brood rearing, and seasonal cover would be a pheasant enthusiast's (and pheasant's) dream; some of this is happening through increases in winter wheat and tall stubble on existing cropland.

It is important that we continue to provide hunter access on private lands through the Walk-In Area Program or similar programs in the future. Private lands make up over 95% of the state's pheasant range and will always be more critical than publicly owned lands for producing pheasants and providing places to hunt. Lastly, it is also a high priority that we continue to recruit young pheasant hunters to help carry on pheasant conservation and pheasant hunting in the future.

Ring-necked pheasants, fall colors, hunting dogs, and friends, it all sounds so appealing and it is still so readily available to hunters. May it still be as great 100 years from now!

APPENDICES

Appendix 1. Common and scientific names used in the text. Only wild or naturalized plants and vertebrates are included. Domestic plants used for crops and livestock are not included unless they have become widely established in the wild (naturalized) in South Dakota.[a]

Grasses and Grass-Like Plants
barnyardgrass (*Echinochloa muricata*)
big bluestem (*Andropogon gerardii*)
blue grama (*Bouteloua gracilis*)
Canada wildrye (*Elymus canadensis*)
cattail (*Typha* spp.)
common reed (*Phragmites australis*)
foxtail (*Setaria* spp.)
green foxtail (*Setaria viridis*)
Indiangrass (*Sorghastrum nutans*)
intermediate wheatgrass (*Elymus hispidus*)
Kentucky bluegrass (*Poa pratensis*)
little bluestem (*Schizachyrium scoparium*)
phragmites (see common reed)
river bulrush (*Scirpus fluviatilis*)
sideoats grama (*Bouteloua curtipendula*)
slender wheatgrass (*Elymus trachycaulus*)
smooth brome (see smooth bromegrass)
smooth bromegrass (*Bromus inermis*)
switchgrass (*Panicum virgatum*)
tall wheatgrass (*Elymus elongates*)
western wheatgrass (*Elymus smithii*)
wild millet (see barnyardgrass)

Forbs and Cactus
alfalfa (*Medicago sativa*)
annual sunflower (*Helianthus annuus*)
buffalo bur (*Solanum rostratum*)
Canada thistle (*Cirsium arvense*)
clover (*Trifolium* spp.)
common dandelion (*Taraxacum officinale*)
fireweed (see kochia)
kochia (*Kochia scoparia*)
leafy spurge (*Euphorbia esula*)
musk thistle (*Carduus nutans*)
partridge pea (*Chamaecrista fasciculata*)
prickly pear (*Opuntia* spp.)
ragweed (*Ambrosia* spp.)
red clover (*Trifolium pretense*)
sunflower (*Helianthus* spp.)
sweetclover (*Melilotus* spp.)
yellow sweetclover (*Melilotus officinalis*)

Shrubs and Trees
Amur maple (*Acer ginnala*)
blue spruce (*Picea pungens*)
boxelder (*Acer negundo*)
caragana (*Caragana* spp.)
chokecherry (*Prunus virginiana*)
common buckthorn (*Rhamnus cathartica*)
common lilac (*Syringa vulgaris*)
eastern redcedar (*Juniperus virginiana*)
green ash (*Fraxinus pennsylvanica*)
Hansen hedge rose (*Rosa* sp.)
hedge cotoneaster (*Cotoneaster lucidus*)
Nanking cherry (*Prunus tomentosa*)

northern hawthorn (*Crataegus chrysocarpa*)
pine (*Pinus* spp.)
plains cottonwood (*Populus deltoides*)
Rocky Mountain juniper (*Juniperus scopulorum*)
Russian olive (*Elaeagnus angustifolia*)
sandbar willow (*Salix exigua*)
Siberian elm (*Ulmus pumila*)
silver buffaloberry (*Shepherdia argentea*)
spruce (*Picea* spp.)
western snowberry (*Symphoricarpos occidentalis*)
wild plum (*Prunus americana*)
willow (see sandbar willow)

Reptiles
prairie rattlesnake (*Crotalus viridis*)

Birds
American crow (*Corvus brachyrhynchos*)
black-billed magpie (*Pica hudsonia*))
blue-winged teal (*Anas discors*)
chickadee (*Poecile* spp.)
Cooper's hawk (*Accipiter cooperii*)
crow (see American crow)
grasshopper sparrow (*Ammodramus savannarum*)
great blue heron (*Ardea herodias*)
great horned owl (*Bubo virginianus*)
greater prairie-chicken (*Tympanuchus cupido*)
greater white-fronted goose (*Anser albifrons*)
gyrfalcon (*Falco rusticolus*)
mallard (*Anas platyrhynchos*)
northern bobwhite (*Colinus virginianus*)
northern goshawk (*Accipiter gentilis*)
northern harrier (*Circus cyaneus*)
northern pintail (*Anas acuta*)
prairie falcon (*Falco mexicanus*)
praire grouse (*Tympanuchus* spp.)
red-tailed hawk (*Buteo jamaicensis*)
rough-legged hawk (*Buteo lagopus*)
ruffed grouse (*Bonasa umbellus*)
sandhill crane (*Grus canadensis*)
sharp-tailed grouse (*Tympanuchus phasianellus*)
snow goose (*Chen caerulescens*)
snowy owl (*Bubo scandiacus*)
upland sandpiper (*Bartramia longicauda*)
Virginia rail (*Rallus limicola*)
western meadowlark (*Sturnella neglecta*)
wild turkey (*Meleagris gallopavo*)

Mammals
American badger (*Taxidea taxus*)
badger (see American badger)
black-tailed prairie dog (*Cynomys ludovicianus*)
common raccoon (*Procyon lotor*)
coyote (*Canis latrans*)
deer (*Odocoileus* spp.)
eastern cottontail (*Sylvilagus floridanus*)

eastern spotted skunk (*Spilogale putorius*)
Franklin's ground squirrel (*Spermophilus franklinii*)
ground squirrel (*Spermophilus* spp.)
meadow vole (*Microtus pennsylvanicus*)
mink (*Mustela vison*)
mule deer (*Odocoileus hemionus*)
northern pocket gopher (*Thomomys talpoides*)
opossum (see Virginia opossum)
plains pocket gopher (*Geomys bursarius*)
prairie vole (*Microtus ochrogaster*)
raccoon (see common raccoon)
red fox (*Vulpes vulpes*)
spotted skunk (see eastern spotted skunk)
striped skunk (*Mephitis mephitis*)
Virginia opossum (*Didelphis virginiana*)

vole (*Microtus* spp.)
weasel (*Mustela* spp.)
white-tailed deer (*Odocoileus virginianus*)

[a] Sources for most common and scientific names were: Johnson, J.R. and G.E. Larson. 2007. Grassland plants of South Dakota and the northern great plains. Bulletin 566 (revised). South Dakota Agricultural Experiment Station, Brookings; American Ornithologist' Union and Cornell Laboratory of Ornithology. 2011. The Birds of North America (online); and K.F. Higgins. E. Dowd Stukel, J.M. Goulet, and D.C. Backlund. 2000. Wild mammals of South Dakota. South Dakota Department of Game, Fish and Parks, Pierre.

Appendix 2. Ring-necked pheasant statistics from 1919 through 2011 from the South Dakota, Department of Game, Fish and Parks.

Ring-necked Pheasant Statistics for South Dakota														
Season Structure					**Licensed Hunters**			**Population Estimates**			**Survey Indices**			
Year	Length (days)	Opening Day	Bag limit	Hen limit	Residents	Nonresidents	Total	Harvest	Pheasants harvested per hunter	Preseason Population	Preseason pheasants per mile	Average brood size	Postseason cocks per 100 hens	
1919	1	30-Oct	2	0	500	500	1,000	200	0.2	100,000				
1920	2	04-Nov	2	0	1,000	1,000	2,000	1,000	0.5	200,000				
1921	7	21-Nov	2	0	10,000	1,000	11,000	7,000	0.6	300,000				
1922	20	09-Nov	2	0	30,000	1,500	31,500	15,000	0.5	500,000				
1923	6	19-Nov	3	0	40,000	1,500	41,500	25,000	0.6	700,000				
1924	15	07-Nov	3	0	50,000	2,100	52,100	250,000	4.8	1,000,000				
1925	15	30-Oct	3	0	75,000	1,100	76,100	500,000	6.6	2,000,000				
1926	52	15-Oct	7	2	82,000	1,400	83,400	1,000,000	12.0	4,000,000				
1927	90	07-Oct	7	3	90,000	2,600	92,600	1,500,000	16.2	6,000,000				
1928	40	25-Oct	5	1	100,000	2,800	102,800	1,250,000	12.2	5,000,000				
1929	16	29-Oct	5	1	95,000	2,700	97,700	1,000,000	10.2	4,000,000				
1930	46	16-Oct	7	2	96,000	2,600	98,600	1,500,000	15.2	7,000,000				
1931	12	15-Oct	3	0	61,000	700	61,700	1,000,000	16.2	5,000,000				
1932	30	20-Oct	4	0	62,000	700	62,700	1,000,000	15.9	5,000,000				
1933	30	10-Oct	5	1	63,000	600	63,600	2,000,000	31.4	8,000,000				
1934	30	21-Oct	5	2	53,000	400	53,400	1,500,000	28.1	7,000,000				
1935	37	21-Oct	6	2	57,000	1,900	58,900	1,500,000	25.5	12,000,000				
1936	20	10-Oct	4	0	61,000	1,600	62,600	1,750,000	28.0	12,000,000				
1937	4	09-Oct	4	0	25,000	800	25,800	75,000	2.9	3,000,000				
1938	14	01-Oct	4	1	44,000	1,800	45,800	1,500,000	32.8	6,000,000				
1939	29	14-Oct	4	1	63,000	2,800	65,800	1,500,000	22.8	6,000,000				
1940	40	01-Oct	5	1	73,000	6,200	79,200	2,500,000	31.6	8,000,000				
1941	50	01-Oct	5	1	83,000	11,000	94,000	3,125,000	33.2	11,000,000				
1942	120	26-Sep	7	2	80,000	16,000	96,000	4,500,000	46.9	15,000,000				
1943	159	25-Sep	7	3	60,000	18,000	78,000	3,168,000	40.6	11,000,000				
1944	163	20-Sep	10	5	77,000	42,000	119,000	6,439,000	54.1	15,000,000				

Ring-necked Pheasant Statistics for South Dakota

	Season Structure				Licensed Hunters			Population Estimates			Survey Indices		
Year	Length (days)	Opening Day	Bag limit	Hen limit	Residents	Nonresidents	Total	Harvest	Pheasants harvested per hunter	Preseason Population	Preseason pheasants per mile	Average brood size	Postseason cocks per 100 hens
1945	153	29-Sep	8	4	88,000	87,000	175,000	7,507,000	42.9	16,000,000			
1946	88	15-Oct	5	2	103,000	84,000	187,000	3,550,000	19.0	11,000,000		6.57	
1947	45	11-Oct	3	0	103,000	13,000	116,000	1,496,000	12.9	7,000,000		7.15	60
1948	55	09-Oct	4	0	123,000	26,000	149,000	2,148,000	14.4	9,600,000		7.63	53
1949	45	15-Oct	4	0	121,000	22,000	143,000	1,864,000	13.0	8,100,000	3.10	7.15	45
1950	10	04-Nov	2	0	88,000	2,000	90,000	507,000	5.6	3,200,000	1.99	6.79	63
1951	25	20-Oct	3	0	95,000	10,000	105,000	1,184,000	11.3	6,000,000	3.69	7.13	55
1952	30	18-Oct	3	0	107,000	13,000	120,000	1,490,000	12.4	6,100,000	5.62	7.89	43
1953	30	17-Oct	3	0	100,000	17,000	117,000	1,210,000	10.3	4,900,000	4.27	6.89	41
1954	30	23-Oct	3	0	105,000	17,000	122,000	1,672,000	13.7	6,200,000	4.84	6.92	37
1955	40	22-Oct	3	0	111,000	19,000	130,000	1,608,000	12.4	6,300,000	6.72	6.90	39
1956	35	27-Oct	3	0	102,000	20,000	122,000	1,221,000	10.0	4,300,000	6.46	6.88	34
1957	37	26-Oct	3	0	102,000	20,000	122,000	1,339,000	11.0	5,900,000	7.31	5.90	43
1958	51	18-Oct	4	0	125,000	36,000	161,000	2,635,000	16.4	11,100,000	11.03	6.80	40
1959	58	17-Oct	5	0	117,000	45,000	162,000	2,212,000	13.7	7,500,000	7.64	5.70	22
1960	42	22-Oct	4	0	130,000	28,000	158,000	2,574,000	16.3	9,500,000	6.73	6.23	28
1961	58	21-Oct	4	0	141,000	51,000	192,000	3,247,000	16.9	11,000,000	11.38	6.34	26
1962	61	20-Oct	4	0	138,000	57,000	195,000	2,790,000	14.3	10,200,000	6.52	5.80	44
1963	74	19-Oct	4	0	144,000	68,000	212,000	3,095,000	14.6	10,000,000	11.24	6.50	23
1964	60	17-Oct	3	0	124,000	23,000	147,000	1,474,000	10.0	5,100,000	3.74	5.91	24
1965	44	16-Oct	3	0	102,000	14,000	116,000	797,000	6.9	3,300,000	2.55	6.28	37
1966	16	15-Oct	3	0	82,000	6,000	88,000	409,000	4.6	2,200,000	2.23	6.30	56
1967	37	21-Oct	3	0	111,000	15,000	126,000	908,000	7.2	2,900,000	2.42	6.30	39
1968	37	19-Oct	3	0	117,000	19,000	136,000	880,000	6.5	3,300,000	2.08	7.17	37
1969	30	18-Oct	3	0	96,000	14,000	110,000	622,000	5.7	2,700,000	1.91	7.60	48
1970	37	17-Oct	3	0	108,000	18,000	126,000	901,000	7.2	3,500,000	2.73	7.50	40
1971	42	16-Oct	3	0	117,000	25,000	142,000	1,106,000	7.8	3,700,000	2.45	7.22	32
1972	49	21-Oct	3	0	120,000	28,000	148,000	1,201,000	8.1	4,100,000	2.75	7.64	39
1973	64	20-Oct	3	0	127,000	37,000	164,000	1,283,000	7.8	4,200,000	3.51	7.04	29
1974	49	19-Oct	3	0	126,000	25,000	151,000	1,071,000	7.1	3,000,000	2.64	7.08	25
1975	23	18-Oct	2	0	100,000	12,000	112,000	497,500	4.4	2,100,000	1.53	7.08	42
1976	30	16-Oct	2	0	89,000	8,000	97,000	372,500	3.8	1,400,000	1.03	6.30	35
1977	44	15-Oct	2	0	90,000	10,000	100,000	518,600	5.2	2,300,000	1.62	7.33	43
1978	44	21-Oct	2	0	82,000	13,000	95,000	558,300	5.9	2,100,000	1.38	7.14	38
1979	51	20-Oct	3	0	105,000	18,700	123,700	934,000	7.6	3,600,000	3.20	7.50	39
1980	53	18-Oct	3	0	107,500	28,500	136,000	1,158,700	8.5	4,200,000	3.70	7.80	21
1981	51	17-Oct	3	0	106,300	33,000	139,300	1,299,100	9.3	4,200,000	3.60	6.84	21
1982	51	16-Oct	3	0	95,300	31,800	127,100	1,070,500	8.4	4,200,000	3.37	6.53	34
1983	51	15-Oct	3	0	102,300	36,400	138,700	1,416,600	10.2	4,800,000	3.80	6.66	21
1984	51	20-Oct	3	0	91,290	35,170	126,460	962,700	7.6	3,300,000	2.23	6.20	28
1985	51	19-Oct	3	0	85,500	34,700	120,200	801,700	6.7	3,200,000	2.27	6.19	31
1986	51	18-Oct	3	0	70,850	24,000	94,850	627,300	6.6	2,100,000	1.81	7.04	34

Ring-necked Pheasant Statistics for South Dakota													
Season Structure					Licensed Hunters			Population Estimates			Survey Indices		
Year	Length (days)	Opening Day	Bag limit	Hen limit	Residents	Nonresidents	Total	Harvest	Pheasants harvested per hunter	Preseason Population	Preseason pheasants per mile	Average brood size	Postseason cocks per 100 hens
1987	51	18-Oct	3	0	83,000	31,900	114,900	929,700	8.1	3,800,000	2.58	7.01	34
1988	51	15-Oct	3	0	79,800	30,000	109,800	782,700	7.1	3,100,000	2.22	6.23	29
1989	51	21-Oct	3	0	71,700	26,100	97,800	687,000	7.0	2,700,000	2.08	6.54	27
1990	51	20-Oct	3	0	71,300	26,501	97,801	777,300	7.9	3,700,000	2.09	6.86	38
1991	65	19-Oct	3	0	91,200	32,127	123,327	1,222,600	9.9	5,000,000	3.25	6.63	31
1992	65	17-Oct	3	0	83,400	42,900	126,300	969,000	7.7	4,200,000	2.77	6.04	35
1993	65	16-Oct	3	0	78,900	45,500	124,400	1,213,800	9.8	5,500,000	2.90	6.33	36
1994	65	15-Oct	3	0	78,800	65,200	144,000	1,370,600	9.5	5,400,000	4.09	6.48	29
1995	65	21-Oct	3	0	75,286	65,361	140,647	1,292,400	9.2	4,900,000	2.66	6.22	26
1996	65	19-Oct	3	0	77,932	65,602	143,534	1,191,700	8.3	4,800,000	2.59	6.86	31
1997	65	18-Oct	3	0	70,573	42,808	113,381	920,700	8.1	3,600,000	2.64	7.63	32
1998	65	17-Oct	3	0	75,083	60,364	135,447	1,186,700	8.8	5,000,000	4.94	7.20	33
1999	65	16-Oct	3	0	84,342	71,956	156,298	1,464,200	9.4	6,100,000	4.51	7.07	32
2000	72	21-Oct	3	0	79,790	70,182	149,972	1,447,700	9.7	6,700,000	4.16	6.31	37
2001	73	20-Oct	3	0	76,772	73,425	150,197	1,361,300	9.1	6,000,000	3.38	6.76	38
2002	74	19-Oct	3	0	70,821	74,873	145,694	1,261,700	8.7	5,500,000	2.69	6.25	37
2003	75	18-Oct	3	0	78,394	83,544	161,938	1,815,000	11.2	8,700,000	6.20	7.55	40
2004	79	16-Oct	3	0	78,984	91,948	170,932	1,653,000	9.7	8,100,000	5.66	6.39	38
2005	79	15-Oct	3	0	79,359	94,959	174,318	1,960,000	11.2	9,200,000	6.63	6.72	39
2006	79	21-Oct	3	0	79,953	98,212	178,165	1,846,400	10.4	8,400,000	6.22	6.06	38
2007	79	20-Oct	3	0	77,879	103,231	181,110	2,122,700	11.7	11,900,000	7.85	6.71	48
2008	79	18-Oct	3	0	75,831	100,349	176,180	1,933,200	11.0	10,300,000	8.56	6.38	47
2009	79	17-Oct	3	0	69,949	97,350	167,299	1,648,200	9.9	8,400,000	6.32	6.03	47
2010	79	16-Oct	3	0	72,465	100,189	172,654	1,831,600	10.6	9,840,000	6.45	6.25	50
2011	79	15-Oct	3	0	69,120	95,077	164,197	1,555,300	9.5	6,600,000	3.55	5.80	42

Appendix 3. Formula used by the South Dakota Department of Game, Fish and Parks to estimate preseason pheasant populations since 1947.

Preseason Population Formula

The variables in the formula are defined as follows:

P_1 = preseason population estimate
f_1 = preseason sex ratio
f_2 = post season sex ratio
K_f = estimated hen harvest (15% of preseason population)
K_t = estimated total harvest

$$P_1 = \frac{(f_2 K_t - K_f)}{(f_2 - f_1)}$$

Preseason population estimate = ((post season sex ratio x estimated total harvest) – (estimated hen harvest)) / (post season sex ratio – preseason sex ratio)

Example (2009 Preseason Population Estimate):

$((0.68 \times 2,370,163) - (309,152)) / (0.68 - 0.53) =$
8,683,720

Note: The post season sex ratio is the estimated proportion of hens in the population. The sex ratio field data for 2009 (Appendix 2) indicated 47 cocks per 100 hens after the hunting season. This means that 32% (47/147 x 100 =32%) of the population was made up of males and 68% of females. Thus, the sex ratio of 0.68 used in the calculation.

LITERATURE CITED

Altieri, M.A. 2009. The ecological impacts of large-scale agrofuel monoculture production systems in the Americas. Bulletin of Science, Technology and Society 29:236–244.

Arnold, T.W., L.M. Craig-Moore, L.M. Armstrong, D.W. Howerter, J.H. Devries, B.L. Joynt, R.B. Emery, and M.G. Anderson. 2007. Waterfowl use of dense nesting cover in the Canadian Parklands. Journal of Wildlife Management 71:2542–2549.

Bahm, M.A. 2009. Conversion of exotic cool-season grassland to restored native plant communities utilizing herbicide treatments. Ph.D. dissertation, South Dakota State University, Brookings.

Bahm, M.A., and T.G. Barnes. 2011. Native grass and forb response to pre-emergent application of imazapic and imazapyr. Natural Areas Journal 31:75–79.

Bahm, M.A., T.G. Barnes, and K.C. Jensen. 2011. Herbicide and fire effects on smooth brome (*Bromus inermis*) and Kentucky bluegrass (*Poa pratensis*) in invaded prairie remnants. Invasive Plant Science and Management 4:189–197.

Bakker, K.K., and K F. Higgins. 2009. Planted grasslands and native sod prairie: Equivalent habitat for grassland birds? Western North American Naturalist 69:235–242.

Bartmann, R.M. 1969. Pheasant nesting on soil bank land in northern Utah. Journal of Wildlife Management 33:1020–1023.

Baskett, T.S. 1947. Nesting and production of the ring-necked pheasant in north-central Iowa. Ecological Monographs 17:1–30.

Basore, N.S., L. B. Best, and J.B. Wooley, Jr. 1986. Bird nesting in Iowa no-tillage and tilled cropland. Journal of Wildlife Management 50:19–28.

Baxter, W.L., and C.W. Wolfe. 1973. Life history and ecology of the ring-necked pheasant in Nebraska. Nebraska Game and Parks Commission, Lincoln.

Bennett, R.S., Jr., and H.H. Prince. 1981. Influence of agricultural pesticides on food preference and consumption by ring-necked pheasants. Journal of Wildlife Management 45:74–82.

Besadny, C.D., and F.H. Wagner. 1963. An evaluation of pheasant stocking through the day-old-chick program in Wisconsin. Technical Bulletin 28. Wisconsin Conservation Department.

Bies, L. 2006. The biofuels explosion: Is green energy good for wildlife? Wildlife Society Bulletin 34:1203–1205.

Blus, L.J., and C.J. Henny. 1997. Field studies on pesticides and birds: unexpected and unique relations. Ecological Applications 7:1125–1132.

Boe, A., R. Bortnem, K.F. Higgins, A.D. Kruse, K.D. Kephart, and S. Selman. 1998. Breeding yellow-flowered alfalfa for combined wildlife habitat and forage purposes. SDAES Bulletin 727. South Dakota State University, Brookings.

Bogenschutz, T.R., D.E. Hubbard, and A.P. Leif. 1995. Corn and sorghum as a winter food source for ring-necked pheasant hens. Journal of Wildlife Management 59:776–784.

Breitenbach, R.P., C.L. Nagra, and R.K. Meyer. 1963. Effect of limited food intake on cyclic annual changes in ring-necked pheasant hens. Journal of Wildlife Management 27:24–36.

Brittas, R., V. Marcstrom, R.E. Kenward, and M. Karlbom. 1992. Survival and breeding success of reared and wild ring-necked pheasants in Sweden. Journal of Wildlife Management 56:368–376.

Brooke, R., G. Fogel, A. Glaser, E. Griffin, and K. Johnson. 2010. Corn ethanol and wildlife: How increases in corn plantings are affecting habitat and wildlife in the prairie pothole region. University of Michigan study published by The National Wildlife Federation (Internet, type in title).

Brown, J.K., and J.K. Smith, eds. 2000. Wildland fire in ecosystems: effects of fire on flora. General Technical Report. RMRS-GTR-42-vol. 2. Ogden, Utah: U.S. Department of Agriculture, Forest Service, Rocky Mountain Research Station.

Carroll, J.P. 1985. Brood defense by female ring-necked pheasants against northern harriers. Journal of Field Ornithology 56:283–284.

Carter, A.V. 1971. Seasonal movements and behavior of ring-necked pheasants in eastern South Dakota. M.S. thesis, South Dakota State University, Brookings.

Carter, A.V. 1973. Pheasant nesting preference study, 1968–1973. Completion Report, Project W-75-R-15. South Dakota Department of Game, Fish and Parks, Pierre.

Chambers, G.D., K.C. Sadler, and R.P. Breitenbach. 1966. Effects of dietary calcium levels on egg production and bone structure of pheasants. Journal of Wildlife Management 30:65–73.

Chesness, R.A., and M.M. Nelson. 1964. Illegal kill of hen pheasants in Minnesota. Journal of Wildlife Management 28:249–253.

Chesness, R.A., M.M. Nelson, and W.H. Longley. 1968. The effect of predator removal on pheasant reproductive success. Journal of Wildlife Management 32:683–697.

Clark, W.R., and T.R. Bogenschutz. 1999. Grassland habitat and reproductive success of ring-necked pheasants in northern Iowa. Journal of Field Ornithology 70:380–392.

Clark, W.R., R.A. Schmitz, and T.R. Bogenschutz. 1999. Site selection and nest success of ring-necked pheasants as a function of location in Iowa landscapes. Journal of Wildlife Management 63:976–989.

Connelly, J.W., K.P. Reese, and M.A. Schroeder. 2003. Monitoring of greater sage-grouse habitats and populations. Station Bulletin 80, College of Natural Resources Experiment Station, University of Idaho, Moscow (Internet).

Cowardin, L.M., D.S. Gilmer, and C.W. Shaiffer. 1985. Mallard recruitment in the agricultural environment of North Dakota. Wildlife Monographs 92.

Dahlgren, R.B. 1962. Pheasant Soil Bank nesting study, 1960. South Dakota Department of Game, Fish and Parks, Pierre, Completion Report, Pittman-Robertson Project W-75-R-3.

Dahlgren, R.B. 1963. Rhythmic fluctuations in South Dakota pheasant populations and associated adult mortality, 1947–1962. Transactions of North American Wildlife and Natural Resources Conference 28:284–297.

Dahlgren, R.B. 1967. Pheasant stocking: why it fails! South Dakota Conservation Digest 34(4):18–21.

Dahlgren, R.B., and R.L. Linder. 1971. Effects of polychlorinated biphenyls on pheasant reproduction, behavior, and survival. Journal of Wildlife Management 35:315–319.

Dahlgren, R.B., and R.L. Linder. 1974. Effects of dieldrin in penned pheasants through the third generation. Journal of Wildlife Management 38:320–330.

Dahlgren, R.B., C.G. Trautman, and G.C. Parikh. 1974. Pheasant mortality and production in South Dakota related to antibodies for western and eastern viral encephalitis. American Midland Naturalist 91:237–241.

Diefenbach, D.R., C.F. Riegner, and T.S. Hardisky. 2000. Harvest and reporting rates of game-farm ring-necked pheasants. Wildlife Society Bulletin 28:1050–1059.

Docken, N.R. 2011. Effects of block predator management on duck and pheasant nest success in eastern South Dakota. M.S. thesis, South Dakota State University, Brookings.

Draycott, R.A.H., A.N. Hoodless, M.N. Ludiman, and P.A. Robertson. 1998. Effects of spring feeding on body condition of captive-reared ring-necked pheasants in Great Britain. Journal of Wildlife Management 62:557–563.

Dumke, R.T., and C.M. Pils. 1979. Renesting and dynamics of nest site selection by Wisconsin pheasants. Journal of Wildlife Management 43:705–716.

Edwards, W.R., P.J. Mikolaj, and E.A. Leite. 1964. Implications from winter-spring weights of pheasants. Journal of Wildlife Management 28:270–279.

Eggebo, S.L., K.F. Higgins, D.E. Naugle, and F.R. Quamen. 2003. Effects of CRP field age and cover type on ring-necked pheasants in eastern South Dakota. Wildlife Society Bulletin 31:779–785.

Engle, D.M., R.L. Mitchell, and R.L. Stevens. 1998. Late growing-season fire effects in mid-successional tallgrass prairies. Journal of Range Management 51:115–121.

Erickson, R.E., and J.E. Wiebe. 1973. Pheasants, economics and land-retirement programs in South Dakota. Wildlife Society Bulletin 1:22–2.7

Fargione, J.E., T.R. Cooper, D.J. Flaspohler, J. Hill, C. Lehman, D. Tilman, T. McCoy, S. McLeod, E.J. Nelson, and K.S. Oberhauser. 2009. Bioenergy and wildlife: threats and opportunities for grassland conservation. BioScience 59:767–777.

Farris, A.L., E.D. Klonglan, and R.C. Nomsen. 1977. The ring-necked pheasant in Iowa. Iowa Conservation Commission, Des Moines.

Fisk, K.J. 2010. An evaluation of duck and ring-necked pheasant nest survival and nest density in relation to patch size and landscape variables in eastern South Dakota. M.S. thesis, South Dakota State University, Brookings.

Flake, L.D., J.W. Connelly, T.R. Kirschenmann, and A.J. Lindbloom. 2010. Grouse of plains and mountains—the South Dakota story. South Dakota Department of Game, Fish and Parks, Pierre.

Fondell, T.F., and I.J. Ball. 2004. Density and success of bird nests relative to grazing on western Montana grasslands. Biological Conservation 117:203–213.

Frey, S.N., S. Majors, M.R. Conover, T.A. Messmer, and D.L. Mitchell. 2003. Effect of predator control on ring-necked pheasant populations. Wildlife Society Bulletin 31:727–735.

Fried, L.A. 1940. The food habits of the ring-necked pheasant in Minnesota. Journal of Wildlife Management 4:27–36.

Gabbert, A.E., and N.A. Schneider. 1998. Spring migration of raptors in Moody County South Dakota. Proceedings of the South Dakota Academy of Sciences 77:145–150.

Gabbert, A.E., A.P. Leif, J.R. Purvis, and L.D. Flake. 1999. Survival and habitat use by ring-necked pheasants during two disparate winters in South Dakota. Journal of Wildlife Management 63:711–722.

Gabbert, A.E., J.R. Purvis, L.D. Flake, and A.P. Leif. 2001. Winter survival and home range of female ring-necked pheasants in relation to food plots. The Prairie Naturalist 33:31–40.

Garrettson, P.R., and F.C. Rohwer. 2001. Effects of mammalian predator removal on production of upland-nesting ducks in North Dakota. Journal of Wildlife Management 65:398–405.

Gates, J.M. 1966a. Renesting behavior in the ring-necked pheasant. Wilson Bulletin 78:309–315.

Gates, J.M. 1966b. Validity of spur appearance as an age criterion in the pheasant. Journal of Wildlife Management 30:81–85.

Gates, J.M. 1970. Recommendations for a scattered wetlands program of pheasant habitat preservation in southeast Wisconsin. Research Report 63. Wisconsin Department of Natural Resources.

Gates, J.M., and J.B. Hale. 1974. Seasonal movement, winter habitat use, and population distribution of an east central Wisconsin pheasant population. Technical Bulletin 76. Wisconsin Department of Natural Resources, Madison.

Gates, J.M., and J.B. Hale. 1975. Reproduction of an east central Wisconsin pheasant population. Technical Bulletin 85, Department of Natural Resources, Madison.

Gates, J.M., and E.E. Woehler. 1968. Winter weight loss related to subsequent weights and reproduction in penned pheasant hens. Journal of Wildlife Management 32:234–247.

Gatti, R.C., R.T. Dumke, and C.M. Pils. 1989. Habitat use and movements of female ring-necked pheasants during fall and winter. Journal of Wildlife Management 53:462–475.

Geaumont, B.A. 2009. Evaluation of ring-necked pheasant and duck production on post-Conservation Reserve Program grasslands in southwest North Dakota. Ph.D. dissertation. North Dakota State University, Fargo.

George, R.R., A.L. Farris, C.C. Schwartz, D.D. Humburg, and J.C. Coffey. 1979. Native prairie grass pastures as nest cover for upland birds. Wildlife Society Bulletin 7:4–9.

George, R.R., J.B. Wooley, Jr., J.M. Kienzler, A.L. Farris, and A.H. Berner. 1980. Effect of hunting season length on ring-necked pheasant populations. Wildlife Society Bulletin 8:279–283.

Gigliotti, L.M. 2004. Pheasant management survey—Evaluation of resident and nonresident pheasant hunting. Report: HD-4-0 AMS, South Dakota Game, Fish and Parks, Pierre.

Giudice, J.H., and J.T. Ratti. 2001. Ring-necked pheasant (*Phasianus colchicus*). *In* The Birds of North America, No. 572 (A. Poole and F. Gill, eds.). The Birds of North America, Inc., Philadelphia, Penn.

Government Accountability Office. 2007. Farm program payments are an important consideration in landowners' decisions to convert grassland to cropland. GAO report 07-1054. Washington, D.C.

Green, C. 2011. Reducing mortality of grassland wildlife during haying and wheat-harvesting operations. NREM-5006. Oklahoma Cooperative Extension Service, Oklahoma State University, Stillwater (Internet, type in title).

Green, W.E. 1938. The food and cover relationship in the winter survival of the ring-necked pheasant, *Phasianus colchicus torquatus Gmelin*, in northern Iowa. Iowa State College Journal of Science 12:285–314.

Greenberg, R.E., S.L. Etter, and W.L. Anderson. 1972. Evaluation of proximal primary feather criteria for aging wild pheasants. Journal of Wildlife Management 36:700–705.

Greenwood, R.J. 1986. Influence of striped skunk removal on upland duck nest success in North Dakota. Wildlife Society Bulletin 14:6–11.

Grier, B. 2003. The bounty of tall stubble. Nebraskaland. 35(4):34–37.

Grondahl, C.R. 1953. Winter behavior of the ring-necked pheasant, *Phasianus colchicus*, as related to winter cover in Winnebago County, Iowa. Iowa State College Journal of Science 27:447–465.

Haensly, T.G., S.M. Meyers. J.A. Crawford, and W.J. Castillo. 1985. Treatments affecting post-release survival and productivity of pen-reared ring-necked pheasants. Wildlife Society Bulletin 13:521–528.

Hankins, J.C. 2007. Evaluation of mixed-vegetation plantings as avian nesting habitats in Eastern South Dakota. M.S. thesis, South Dakota State University, Brookings.

Hanson, L.E., and D.R. Progulske. 1973. Movements and cover preferences of pheasants in South Dakota. Journal of Wildlife Management 37:454–461.

Harmon, K.W., and M.M. Nelson. 1973. Wildlife and soil considerations in land-retirement programs. Wildlife Society Bulletin 1:28–38.

Haroldson, K.J., R.O. Kimmel, M.R. Riggs, and A.H. Berner. 2006. Association of ring-necked pheasant, gray partridge, and meadowlark abundance to conservation reserve program grasslands. Journal of Wildlife Management 70:1276–1284.

Havasi, A.G. 1992. Seasonal changes in the diet and body weight of adult pheasants *Phasianus colchicus L.* in agrohabitats of Hungary. Transactions of the Congress, International Union of Game Biologists 18:591–594.

Hessler, E., J.R. Tester, D.B. Siniff, and M.M. Nelson. 1970. A biotelemetry study of survival of pen-reared pheasants released in selected habitats. Journal of Wildlife Management 34:267–274.

Hickey, J.J. 1955. Some American population research on gallinaceous birds. Pages 326–396 *in* Recent studies in avian biology (A. Wolfson, ed.). University of Illinois Press, Urbana.

Higgins, K.F. 1986. Interpretation and compendium of historical fire accounts in the northern Great Plains. Resource Publication 161. U.S. Department of Interior, Fish and Wildlife Service.

Higgins, K.F., and W.T. Barker. 1982. Changes in vegetation structure in seeded nesting cover in the prairie pothole region. Special Scientific Report-Wildlife 242. United States Department of Interior, Fish and Wildlife Service, Washington, D.C.

Higgins, K.F., A.D. Kruse, and J.L. Piehl. 1989. Effects of fire in the northern great plains. U.S. Fish and Wildlife Service and Cooperative Extension Service, South Dakota State University. (Available on web site: Department of Wildlife and Fisheries Sciences, South Dakota State University, Department Publications).

Hill, D.A. 1985. The feeding ecology and survival of pheasant chicks on arable farmland. Journal of Applied Ecology 22:645–654.

Hill, D.A., and P.A. Robertson. 1988a. Breeding success of wild and hand-reared ring-necked pheasants. Journal of Wildlife Management 52:446–450.

Hill, D.A., and P.A. Robertson. 1988b. The pheasant: ecology, management, and conservation. BSP Professional Books, Oxford, UK.

Hinkson, R.S. Jr., L.T. Smith, and A.G. Kese. 1970. Calcium requirement of the breeding pheasant hen. Journal of Wildlife Management 34:160–165.

Hissa, R., S. Saarela, H. Rintamaki, H. Linden, and E. Hohtola. 1983. Energetics and development of temperature regulation in *Capercaillie tetrao urogallus*. Physiological Zoology 56:142–151.

Hodne-Fischer, E.A. 2009. Anthraquinone corn seed treatment (Avitec™) as a feeding repellent for ring-necked pheasants (*Phasianus colchicus*) on newly planted corn in eastern South Dakota. M,S. thesis, South Dakota State University, Brookings.

Holechek, J.L. 1994. Financial returns from different grazing management systems in New Mexico. Rangelands 16:237–240.

Holechek, J.L., H. Gomes, F. Molinar, D. Galt, and R. Valdez. 2000. Short-duration grazing: the facts in 1999. Rangelands 22:18–22.

Homan, H.J., G.M. Linz, and W.J. Bleier. 2000. Winter habitat use and survival of female ring-necked pheasants (*Phasianus colchicus*) in southeastern North Dakota. American Midland Naturalist 143:463–480.

Ignatiuk, J.B., and D.C. Duncan. 2001. Nest success of ducks on rotational and season-long grazing systems in Saskatchewan. Wildlife Society Bulletin 29:211–217.

Jarvis, R.L., and J. Engbring. 1976. Survival and reproduction of wild game-farm pheasants in western Oregon. Northwest Science 50:222–230.

Johnsgard, P.A. 1986. The pheasants of the world. Oxford University Press, New York.

Johnson, W.C., B. Werner, G.R. Guntenspergen, R.A. Voldseth, B. Millett, D.E. Naugle, M. Tulbure, R.W.H. Carroll, J. Tracy, and C. Olawsky. 2010. Prairie wetland complexes as landscape functional units in a changing climate. BioScience 60:128–140.

Joselyn, G.B., and G.I. Tate. 1972. Practical aspects of managing roadside cover for nesting pheasants. Journal of Wildlife Management 36:1–11.

Keyser, E.J. III. 1986. Pheasant nesting and vegetation development in dense nesting cover established under the South Dakota Pheasant Restoration Program. M.S. thesis, South Dakota State University, Brookings.

King, J.W., and J.A. Savidge. 1995. Effects of the Conservation Reserve Program on wildlife in southeast Nebraska. Wildlife Society Bulletin 23:377–385.

Kirkpatrick, C.M. 1944. Body weights and organ measurements in relation to age and season in ring-necked pheasants. Anatomical Record 89:175–194.

Kopischke, E.D., and M.M. Nelson. 1966. Grit availability and pheasant densities in Minnesota and South Dakota. Journal of Wildlife Management 30:269–275.

Krapu, G.L., D. A. Brandt, and R.R. Cox, Jr. 2004. Less waste corn, more land in soybeans, and the switch to genetically modified crops: trends with important implications for wildlife management. Wildlife Society Bulletin 32:127–136.

Krausman, P.R., D.E. Naugle, M.R. Frisina, R. Northrup, V.C. Bleich, W.M. Block, M.C Wallace, and J.D. Wright. 2009. Livestock grazing, wildlife habitat, and rangeland values. Rangelands 31:15–19.

Krauss, G.D., H.B. Graves, and S.M. Zervanos. 1987. Survival of wild and game-farm cock pheasants released in Pennsylvania. Journal of Wildlife Management 51:555–559.

Kuck, T.L., R.B. Dahlgren, and D.R. Progulske. 1970. Movements and behavior of hen pheasants during the nesting season. Journal of Wildlife Management 34:626–630.

Kuehl, A.K., and W.R. Clark. 2002. Predator activity related to landscape features in northern Iowa. Journal of Wildlife Management 66:1224–1234.

Kuehl, A.K., and L.D. Flake. 1998. Pheasant habitat: finding refuge during a severe winter. South Dakota Conservation Digest 65(5):10–12.

Labisky R.F., and R.W. Lutz. 1967. Responses of wild pheasants to solid-block applications of Aldrin. Journal of Wildlife Management 31:13–24.

Larsen, D.T. 1992. Food plot and habitat characteristics associated with ring-necked pheasant use of winter food plots in east-central South Dakota. M.S. thesis, South Dakota State University, Brookings.

Larsen, D.T., P.L. Crookston, and L.D. Flake. 1994. Factors associated with ring-necked pheasant use of winter food plots. Wildlife Society Bulletin 22:620–626.

Leathers, R.J. 2003. Relative invertebrate availability in Nebraska's Conservation Reserve Management Access Program. M.S. thesis, South Dakota State University, Brookings.

Leif, A.P. 1993. Survival and productivity of wild and pen-reared ring-necked pheasants in South Dakota, 1990–92. Completion Report 93-02. South Dakota Department of Game, Fish and Parks, Pierre.

Leif, A.P. 1994. Survival and reproduction of wild and pen-reared ring-necked pheasant hens. Journal of Wildlife Management 58:501–506.

Leif, A.P. 1996. Survival and reproductive chronology of female ring-necked pheasants in South Dakota. Prairie Naturalist 28:189–198.

Leif, A.P. 2003. Survival, spatial ecology and habitat use of male ring-necked pheasants in South Dakota. Completion Report 2003–08. South Dakota Department of Game, Fish and Parks, Pierre.

Leif, A.P. 2005. Spatial ecology and habitat selection of breeding male pheasants. Wildlife Society Bulletin 33:130–141.

Leif, A.P. 2007. Pheasant history. South Dakota Conservation Digest 74(4):12–13.

Linder, R.L., D.L. Lyon, and C.P. Agee. 1960. An analysis of pheasant nesting in south-central Nebraska. Transactions of the North American Wildlife Conference 25:214–230.

Low, J.B. 1954. Game farm pheasant returns to the hunters' bag, Weber County, Utah, 1946–1951. Journal of Wildlife Management 18:419–423.

Lusk, J.J., S. Taylor, M. Feeney, M. Bresley, and B. Meduna. 2009. An evaluation of the Surrogator captive propagation system for ring-necked pheasants. Nebraska Game and Parks Commission, Lincoln, unpublished report.

Marcstrom, V., R.E. Kenward, and M. Karlbom. 1989. Survival of ring-necked pheasants with backpacks, necklaces, and leg bands. Journal of Wildlife Management 53:808–810.

Martinson, R.K., and C.R. Grondahl. 1966. Weather and pheasant populations in southwestern North Dakota. Journal of Wildlife Management 30:74–81.

Masters, R.A., S.J. Nissen, R.E. Gaussoin, D.D. Beran, and R.N. Stougaard. 1996. Imidazolinone herbicides improve restoration of Great Plains grasslands. Weed Technology 10:392–403.

Mayfield, H. 1975. Suggestions for calculating nest success. Wilson Bulletin 87:456–466.

McCann, L.J. 1939. Studies of grit requirements of certain upland game birds. Journal of Wildlife Management 3:31–41.

McClure, H.E. 1948. Factors in winter starvation of pheasants. Journal of Wildlife Management 12:267–271.

McCoy, T.D., E.W. Kurzejeski, L.W. Burger, Jr., and M.R. Ryan. 2001. Effects of conservation practice, mowing, and temporal changes on vegetation structure on CRP fields in northern Missouri. Wildlife Society Bulletin 29:979–987.

Messick, J.P., E.G. Bizeau, W.W. Benson, and W.H. Mullins. 1974. Aerial pesticide applications and ring-necked pheasants. Journal of Wildlife Management 38:679–685.

Mezquida, E.T., S.J. Slater, and C.W. Benkman. 2006. Sage-grouse and indirect interactions: potential implications of coyote control on sage-grouse populations. Condor 108:747–759.

Murphy, R.K., D.J. Schindler, and R.D. Crawford. 2004. Duck nesting on rotational and continuous grazed pastures in North Dakota. The Prairie Naturalist 36.

Musil, D.D., and J.W. Connelly. 2009. Survival and reproduction of pen-reared vs. translocated wild pheasants *Phasianus colchicus*. Wildlife Biology 15:80–88.

National Agricultural Statistics Services (NASS). 2010. United States Department of Agriculture. www.nass.usda.gov/

Naugle, D.E., K.F. Higgins, and K.K. Bakker. 2000. A synthesis of the effects of upland management practices on waterfowl and other birds in the northern great plains of the U.S. and Canada. Wildlife Technical Report 1. College of Natural Resources, University of Wisconsin-Stevens Point.

Nelson, B.A., and R.G. Janson. 1949. Starvation of pheasants in South Dakota. Journal of Wildlife Management 13:308–309.

Nelson, D.R., R.O. Kimmel, and M.J. Frydendall. 1990. Ring-necked pheasant and gray partridge brood habitat in roadsides and managed grasslands. Perdix V:103–112.

Nielson, R.M., L.L. McDonald, J.P. Sullivan, C. Burgess, D.S. Johnson, and S. Howlin. 2006. Estimating response of the ring-necked pheasant (*Phasianus colchicus*) to the Conservation Reserve Program. Technical report prepared for US Department of Agriculture Farm Service Agency, Contract Number 53-3151-5-8059, Western EcoSystems Technology, Inc., 2003 Central Avenue, Cheyenne, Wyo.

Norton, M.A. 2005. Reproductive success and brood habitat use of greater prairie chickens and sharp-tailed grouse on the Fort Pierre National Grassland of central South Dakota. M.S, thesis, South Dakota State University, Brookings.

Nusser, S.M., W.R. Clark, J. Wang, and T.R. Bogenschutz. 2004. Combining data from state and national monitoring surveys to assess large-scale impacts of agricultural policy. Journal of Agricultural, Biological, and Environmental Statistics 9:381–397.

Ohlsson, T., and H.G. Smith. 2001. Early nutrition causes persistent effects on pheasant morphology. Physiological and Biochemical Zoology 74:212–218.

Ohlsson, T., H.G. Smith, L. Raberg, and D. Hasselquist. 2001. Pheasant sexual ornaments reflect nutritional conditions during early growth. Proceedings Royal Society of London-Biological Sciences 269:21–27.

Olson, R.A., and L.D. Flake. 1975. Nesting of ring-necked pheasants in eastern South Dakota. Proceedings of the South Dakota Academy of Sciences 54:126–136.

Paine, L., D.J. Undersander, D.W. Sample, G.A. Bartelt, and T.A. Schatteman. 1996. Cattle trampling of simulated ground nests in rotationally grazed pastures. Journal of Range Management 49:294–300.

Paulik, G.J., and D.S. Robson. 1969. Statistical calculations for change-in-ratio estimators of population parameters. Journal of Wildlife Management 33:1–27.

Pedlar, J.H., L. Fahrig, and H.G. Merriam. 1997. Raccoon habitat use at 2 spatial scales. Journal of Wildlife Management 61:102–112.

Perkins, A.L., W.R. Clark, T.Z. Riley, and P.A. Vohs. 1997. Effects of landscape and weather on winter survival of ring-necked pheasant hens. Journal of Wildlife Management 61:634–644.

Petersen, L.R. 1979. Ecology of great horned owls and red-tailed hawks in southeastern Wisconsin. Technical Bulletin 111. Wisconsin Department of Natural Resources, Madison.

Petersen, L.R., R.T. Dumke, and J.M. Gates. 1988. Pheasant survival and the role of predation. Pages 165–196 in Pheasants: Symptoms of Wildlife Problems on Agricultural Lands (D.L. Hallett, W.R. Edwards, and G.V. Burger, eds.). North Central Section of The Wildlife Society, Bloomington, Ind.

Purvis, J.R., A.E. Gabbert, and L.D. Flake. 1999a. Nest site characteristics of ring- necked pheasants in eastern South Dakota. The Prairie Naturalist 31:1–7.

Purvis, J.R., A.E. Gabbert, L.D. Flake, and A.P. Leif. 1999b. Over-winter condition changes in female ring-necked pheasants during two mild winters. Proceedings of the South Dakota Academy of Science 78:177–183.

Riley, T.Z. 1995. Association of the Conservation Reserve Program with ring-necked pheasant survey counts in Iowa. Wildlife Society Bulletin 23:386–390.

Riley, T.Z., and J.H. Schulz. 2001. Predation and ring-necked pheasant population dynamics. Wildlife Society Bulletin 29:33–38.

Riley, T.Z., W.R. Clark, D.E. Ewing, and P.A. Vohs. 1998. Survival of ring-necked pheasant chicks during brood rearing. Journal of Wildlife Management 62:36–44.

Riley, T.Z., J.B. Wooley, Jr., and W.B. Rybarczyk. 1994. Survival of ring-necked pheasants in Iowa. Prairie Naturalist 26:143–148.

Robel, R.J., and S.M. Arruda. 1986. Energetics and weight changes of northern bobwhite fed 6 different foods. Journal of Wildlife Management 50:236–238.

Robertson, C. 2010. Hunting safety—It's no accident. South Dakota Conservation Digest 77(5):4–5.

Robertson, P.A. 1996. Does nesting cover limit abundance of ring-necked pheasants in North America? Wildlife Society Bulletin 24:98–106.

Robertson, P.A. 1997. Pheasants. Voyageur Press, Inc, Stillwater, Minn.

Rock, M.E. 2006. Avian nesting density and success in alfalfa, cool season CRP, and warm-season CRP planting in eastern South Dakota. M.S. thesis, South Dakota State University, Brookings.

Rodgers, R.D. 1983. Reducing wildlife losses to tillage in fallow wheat fields. Wildlife Society Bulletin 11:31–38.

Rodgers, R.D. 2002. Effects of wheat-stubble height and weed control on winter pheasant abundance. Wildlife Society Bulletin 30:1099–1112.

Rodgers, R.D. 2005. A century of ringnecks. Kansas Wildlife and Parks 62:2–7.

Rohlfing, M.B. 2004. Avian nest densities and success in introduced cool-season grass-legume plantings versus warm-season native grass plantings in South Dakota, 2002–2003. M.S. thesis, South Dakota State University, Brookings.

Ryser, F.A., and P.R. Morrison. 1954. Cold resistance in the young ring-necked pheasant. Auk 71:253–266.

Sather-Blair, S., and R.L. Linder. 1980. Pheasant use of South Dakota wetlands during the winter. Proceedings of the South Dakota Academy of Sciences 59:147–155.

Schilowsky, R.D. 2007. Habitat selection and use by breeding hen pheasants in eastern South Dakota, 1999–2001. M.S. thesis, South Dakota State University, Brookings.

Schmitz, R.A., and W.R. Clark. 1999. Survival of ring-necked pheasant hens during spring in relation to landscape features. Journal of Wildlife Management 63:147–154.

Sedivec, K.K., D.A. Tober, W.L. Duckwitz, D.D. Dewald, and J.L. Printz. 2007. Grasses for the Northern Plains, growth patterns, forage characteristics, and wildlife value, vol I, Cool-season, R-1323. North Dakota State University Extension Service. U. S. Department of Agriculture Natural Resource Conservation Service, Bismarck Plant Materials Center (available on Internet).

Sedivec, K.K., D.A. Tober, W.L. Duckwitz, D.D. Dewald, J.I. Printz, and D.J. Craig. 2009. Grasses for the Northern Plains: growth patterns, forage characteristics, and wildlife value, vol. II, Warm-season, R-1390. North Dakota State University Extension Service, U. S. Department of Agriculture, Natural Resource Conservation Service, Bismarck Plant Materials Center (available on Internet).

Shick, C. 1947. Sex ratio—egg fertility relationships in the ring-necked pheasant. Journal of Wildlife Management 11:302–306.

Smith, A., and T. Leif. 2002. Small Game, Upland Bird and Migratory Game Bird Harvest Projections, 2000 Annual Report. Report Number 2001–03. South Dakota Department of Game, Fish and Parks Game, Pierre.

Smith, J.K., ed. 2000. Wildland fire in ecosystems: effects of fire on fauna. General Technical Report, RMRS-GTR-42, vol. 1. Ogden, Utah: U.S. Department of Agriculture, Forest Service, Rocky Mountain Research Station.

Smith, W.K., K.E. Church, J.S. Taylor, D.H. Rusch, and P.S. Gibson. 2002. Modified decoy trapping of male ring-necked pheasant (*Phasianus colchicus*) and northern bobwhite (*Colinus virginianus*). Game and Wildlife Science 18:581–586.

Snyder, W.D. 1984. Ring-necked pheasant nesting ecology and wheat farming on the high plains. Journal of Wildlife Management 48:878–888.

Snyder, W.D. 1985. Survival of radio-marked hen ring-necked pheasants in Colorado. Journal of Wildlife Management 49:1044–1050.

Solomon, K. 1982. Pheasant restoration band returns. South Dakota Department of Game, Fish and Parks, unpublished report.

Sovada, M.A., A.B. Sargeant, and J.W. Grier. 1995. Differential effects of coyotes and red foxes on duck nest success. Journal of Wildlife Management 59:1–9.

Stafford, J.D., L.D. Flake, and P.W. Mammenga. 2002. Survival of mallard broods and ducklings departing overwater nesting structures in eastern South Dakota. Wildlife Society Bulletin 30:327–336.

Swenk, W.H. 1930. The food habits of the ring-necked pheasant in central Nebraska. Research Bulletin 50:1–33. University of Nebraska, Lincoln.

Switzer, C.T. 2009. Empire of the ringneck: a century of pheasants in South Dakota. South Dakota Conservation Digest 76(1):10–13.

Switzer, C.T. 2010. Ring-necked pheasant management plan for South Dakota 2009–2014. Version 09-02. South Dakota Game, Fish and Parks, Pierre.

Taber, R.D. 1949. Observations on the breeding behavior of the ring-necked pheasant. Condor 51:153–175.

Tilman, D., J. Hill, and C. Lehman. 2006. Carbon-negative biofuels from low-input high-diversity grassland biomass. Science 314:1598–1600.

Trautman, C.G. 1952. Pheasant food habits in South Dakota and their economic significance to agriculture. Technical Bulletin 1. South Dakota Department of Game, Fish and Parks.

Trautman, C.G. 1960. Evaluation of pheasant nesting habitat in eastern South Dakota. Transactions of the North American Wildlife and Natural Resources Conference 25:202–213.

Trautman, C.G. 1982. History, ecology and management of the ring-necked pheasant in South Dakota. Wildlife Research Bulletin 7. South Dakota Department of Game, Fish and Parks, Pierre.

Trautman, C.G., L.F. Fredrickson, and A.V. Carter. 1974. Relationship of red foxes and other predators to populations of ring-necked pheasants and other prey, South Dakota. Transactions of the North American Wildlife Conference 39:241–252.

U.S. Department of the Interior and U.S. Department of Commerce. 2006. National Survey of Fishing, Hunting and Wildlife-Associated Recreation (Internet, search under title).

Vance, D.R. 1971. Physical and chemical alterations of grit consumed by pheasants. Journal of Wildlife Management 35:136–140.

Randel, G.M. III. 1980. Land use changes and pheasant declines in eastern South Dakota. M.S. thesis. South Dakota State University, Brookings.

Randel, G.M. III, and R.L. Linder. 1981. Pheasants decline but cover-type acreages unchanged on South Dakota study area. Wildlife Society Bulletin 9:299–302.

Warner, R.E. 1979. Use of cover by pheasant broods in east-central Illinois. Journal of Wildlife Management 43:334–346.

Warner, R.E. 1984. Effects of changing agriculture on ring-necked pheasant brood movements in Illinois. Journal of Wildlife Management 48:1014–1018.

Warner, R.E., and L.M. David. 1982. Woody habitat and severe winter mortality of ring-necked pheasants in central Illinois. Journal of Wildlife Management 46:923–932.

Warner, R.E., and S.L. Etter. 1983. Reproduction and survival of radio-marked hen ring-necked pheasants in Illinois. Journal of Wildlife Management 47:369–375.

Warner, R.E., S.L. Etter, G.B. Joselyn, and J.A. Ellis. 1984. Declining survival of ring-necked pheasant chicks in Illinois agricultural ecosystems. Journal of Wildlife Management 48:82–88.

Warner, R.E., P. Hubert, P.C. Mankin, and C.A. Gates. 2000. Disturbance and the survival of female ring-necked pheasants in Illinois. Journal of Wildlife Management 64:663–672.

Warner, R.E., G.B. Joselyn, and S.L. Etter. 1987. Factors affecting roadside nesting by pheasants in Illinois. Wildlife Society Bulletin 15:221–228.

Warner, R.E., P.C. Mankin, L.M. David, and S.L. Etter. 1999. Declining survival of ring-necked pheasant chicks in Illinois during the late 1900s. Journal of Wildlife Management 63:705–710.

Warnock, J.E., and G.B. Joselyn. 1964. Nesting of pheasants in soybean fields. Journal of Wildlife Management 28:589–592.

Washburn, B.E., and T.G. Barnes. 2000. Native warm-season grass and forb establishment using imazapic and 2,4-D. Native Plants Journal 1:61–69.

West, R.R., R.B. Brunton, and D.J. Cunningham. 1969. Repelling pheasants from sprouting corn with a carbamate insecticide. Journal of Wildlife Management 33:216–219.

Westemeier, R.L., J.E. Buhnerkempe, W.R. Edwards, J.D. Brawn, and S.A. Simpson. 1998. Parasitism of greater prairie-chicken nests by ring-necked pheasants. Journal of Wildlife Management 62:854–863.

Westerskov, K. 1957. Growth and moult of pheasant chicks. Wildlife Publication 47. New Zealand Department of Internal Affairs.

Weston, H.G. Jr. 1954. The winter-spring movements of the ring-necked pheasant in northern Iowa. Iowa State College Journal of Science 29:39–60.

Whitmore, R.W., K.P. Pruess, and R.E. Gold. 1986. Insect food selection by 2-week-old ring-necked pheasant chicks. Journal of Wildlife Management 50:223–228.

Wilson, R.J., R.D. Drobney, and D.L. Hallett. 1992. Survival, dispersal, and site fidelity of wild female ring-necked pheasants following translocation. Journal of Wildlife Management 56:79–85.

Wishart, W. 1969. Age determination of pheasants by measurement of proximal primaries. Journal of Wildlife Management 33:714–717.

Woehler, E. E. and J. M. Gates. 1970. An improved method of sexing ring-necked pheasant chicks. Journal of Wildlife Management 34:228–231.

Zouhar, K., J.K. Smith, J. Kapler; S. Sutherland, and M.L. Brooks. 2008. Wildland fire in ecosystems: fire and nonnative invasive plants. General Technical Report, RMRS-GTR-42-vol. 6. Ogden, Utah: U.S. Department of Agriculture, Forest Service, Rocky Mountain Research Station.